... upon the upper barn wants new ... ... part of the thatch - the adjoining ... ...ble barn with two floors wants tho... ...ny places and the ridge wants new ... ...wet from rotting the Timbers - The back side of the ...se and one end is nearly all tumbling down being ...y much decayed for want of being attended to in prop... ...re - The end of the Cart house wants a considerabl... ...l of new weather boarding the old being in part do... ...d the remainder much decayed and broke - The Co... ...use and Carpenters Shop in Nettus Meadow wants ...ne weather boarding put up - The lower barn in ...uttus Meadow - the North end of the weather board... ...in a very bad state being a good deal down and ... ...cayed and rotten state also the south end wants ... ...pairs - The Thatch in bullock sheds in Gravel Pitt ...ld at the end of this barn wants repairing to preve... ...e Timbers rotten from the wet - The Man that occupie... ...is farm was Mr Revetts Game keeper but since Mr Re... ...ath there is scarcely five brace of Pheasants to be found ...r all the three Manors when at one time he says ... ...mself 50 Brace might be found in one grove of 8 acr... ...our his farm and he accounts for this in a very stra... ...anner and yet he says he has been the Game keeper ...rs Revett ever since Mr Revetts death -

Farm in the occupation of Mr Garnham - State of H... ...ildings - The underpins of the Pigsties nearly all go... ...d the Weather boarding totally decayed - Hog pound... ...ants new railing all round - Cheese room windows ...uch out of repair - the North end of the house the ...astering nearly all down - the tiling wants fresh poin...

A HISTORY OF BRANDESTON HALL

HONOURING THE PAST, BUILDING THE FUTURE

Norman Porter

First Published in 2009 by Albert Publications
in association with The Society of Old Framlinghamians
www.oldframlinghamian.com

Albert Publications
Rill Cottage, Kiln Lane, Great Bealings, Woodbridge, IP13 6NJ
© Norman Porter 2009

ISBN 978-0-9562872-0-5

DESIGNED BY CHRIS KEEBLE, KEEBLE+HALL
PRINTED IN SUFFOLK ON ELEMENTAL CHLORINE-FREE PAPER,
SOURCED FROM SUSTAINABLE FORESTS.

Delightfully situated in the Parish of Brandeston in the County of
Suffolk and only ten miles from the Shipping Port of Woodbridge
abounding with good roads...

An elegant lawn and pleasure ground, thriving plantations and
umbrageous walks, large gardens and orchards enclosed and
clothed with choice fruit trees and comprising 35 acres of Rich
Meadow Land and near 3 acres of Grove, Ornamented with a great
variety of full grown and stately Timber Trees pleasingly diversified
forming a complete Park and several beautiful Groves ornamented
with a handsome sheet of water streaming through the middle of
the grounds, well stocked with fish, the whole commanding the
most delightful and enchanting views in various directions to the
eye from the House known as the Manor House.

From the 1820 Survey... so how much have things *really* changed?

CONTENTS

FOREWORD BY ANDREW FANE,
CHAIRMAN OF GOVERNORS

The building pre-dates my Chairmanship by some 450 years. The school pre-dates my Chairmanship by some 50 years. So I am a relatively recent arrival on the scene. My perspective is that of Chairman since 2001, and a Governor since from 1995.

One of the delights of being Chairman of Governors of Framlingham College is the way that Brandeston Hall Prep School is seamlessly conjoined into the whole enterprise. This means that we can enjoy attending a cricket match, a school play, or Speech Day at Brandeston and marvel at the enthusiasm, skill and charm of the young people, in full anticipation of enjoying their growing contributions to all aspects of life at the College as they move on up. I have been Chairman for long enough to know that a young star in whatever field at Brandeston has every chance of maturing into a super star in many fields when at the College.

It brings me to the seamlessness of an ideal educational process and above all to the grounding young people need, be it in academia, sport or music, if they are to give of their ultimate potential at their Senior School. It is hugely valuable for them to have the benefit of a first class and planned preparation during those vital early school years.

Ultimately it is the teachers who are the biggest influence on turning out that honed and prepared 18 year-old armed with his or her 'A' levels, their certificates of other achievements, and their comprehensive personal statements for university entry. Brandeston's greatest strength has been the skill and dedication of its staff, who work their magic with all their pupils, whether they go on to the College or to other schools. The quality of the grounding they receive serves them throughout life. The role of a wise and hugely experienced Head of the College, giving ultimate leadership to all that goes on at Brandeston, must not be understated, and, for the last 15 years Gwen Randall has delivered that with her customary passion.

Tony Lawrence, who has become such a dominant personality at the College, not least in producing a series of plays and musicals to a West-End standard along with all his other duties, started out his teaching life at Brandeston. Martin Myers-Allen, who is now giving such vigour and passion to the Mastership at Brandeston honed his schoolmastering skills in the 15 years that he spent at the College. Exchanges like that are not uncommon, and in addition there are also the bursarial and other specialist skills that enable the success of Brandeston. All of these come together to provide a Prep School that is disproportionately well served in expertise and resources when compared to its freestanding competitors.

After mentioning the pupils and staff, I have to recognise that the exceptional setting of the school and its facilities is an attribute that puts it firmly into a leading position. Our predecessors in the post-war years must have been a very wise and clear sighted group of governors and OFs to have foreseen the potential in the Brandeston site and to have had the confidence to acquire it for such a worthwhile purpose. It is a memorial to all those from the College who so tragically lost their lives in two world wars, but it is living evidence too, of all those features of a truly outstanding school and its capacity to alter greatly for the good the lives of all those young people who come through on their way to becoming happy, rounded and valued adults. Brandeston has done so much for so many people and all involved can be rightly proud.

Andrew Fane

Andrew Fane,
Chairman of Govenors

Andrew Fane has lived locally to Brandeston since he was a boy, and has farmed in the adjacent village of Hoo for 25 years. As well as his local interests, he has been extensively engaged outside Suffolk. His first career was as a chartered accountant, working in corporate finance and fund management in the City. That led progressively to a range of other roles including 8 years as a councillor in local government in London. He was invited to join the board of English Heritage where he chaired the Historic Buildings Council and the London Committee for a number of years, dealing with listed building consent issues on many of the great buildings of England, including the British Library and St Pancras station, and closer to home at Heveningham Hall. This gave him an abiding enthusiasm for heritage buildings, and a particular commitment to Brandeston Hall. He has also worked as a non-executive director for 10 years at Gt Ormond Street Hospital, where he is now deputy chairman of the NHS Trust board.

INTRODUCTION BY NORMAN PORTER,
AUTHOR/EDITOR

Brandeston Hall is a building of distinction. That building has had an ever-evolving history, firstly as a grand house, then, for a brief interlude, a military Headquarters, and finally as a school. That school has, at the time of writing, just celebrated its 60th birthday – reason enough in itself for writing this history. There is, however, an even more compelling motivation for this enterprise.

Brandeston Hall, the school, is not simply a school – it is a living war memorial, a school made possible by the generosity of Old Framlinghamians who wished to pay tribute to those of their friends who had given their lives in battle, and who wished to perpetuate the memory of those friends by enabling future generations to enjoy the kind of education that they, and their lost friends had received. Their way of honouring the past was to set up a school which would help to build the future.

It was a meeting with John Pemberton, then a sprightly 87, and one of the original teachers at the school, which triggered off my awareness that Brandeston had no full and fitting history. Historical surveys and theses – yes – but nothing which captured the rich complexities of the school or its human dimension. The first generation of Brandestonians were into their seventies; some had already departed this life, and, rather in the way that impressionist painters try to capture the fleeting moment, it seemed important that the nostalgia of childhood memories be articulated and captured while the very first Brandestonians were still capable of putting their distant memories into words.

For many of the contributors this is a chronicle of childhood, a chronicle of enduring impressions and memories, inevitably both good and bad, but all part of the fabric of growing up. Walls have no memories. It needs the people who have lived and worked within those walls and grounds to articulate that history which the walls have silently witnessed.

This book does not pretend to be a serious historical work. There is little that is based on primary research. It does include elements based on the scholarly historical research of others, particularly John Booth, Wilda Woodland, the late Simon Fuller and Carole Maran. I am also greatly indebted to Bob Williams for his research into school records and for his collation of much information. Beyond that, the book does also aim to put the school into a broader historical and geographical context, but it is really about people, an attempt to get inside the hearts and minds of those who have lived and worked there, and to understand how the place has impacted on their lives.

There are bound to be serious omissions – all were invited to contribute – many have – but it is impossible to cover the many hundreds of staff and pupils who have passed through the school. Even if the book covers only a representative number of them, it will hopefully serve to remind new generations of Brandestonians of the wealth and richness of their heritage – a heritage recalled every Remembrance Sunday at the College as hundreds of poppies are laid upon the altar in memory of those who perished. That is the wider purpose of this book. Hopefully it will help to sustain a sense of continuity, and bring young Brandestonians (and their parents) to understand how a grand Hall became a school, and how their own experiences, despite the fluctuations of educational practice, continue to evolve from what has gone on before.

It is the setting and the grounds of Brandeston Hall which inspire so many childhood memories, but that would mean little were it not for the efforts of so many teachers over so many years, who have ensured that Brandeston is chiefly remembered for being a happy school.

This book is dedicated to all who, in their manifold ways, have made Brandeston Hall what it is.

Norman Porter

Norman Porter (right) in conversation with
David Mallett – an ex-head boy of
Brandeston Hall – at the East India Club,
London SW1, March 2009

The author/editor joined Brandeston Hall as an 11+ Direct Grant student in the early 1950s. Brandeston, Framlingham College and St Andrews University implanted the seeds that were to grow into a life-time teaching career – one which embraced primarily modern foreign languages and sports coaching. That career took him to Loretto School, Dulwich College, and Wellington College before it tapered gently away into a part-time, semi-retirement post at Woodbridge School on his return to Suffolk in 1997.

In this book he brings together the varied perspectives of pupil, teacher, parent, sports coach, College Governor and Secretary of the Old Framlinghamians. He is well qualified to recognise qualities which make schools special. He also writes as one who has had a lifelong love of the county of Suffolk, together with a burgeoning interest in the history of the county. He has undertaken to write this book as a mark of affectionate gratitude to the school which started him off on his path through life.

PART 1
EARLY YEARS

December 21st 1874 was a gloomy day for the village of Brandeston, when
Mr Austin finished a most successful and brilliant career in the 75th year of his age.
– CHARLES AUSTIN ESQ QC (from Lambert's Family Almanac 1875)

August 1898

THE HALL BEFORE 1939

There were Lords of the Manor before the Hall was built in the mid-sixteenth century, but this is not the place to chart them in great detail. A brief survey must suffice. For more detailed information on the various Lords of the Manor see the late *Simon Fuller's* excellent History – Simon was Head of History at Brandeston Hall from 1987-1994 and the value of his work as a source of information is hereby acknowledged.

EARLY ABSENTEE LORDS OF THE MANOR

It is easy to think of the Manor as synonymous with the Manor House and its incumbent. This is not always the case. Even before the Hall was built, Brandeston was indeed part of a Manor, in the sense that it was part of an agricultural estate, including the village, the Lord's estate and houses for his tenants who provided labour and paid rents. The Lord of the Manor was himself either a tenant of the crown or held his estate from a superior feudal lord. Brandeston was administered within a *Hundred*. The Hundred was a unit of local administration from the 10th to the 19th century. It was a sub-division of a shire, with its own court. Each Hundred included a number of Manors. Brandeston was in the Loes Hundred. This comprised some 18 parishes, with the River Deben winding through them. Until the mid-16th century the Lords of the Brandeston Manor lived away from the estate.

Before the Norman Conquest and at the time of Edward the Confessor in 1065, the Manor in the broad sense of the word, was held by *Edmund the Priest*. He held it from St Etheldreda's at Ely Abbey which was his base. The Brandeston Manor then consisted of only 60 acres. Following the Conquest in 1066 the Manor was awarded to *William de Arques*, an uncle of William the Conqueror and the builder of the famous castle of Arques on a hill-top above the Normandy coast. The Manor grew in size, perhaps reflecting the status and acquisitive intent of those Lords. They were well connected. Suffolk appears to have been at the forefront of history: either the land was viewed as being of particular value, or, as it is suggested, the East Anglians were somewhat fractious, and William sent in his senior relatives to keep the locals in check. These were, of course, the times before the discovery of the New World. England necessarily looked eastwards towards the continent (and the Hanseatic League) from which direction all the trade and invasions came. Hence the importance of the East coast, and the relative insignificance of the ports on the West coast of England.

At the time of the Doomsday Book of 1086, the Manor had passed to *Odo*, whose wife, Adelize, was half-sister to William. Henry III granted the Manor to *Alan Baron Burnell* who in turn granted it, together with the rents from the church to *Sir John de Weyland* in 1259. From the 13th-16th century Sir John de Weyland and his descendants, the *Weylands, Tuddenhams, and Bedingfields* were Lords of the Manor. They can be considered as absentee Lords of the Manor, receiving rents, but not living amongst their tenants.

THE REVETTS AND THE BUILDING OF BRANDESTON HALL

In 1543 *Andrew Revett* purchased the Manor from Henry Bedingfield. He previously held the Manor of Monewden. He made Brandeston his seat and started to build the Hall in 1543 and completed it in 1550, straddling the rules of Henry VIII and Edward VI. This was just 25 years after the building of Hampton Court. Andrew Revett, founder of a 300 year dynasty based on Brandeston Hall, was a country gentleman and government official who lived during the reigns of Henry VIII, Edward VI, Mary I and Elizabeth I. Revett was also Escheator for the two counties of Norfolk and Suffolk. An Escheat was the falling of land to the Crown on the death of the owner, intestate or without heirs. The Escheator's office had to take notice of such incidents in the affairs of his neighbours and notify the Exchequer. He it was who bought the Manor of Cretingham. He died in 1572, having been for many years involved in a dispute over land, even to the extent of being imprisoned in the Tower of London for 15 weeks. He was finally pardoned in 1558. He is buried in the chancel of *All Saints Church, Brandeston*.

John Revett, second Lord of the Manor of Brandeston of the Revett line, increased the importance of the family by his marriage with Anne, a niece of Sir Nicholas Bacon, Lord Keeper of the Great Seal under Elizabeth I. The Lord Keeper entertained his sovereign at his Manor of Redgrave, only half a day's journey on horseback from Brandeston. Of Mistress Bacon's cousins, the Lord Keeper's five sons, one was Sir Francis Bacon, Baron Verulam, Lord Chancellor, natural philosopher and man of letters; of the others, one was the first Baronet of England, and three were members of Parliament for either Norfolk or Suffolk, and received the honour of knighthood. Anne bore her husband twelve children, whose names may be read on a monument in Brandeston Church. John Revett was certainly well connected. He died in 1616 and his memorial tablet is on the North wall of the chancel.

Memorial Tablet in All Saints Church in memory of John Revett (d 1616) and his wife Anne.

John Revett's eldest son, *Nicholas Revett* succeeded him. He died in 1643 and he, too, is buried in the chancel. Nicholas's eldest son, *John Revett II* succeeded him. This was during the English Civil War, the rule of Oliver Cromwell, and the time of the execution of Charles I. He managed to survive, reputation intact, and was made Justice of the Peace on the Restoration of Charles II. It was during this period that *John Lowes* (see p16) was executed for witchcraft. John Revett II died in 1671. *Thomas Revett*, John's fourth son, inherited the Hall. He died in 1704 and his memorial plate is on the north chancel wall. His wife became the guardian of their eldest son *John Revett III* until he was 21. John Revett III moved to Framlingham but missed Brandeston. He died in

Nicholas Revett's drawing for the West Portico for West Wycombe House, Buckinghamshire, c1770, for Sir Francis Dashwood

1756. His younger son, *Nicholas Revett* (1720-1804) was born at the Hall. He was an artist and antiquary and a member of the polite Society of Dilettanti. He travelled in Italy and Greece. He also had the reputation of being one of the first Englishmen to travel in Asia Minor. The drawings he brought home of the architectural antiquities of the countries he had visited attracted the admiration of 18th Century connoisseurs. He wrote, in collaboration with James Stuart, the first volume of *'The Antiquities of Athens'* – the book which introduced Greek architecture to the English public. Nicholas Revett died in 1804 and was buried in Brandeston churchyard. The Manor passed to *John Revett IV*, and then on to his eldest son, *John Revett V*.

Marriage then brought the name of *Pytches* into the line of succession but essentially the Manor passed from father to son in unbroken succession for eight generations. In all, the succession from the Revetts, and their occupation of the Hall, lasted three hundred and one years.

They were indeed a distinguished family, and there are many Revetts buried in the chancel of All Saints Church, as evidenced by their memorial tablets. The Revetts cycle business in Ipswich came from a branch of this family, and gave money for the repair of Nicholas Revett's tomb in the churchyard. The Revett name lives on.

On a less flattering note it was said that the "old squires" liked to keep hounds, lived hard and were very liberal. The last of the line was heavily in debt and it was feared, so it was said, that his body which lay in the Parlour of the Hall might be seized by his creditors. As a security measure some of the tenants and servants secretly carried off the body in the middle of the night to the safety of the church.

BRANDESTON AND WITCHCRAFT

One of the most memorable chapters in Brandeston's history revolved around the fate of *Rev John Lowes*. The church and the Hall were clearly closely connected with one another, and the affairs of the church were inevitably the concern of the Lord of the Manor. The close proximity of the two buildings is not without significance. The Vicarage too, The Broadhurst, was close by.

In 17th century Suffolk there was a strong belief in witchcraft. Persecution was rife. Allegedly, of the 109 people convicted in England for witchcraft, 60 were hanged in Suffolk. Much of this was probably due to the determined efforts of witch-hunter-in-chief, *Matthew Hopkins*, who was based in Manningtree, and who was actually paid by Parliament to hunt out witches – at the rate of twenty shillings per conviction. In 1642 John Lowes was the priest at All Saints and was approaching 80 when he fell under suspicion. Lowes had become vicar in 1596 and by the 1640s the village, like much of Suffolk, had turned very puritan. Lowes was rightly suspected of being a supporter of Charles and Archbishop Laud. He was therefore an anachronism in the early years of the English Civil War in East Anglia. His own parishioners accused him of having Papist tendencies and also considered him to be vexatious.

As a consequence the parishioners tried to have him removed. They failed, but did manage to bring him to the attention of the Witch-Hunter General whereupon John Lowes was accused of being in league with the devil. The unfortunate man was duly bound and thrown into Framlingham Mere to see if he would float. He was also accused of sinking ships off Felixstowe. He was eventually found guilty and convicted. The penalty for witchcraft was death by hanging, and he was executed, but not until he had read his own burial service, to ensure a Christian departure from this world. His death is still commemorated, somewhat gruesomely, on the village sign and was featured in the film *The Witchfinder General*, based on the Brandeston story. In All Saints Church there is a plaque in memory of the wronged vicar.

John Lowes was not condemned on the evidence of the Lord of the Manor, but on the evidence of outsiders. Indeed, Thomas Revett subsequently endeavoured to clear the priest's name and reputation. The Broadhurst, into which Charles Austin II moved when he left the Hall, was formerly the Vicarage and, as such, the vicarage of John Lowes. (The Old Vicarage was built in 1857 because Charles

Far Left: Detail of the Brandeston Village sign showing the executed vicar, John Lowes.
Left: Poster promoting the film 'Witchfinder General', subsequently re-titled 'Conqueror Worm' featuring the Brandeston story of witchcraft.
Right: The Broadhurst, formerly the Brandeston Vicarage, in the early 20th century.
(Photograph courtesy Lord and Lady Cunliffe)

Austin II had appropriated the Vicarage and needed to give the Vicar another place in which to live. In 1982 the Vicarage was sold by the Church and thereafter became The Old Vicarage).

19TH CENTURY BRANDESTON

In the days before communications with the outside world became easier and faster, many villagers would spend the greater part of their lives in or around the village, with outings to the local town or market their only glimpse of the world beyond. It is easy to forget that these developments did not occur until well into the 19th century. From the mid-19th century, the beginning of the great age of the railways, we have the following description of the village, together with a reference to Charles Austin:

"BRANDESTON, a parish in the hundred of Loes, in the county of Suffolk, 4 miles to the S.W. of Framlingham, 5 from Wickham Market, its post town, and 12 N.E. of Ipswich. It is situated on the banks of the river Deben. A branch of the Great Eastern Railway runs from Wickham Market to Framlingham. The living is a vicarage in the dioc, of Norwich, value £100, in the patronage of the Rev. T. Smythe. The church, dedicated to All Saints, is a Gothic building, with square tower. There is an Independent chapel, built in 1836, capable of accommodating 400 persons. The school is supported by Charles Austin, Esq., J.P., who is lord of the manor and principal landowner. There are some poors' land and other charitable endowments of small value. A new vicarage has lately been built."
From The National Gazetteer of Great Britain and Ireland (1868).

The above description suggests that the owner of Brandeston Hall played a significant role in the lives of the villagers in the 19th century. The Lord of the Manor owned most of the land and the estate had grown to close on 2000 acres by this time. For much of this century and on into the 20th century, the Hall itself was owned by another dynasty, the Austins.

THE AUSTINS

In 1845 the Manor was bought by *Charles Austin*. He was one of the most eminent lawyers of his time. He was born in 1799 in Ipswich in Handford Mill, presumably in the vicinity of Handford Road. There is no record of the mill – it probably disappeared in the mid-19th century. He was educated at Ipswich School and Bury St Edmunds School. He went up to Jesus College, Cambridge and thence to the Middle Temple. Stories are told of his cogent advocacy and spectacular success at the Parliamentary Bar. He apparently rejected a proposal that he should fill the office of Solicitor-General in Sir Robert Peel's second administration, although, when the offer was made to him, he had no seat in the House of Commons, and had never even contested an election. "He recoiled from the drudgery of political life, and viewed with no favour the exacting demands of a certain class of voters." He is said to have read widely, and to have been a fine Latin scholar.

Austin had his chambers in the Temple, and continued to live in London until he retired from practice in 1848. He had not taken up residence at the time of the fire which severely damaged the Hall in 1847. For a detailed description of his work on restoring the building see p37 (The Building).

When he had retired from professional practice he found great pleasure at Brandeston in renewing his study of classical authors.

Left: A sampler produced by Emma Nunn in 1878 at Brandeston Hall
National School, supported by Charles Austin.
Below left: Pupils at Brandeston Hall National Voluntary School c1901.

He is also said to have had a fine gift for conversation when in the company of his friends. His circle, first formed when Austin was at university, included some of the most cultivated minds and most powerful intellects amongst the Victorians. *Lord Macaulay*, historian, was one of the first of his friends. *John Stuart Mill*, philosopher, was another member of this group of intellectual luminaries. The Second Earl of Stradbroke, Lord Lieutenant of Suffolk, first President of Framlingham College, *Sir Fitzroy Kelly*, Lord Chief Baron of the Exchequer and one of the founders of the College, and the *Venerable Robert Hindes Grome*, Archdeacon of Suffolk and friend and correspondent of *Edward Fitzgerald*, could also be counted amongst Austin's friends in his later years.

Charles Austin is said to have given thirty five thousand pounds for Brandeston Manor, though his obituary notice in 'The Ipswich Journal' quoted the price as thirty thousand guineas. It stated that a friend at the Bar, to whom Austin was relating the negotiations leading to the purchase, asked him: "Well, after all, was it one year's earnings?" and the new Lord of the Manor replied "Not quite". Sceptical questions were asked about how Charles Austin managed to lavish so much money on the rebuilding of the Hall. He did make a great deal of his money as a lawyer during the railway boom of the 1830s and 40s. (When railway schemes were quoted by the score, and when Mr Austin was in constant request, he made money by handfuls" – *Lambert's Family Almanac 1875*.) However he managed to do it, his achievement and devotion to the rebuilding project have given subsequent generations cause to be grateful. What could have been a heap of burnt rubble was recreated as the splendid building which we can continue to enjoy today.

For more than twenty years during that time he engaged in public work in the county. Charles Austin was High Steward of Ipswich, and in that capacity took part in the reception of *Albert, the Prince Consort*, when he visited Suffolk in 1851. He was a Justice for the County and Chairman of the East Suffolk Quarter Sessions. He re-united the Manor of Monewden with Brandeston. Charles Austin honoured his educational obligations to the village by assuming responsibility for the Village School in Mill Lane. White's Directory of 1855 notes that it was: *"a commodious school, erected in 1852 by C Austin Esq., and chiefly supported by him, for the children of this parish and the adjacent parishes of Cretingham and Kettleburgh".*

Charles Austin paid for the furnishings, and paid the teachers (probably two of them). Such were the perceived obligations of the owner of The Hall. The school's Log Book starts on September 13th 1875 when the building is called the Brandeston Hall National School.

Charles Austin was also one of the founders of *Framlingham College*, named in the Royal Charter of 1864 as one of the original members of the College Corporation. Austin presided, and distributed the prizes at the first-ever Speech Day at Framlingham. This man was responsible for the beautiful re-creation of the Hall after catastrophe. He was married to Harriet née Ingleby and her initials are to be seen on the ceiling of the Entrance Hall. He was a key figure in the foundation of Framlingham College. He was also closely associated with education in the village. It is therefore fitting that he should, posthumously, have been reunited with education and with the College when his former and lovingly restored home was purchased by the Framlingham College Governors from his grandson to house the new Junior School. Charles Austin I died at Brandeston on 21st December 1874, aged seventy five years, and was buried there the day after Christmas Day.

The first Charles Austin (also known as 'The Old Squire'), was a major Victorian figure and restorer of the fire-ravaged Hall. He was

Right: Brandeston 1896 – Amy Holt, A Waters, Nora Boyd, Marjory Brooke, N Waters and Guy Boyd, with Laddie.
Below right: Charles Austin II (1858-1937) with his first wife Harriet (née Richer, 1866-1910).

a dominant figure: it is said that, as well as building the new Vicarage to allow his son to move into The Broadhurst, he also realigned the river, moved the road from between the river and the Hall to North of the Hall, and built the Mortuary Chapel on the North side of the village as he didn't like people being buried in his 'garden' (ie the churchyard). When Brandeston Hall was opened as a school in 1948, it was some 100 years after Austin's Hall had risen, phoenix-like, from its ashes.

He was succeeded by Charles Austin II. Charles Austin II was born in 1858 and died in 1937. He was Lord of the Manor for 62 years and the last Lord of the Manor to reside in the Hall. During the early twentieth century over two thousand acres of the estate were sold. When the Manor was sold in 1920 it consisted of 1600 acres, some 20 farms and many other assorted premises. Charles Austin II lost the Hall in a gambling bet with the Duke of Hamilton but it is said that the winner of the wager would not accept the deeds. Equally controversial was the Radio play broadcast in 2005 entitled 'Death of a secret wife'. The play was based on a local inquest in 1910 into the mysterious death of Mrs Harriet Austin, wife of the dissolute Lord of the Manor. Harriet was Charles Austin's first wife – 'the secret wife' – she had been a servant, and a divorcee. Her husband was too terrified of his aristocratic mother's disapproval to admit that he had married her. It was Charles Austin II and Harriet (née Richer) who moved out of the Hall to The Broadhurst in 1906, and who then rented out the house to tenants on 7 year leases. Charles Austin II did remarry, very shortly after the death of his first wife, and a child (Charles Austin III) was born shortly afterwards.

This Charles Austin, (1912-1993), completed a dynasty of three generations: father, son and grandson. The Austins owned The Broadhurst (named after Rev Broadhurst, Vicar of Brandeston 1815-1856) and wanted to move out of The Hall, so had to build a new vicarage. Charles Austin III lived in The Broadhurst all his life until he sold the property to Lord and Lady Cunliffe and moved to Rendham.

Charles Austin III (usually known as Bunny) looked after the remains of the Manor and divided it up into three parts amongst his family. The land which is now Cretingham Golf Course was part of this. Charles Austin's nephew, John, was instrumental in setting up the course from 1984 onwards.

After the Austins had moved out into the Broadhurst, the Hall's tenants were primarily *Sir Tom Talbot Leyland Scarisbrick, Bt*, the first to move in, followed by the *Wentworth Reeves* (21-28), the *Scrimgeours* (stockbrokers, 28-36) who moved on to Monewden

Hall. The proceeds from a village fete held by them provided the funds for heating the church. The last family to be tenants were the *Leonards* who are said to have fled to South America at the outbreak of WWII.

During these latter years the Hall remained the seat of gentry, albeit tenants, with appropriate staff.

Ownership of the land, alongside the title of Lord of the Manor has evolved, and the two seem to have diverged. Lord and Lady Cunliffe, the present owners of The Broadhurst, the farm and surrounding woods, purchased the property in 1979 from Charles Austin III, with no mention of the Lordship of the Manor. Despite owning the land around the Hall (In Lady Cunliffe's colourful phrase Brandeston Hall is "the hole in the doughnut!"), Lord Cunliffe is not the Lord of the Manor. After the sale of the Manor in 1920, the concept of Lord of the Manor faded in significance. John Austin, nephew of Charles Austin III appears to be nominal Lord of the Manor. A bachelor, he sees himself as the end of the Austin line.

So – an inverted symmetry appears: in medieval times the Manor was in the possession of absentee landlords who had no seat in the village. Conversely, by the early 20th century, a splendid Hall remained, but there was no Lord of the Manor resident in it.

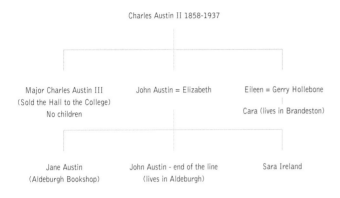

Charles Austin II 1858-1937

Major Charles Austin III (Sold the Hall to the College) No children	John Austin = Elizabeth	Eileen = Gerry Hollebone Cara (lives in Brandeston)
Jane Austin (Aldeburgh Bookshop)	John Austin - end of the line (lives in Aldeburgh)	Sara Ireland

Above: John Durrant, Butler, in the Dining Room, 1930s. After the war he restarted a shoe repair business in Otley, and on Mondays would ride out to local villages seeking custom. One of the places he collected from was Brandeston Hall, where he had worked as a butler before the war and where he had met his wife, who was a housemaid.

DATES

Andrew Revett	d.1572
John Revett I	d.1616
Nicholas Revett	d.1643
John Revett II	d.1671
Thomas Revett	d.1704
John Revett III	d.1756

(Second son: **Nicholas Revett** b. BH 1720, d.1804 – Edited Antiquities and Ruins of Athens)

John Revett 1V	d.1773
John Revett V	d.1829

John Pytches (assumed the name Revett) inherited the Manor 1829. His son John Pytches, inherited the Manor in 1830 but died childless in 1897.

Charles Austin I d.1874, b.1799. Ipswich School, Jesus College, Cambridge and Middle Temple; QC; High Steward of Ipswich d.1874. Married to Harriet née Ingleby c1830-1902.

Charles Austin II d.1937, b.1858. Last Lord to live in the Hall but moved out in early 20th century to the Broadhurst. Twice married. First Harriet (née Richer)– the 'secret wife') (1866-1910) then Eileen, née O'Callaghan (1881-1974)

The Hall was then rented out to tenants:

Cosmo Gordon Paterson – d.1906, and his wife.

Stanley George Harding – new tenants in 1908.

Sir Thomas and Lady Talbot Legland Scarisbrick – from 1915.

Charles and Beatrice Wentworth-Reeve – from 1922.

Hugh Carron and Oonah (née O'Callaghan) **Scrimgeour** – from 1926. They moved to Monewden Hall and the last private tenants were:

Albert and Marguerite Leonard – from 1937-39.

Major Charles Austin III (Bunny) – sold Brandeston Hall to the Governors of Framlingham College in 1947. Unmarried. Had a sister Eileen (1913-1996) and brother, John Austin Senior, father of John Austin, now the last in the Austin line.

Facing page:
Top row from left: Joachim Von Ribbentrop – said to have dined with the Leonards, the last tenants of the Hall pre-war. Dorothy and Marjorie Brooke – grandchildren of Charles and Harriet Austin – 1890s – with their Grandmother. Scrimgeour staff: Frank Sykes (butler), unnamed 'wireless' installer, John Durrant(2nd footman), Jimmy Durrant(1st footman).
Middle row: John Durrant with his bride Ruth Robinson. Mrs Beatrice Wentworth-Reeve and Mr Charles Wentworth-Reeve, 1920s.
Bottom row: Hugh Scrimgeour (5th from left, standing), with the Rifle Club. John Austin Senior next to him.

The East Anglian coast has, through the centuries, been of strategic significance for the defence of our country from would-be European invaders. Suffolk's surviving medieval castles and Martello towers (*pictured right*) bear witness to threats down the ages. What follows is based on descriptions of the Hall, prepared by John Booth for the revised Appeal Booklet, research into the military units which were accommodated in the Hall, information supplied by the Tank Museum in Dorset and local historical background from Wilda Woodland.

During the Second World War Suffolk not only had to defend its coast line, but it was well placed, and had the appropriate terrain, for training the forces, both land-based and airborne, which were to take the fight against Hitler back across the Channel. For some time after the end of the war, the beaches remained unsafe because of unexploded mines, and entanglements of barbed wire. WWII relics can still be seen along the beaches and further inland. There are concrete blocks designed to keep tanks at bay and pill boxes designed to house machine guns overlooking expanses of land which would have been crossed by invading troops. There were 29 of Churchill's Secret Army bunkers in Suffolk, and a visit to Parham Museum, and the bunker there, reveals how secret forces would have been deployed to sabotage enemy efforts in the early days of an invasion. Later on in the war many airfields were built on the flat East Anglian acres, and thousands of bombing raids were launched from these airfields. Suffolk was in the thick of the war effort, both in the repelling of potential enemies during the early stages of the war and in the preparation of troops for the winning back of the mainland of Europe.

Brandeston Hall fitted into this complex war-time structure in a way which is rather more significant than might be envisaged by those young boys who simply remember the old army Nissen huts, lengths of barbed wire and a few crates of undetonated bombs which were what remained in 1948 when Brandeston Hall opened as a school.

Under the Emergency Powers Act of 1939 scores of country houses were requisitioned by Government departments, but few had the distinction of Brandeston Hall – that of becoming HQs of 2 divisions, together with a number of other units. The East Anglian coast, not for the first time in history, was in the forefront of an expected invasion. The requisition period began on November 1st 1940 and continued until 10th February 1947. Nine units and troop formations were based successively at Brandeston. The Hall was never empty for more than a few weeks at a time. Some of the kneelers in All Saints Church identify units which served at the Hall.

The early units were primarily concerned with defence. The first troops to be based in the area were units of the Royal Searchlight Batteries. One searchlight battery operated at Lampard Brook between Kettleburgh and Framlingham. There were three searchlight batteries with Headquarters at Brandeston Hall until 22nd September 1942.

Gerard (Gerry) Hollebone, still living in Brandeston in 2009, aged 95, was Adjutant to one of the first units to be posted there. He recalls that his Commanding Officer was Colonel Woolley. The unit, the 32nd Regiment, was initially housed in the requisitioned Crown Hotel in Framlingham, but the Colonel wanted his men out of there, and they were moved into the Hall. This was an 'Ack Ack and Mortar' unit, responsible for air defence. Gerry recalls how they picked up German airmen from shot-down planes. Eventually the Regiment moved to Manningtree, and other units took its place.

Subsequently the Hall was the Headquarters of two Divisions. The first was the 54th Infantry Division, commanded by **General (then Major General) Sir Evelyn Barker KBE CB DSO MC**. The division came from Thorndon near Eye, the seat of Lord Henniker, and its occupation lasted from March 20th until 17th Aug 1943. The Division remained in the United Kingdom as a local defence formation, responsible for the tactical work of the Home Guard. It was disbanded and broken up on 14 December 1943. Its component units would later take part in the Normandy campaign as support units. The 3rd Earl of Stradbroke, Lord Lieutenant of Suffolk, visited the Division several times. The HQ staff consisted of some 40 officers. The General's personal staff lived in the Hall. Gunner and Signals HQs were accommodated in huts built in the park after the War Office assumed control. The General used the morning room as his office and slept in the room over it – these later became a classroom and dormitory respectively.

The South Room, which became DD Kittermaster's study, was occupied by **Major General (then Lieut Colonel) G L Watkinson DSO** who was GSO. The billiard room was the main office. The Library was the mess ante-room and the officers dined in the former dining room which became part of the School Hall. The

Dining Room was the Map Room, and the telephone switchboard, with direct lines to the War Office, was placed in what had been the Housekeeper's room in the time of the Austins.

Sir Evelyn thought no day well begun unless it included a lengthy run before breakfast. As a Major General he continued at Brandeston the practice he had begun as a young officer. So it came about that each morning, men and women going early to work in the fields – food production was an essential part of the national effort – paused to salute the Divisional Commander taking energetic exercise. This was the first Division to have its Headquarters in the Hall.

The second of the two Divisions to have Headquarters there, was the **79th Armoured Division**. This was a unique formation, being all armoured and having every form of specialised tank. It survived in the Specialised Armour Establishment, Royal Armoured Corps. Its members wore a special badge. The Commander was **Major General Sir Percy Hobart, KBE, CB, DSO, MC**, (known as "Hobo" to his friends and superiors) a distinguished soldier who had had nearly 40 years service before he came to Brandeston, and who later became Colonel Commandant of the Royal Tank Regiment. His name is especially associated with armour, and with good reason. Thanks to the **Tank Museum** at Bovington in Dorset we have the following authoritative account:

"The situation regarding 79th Armoured Division is a bit curious because it was not a normal armoured division, even by British standards – at least not after September 1943. By its very nature the 79th Division was designed to be fragmented so that special purpose tanks could be distributed to other fighting formations, as required. As such, it never fought as an entity, even though constituent elements could be assigned to other fighting formations. It was designed specifically to operate in North West Europe and to develop ways of attacking Rommel's Atlantic Wall. From September 1943 the division was dedicated to the use of special purpose tanks such as mine flails, engineer tanks and flame-throwers, amongst others. Even after D Day, in order to maintain interest in Specialised Armour or "The Funnies", a truncated organisation remained, known as the Specialised Armour Development Establishment (SADE), still under Hobart and still at Brandeston Hall and Woodbridge. During that time it certainly occupied a fair amount of Suffolk countryside. It later became the Specialised Armour Establishment and ended up at Tidworth on Salisbury Plain. Hobart died on 19th February 1957."
(There is a biography of Hobart by Major K J Macksey entitled 'Armoured Crusader' published by Hutchinson in 1967)

Hobart was a demanding task-master, and on good terms with Churchill. He drove his men hard to get results. This Division was at Brandeston from 30th August 1945 to 12th December 1946. Previously a constituent part of it had been there from September 1943 until shortly before going to France in 1944.

Top: Buffalo Amphibian (landing tracked vehicle) – crossing the Rhine in 1945.
Centre: Churchill Crocodile. One of the more notable Churchills, it was a Churchill VII which replaced the hull machine gun with a flame-thrower. The fuel was in an armoured wheeled trailer towed behind. It could fire several one-second bursts over 150 yards. The Crocodile was one of 'Hobart's Funnies'. A working example can still be seen at the Cobbaton Combat Collection in North Devon.
Bottom: A Sherman Crab Flail – an anti-mine tank which has got itself bogged down.

There is an interesting personal link to Major General Hobart. In 1942/3 a young Captain serving with the Royal Norfolk Regiment was part of an inspection by the Major General. The young 22 year old Captain was particularly interested in the "Funnies" as his own role was in an anti-tank capacity. That young Captain was (later to become Major General) **Jack Dye**, Governor, and currently Vice President of the Corporation.

LIFE IN WARTIME

For a view of someone who lived in the village we turn to **Peter Arbon**. Peter lived in the village for all of his life and was still living there, sharing his memories in 2009. He was a gardener at Brandeston Hall for most of his working life. Peter recalls life in Brandeston before and during the war. In 1936 Mr Carron Scrimgeour, a stockbroker renting the Hall, had moved to Monewden Hall, and the Leonards moved in. They were believed to have Nazi sympathies and it is thought that they dispersed when the Hall was requisitioned, possibly to avoid internment. There is a story of would-be dinner guests arriving on the doorstep to find the Hall empty – the Leonards having hurriedly left. By way of corroboration of their allegiances, there is a story, unsubstantiated, that the German Ambassador, von Ribbentrop visited the Hall in 1938 for a spot of pheasant shooting. Charles Austin III was then living in 'The Broadhurst' in the village, but still owned the Hall.

Peter's memories include his recollection of how fuel was needed at the Hall and how coal first came in from Framlingham via the branch line. It then arrived direct in the shape of coke from Mansfield. He recalls one incident when a delivery lorry swung across as it entered the main gates and hit one of the entrance pillars. The damage remained unrepaired for some time. There was very little petrol, so the villagers had not much choice apart from staying at home, digging for Britain and watching what was going on.

The skies overhead were crowded. The bomber formations flew off to Germany and came straggling back. Peter remembers hedge-hopping planes, coming in and trying to avoid the ack-ack.

The NAAFI shop became the original school changing rooms. It was staffed by local girls. Villagers were not normally allowed into the grounds during the war, but the army did employ one man to look after the grounds. The kitchen garden was kept going. John Turner from Yoxford was in charge of the gardens and greenhouse. What are now the top two pitches on the main playing field had been ploughed up to grow potatoes.

The troops paraded up and down the road, and the meadow opposite was full of army vehicles. Elm Row (the elms now all gone –killed off by Dutch Elm disease) was covered with metal tracks. The soldiers, of course, needed relaxation and were regular visitors to the pub, normally causing no trouble. The local girls did not go short of company. A dance was held most weeks in the old Village Hut. There were as many as 400 officers and men, the officers living in the Hall and the men in Nissen huts. Conditions must have been cramped.

It is easy to revert to objective descriptions of these times and to forget that real people, leading real, often perilous lives were involved. **Wilda Woodland**, the Brandeston Historical Recorder, has kindly supplied us with images of this time. The men serving in the Hall came from all over the country. Thanks to Wilda's archive we can personalise this period of requisition with pictures, showing soldiers who served, who, embarked on enduring relationships, or indeed, were later killed in action.

On March 6th 1942 a war wedding took place **between Captain Gerard Hollebone** (see above) and **Eileen Mary Austin**. Eileen's brother was Lieut (later Major) Charles Austin (here seen with the bridesmaids) – later to become the vendor of the Hall to the College. Members of the **32nd Searchlight Regiment** pulled the newly weds' car from the Church to the Hall for the reception.

Left: Major General Sir Percy Hobart.
Above: (l-r) Captain Jack Dye in the early 40s. Wedding on March 6th 1942 between Captain Gerard Hollebone and Eileen Mary Austin. Eileen's father, Lieut. Charles Austin (with the bridesmaids) – later sold the Hall to the College. Members of the 32nd Searchlight Regiment pulled the newly weds' car from the Church to the Hall for the reception.

In 1944 another villager was married at All Saints – Barbara Norman of Hill Farm, Friday Street, married Leslie Brock, with the 32nd Searchlight Regiment and at some time stationed at the Hall (pictured right). Despite the many restrictions of wartime, and its uncertainties, life went on.

The village, of course, had its own Home Guard. The photo below has some familiar names: three **Arbons** – **Peter** was too young for the army; **Will Cable** grandfather of **Jonathan Cable** (a groundsman at the College, aka Old Fred on Radio Suffolk); **Ted Peck** who worked at Brandeston in the 70s/80s; **Goff Harvey** whose daughter Mary married Rodney Carter OF, Stuart Patterson, father of **Andrew Patterson** OF, **Gilbert Bedwell**, brother of **Frank Bedwell** who looked after boilers and maintenance at the Hall for some 50 years; **David Risk**, Snr, farmer, who delivered milk to the school. The names and the connections show very clearly the close links between the Hall and the village.

BACK ROW   Cliff Hughes   Gilbert Bedwell   ?   Geoff Arbon   Dennis Cable
Jim Arbon   Goff Harvey   Vic Read   Fred Adams   ?   Peter Arbon   Ted Peck

Will Cable   ?   Tom Girling   Jack Adams   David Risk   Stuart Patterson   Paul Stearn   Hub Meadows

THE AFTERMATH

Before the sale of the Hall finally went through there was protracted wrangling with the War Office as the would-be purchasers endeavoured to reduce the purchase price to compensate for damage incurred during the requisition period.

Even when the Hall became a school in 1948 there was still much evidence of its wartime use. Many of the Nissen huts remained standing and were converted. The NAAFI had been a long 60x20 Nissen hut and this was converted into the first changing room. There was a combustion stove with an iron guard around it – the only means of drying clothes. The Cookshop became "Doody" Day's carpentry shop. One Nissen hut housed a saw bench, to keep

The lids inside the boxes were ideal for use as tractor number plates and were recycled! Remnants of barbed wire were to be found all around. **John Pemberton** spent much time cleaning it up. One unfortunate consequence of the military occupation was the damage to the study ceiling, possibly caused by an overflowing bath above.

As recently as September 2008 war-time remnants were being turned up in the grounds. A .472 (12mm) heavy machine gun bullet was found by **Lewis Myers-Allen** in a ditch in the NW corner of the grounds whilst playing golf. It was fortunate that he didn't whack it too hard whilst foraging in the undergrowth for his ball. His father, **Martin Myers-Allen**, the CCF-hardened Headmaster, rang a policeman friend of his who suggested it was from a .50

all the open fires going. Another one was used for tuck boxes; another, the tuck shop; two were used as classrooms. **Alan Manthorpe** used one for his art class every Friday. The Sports Pavilion was another Nissen hut.

When the army left, much unwanted detritus had been dumped in the pond, anything from phosphorous bombs to old boots. **David Risk** recalls how the phosphorous bombs were dumped in the pond in wooden boxes. His father was in the Home Guard, (see photo on previous page) and a whole heap of these bombs was also found at the back of the garage.

Above left: They served at Brandeston – Tommy Tucker (killed in action); Ralph Porter; Dick Parry. Centre: Peter Arbon in the Vinery at the Hall. Right: Lewis Myers-Allen's bullet – found in the grounds in 2008 – the orange gives an idea of scale.

Browning machine gun used in WWII on the Flying Fortresses flown by the Americans stationed at places like Parham. It could be that some of the ammunition was stored or in transit at Brandeston Hall when it was requisitioned by the MOD 1940-47.

The past can still suddenly re-emerge in the present, but nowadays a fertile imagination is needed to envisage life at Brandeston Hall during the period of its requisition. Stories of the early years do, however, live on in the minds of the first generations of boys, whose childhood adventures could still be played out amidst vestiges of a more dangerous era, just past.

THE HALL AND EDUCATION

Lest it should be thought that Brandeston Hall and its owners had been completely aloof from education before the opening of the Hall in 1948, it should be recalled that, in 1852, **Charles Austin** had established a school for children

from the parishes of Brandeston, Kettleburgh and Cretingham, (*see photo above*), and that he had also been one of the original founders of Framlingham College, seconding **Sir Edward Kerrison** in his proposal for "the setting up of a School or College for Scientific and Practical Instruction of the Middle Classes at a moderate cost". So there was an element of educational continuity in the move of the Junior House of Framlingham College to Brandeston Hall.

A JUNIOR HOUSE

The establishment of a separate house had been suggested before – in 1866, by Headmaster, Scott-White. It had not been a propitious time for this suggestion, as numbers had fallen to less than 100 and the school was £3000 in debt. Numbers sank even further to 65 and Scott-White resigned. The idea of a separate Junior House perished with him for the next eighty years.

The problems in the immediate post-war period were of a different order. This time there were too many pupils and too little accommodation. To understand the reasons for this, we need to understand the educational system at the time and what it meant

for Framlingham to be a Direct Grant School. One of the provisions of Butler's 1944 Education Act was the opening up of the possibility for independent schools to accept a 'Direct Grant' from Government, in exchange for accepting a proportion of pupils sponsored by Local Education Authorities, as well as reduced independence. Framlingham chose to go down this route, and this led, inevitably, to increased numbers. Governors were wrestling with the problem of accommodating them all. Plans were already on the table for the building of a new Junior House in the grounds of the College – on the site where the Athlone Hall now stands. It was in the Summer of 1946 that the Governors were made aware of the attractive alternative of purchasing a ready-made building, off-site, and not yet equipped as a school, but with all the potential of meeting their requirements. This was, of course, Brandeston Hall.

NEGOTIATIONS

There was a period of uncertainty while the War Office went through the necessary preliminaries of offering the accommodation to other Ministries. No alternative bid transpired. The Hall was declared redundant and available for purchase. Notification was received that the Hall would be vacant on 20th December 1946.

JUSTIFICATION OF THE MOVE

The College was overcrowded and extra accommodation was clearly needed, but the Ministry of Education had to be persuaded of the merits of the case, and of the suitability of the Hall for educational purposes. A letter from the Bursar to the Ministry dated July 12th 1946 makes the case:

1 – The present buildings are much overcrowded; the boarding accommodation was designed for 200-220. There are now 250 boarders. This situation, though accepted during the war emergency, cannot be contemplated as a permanency.

2 – There is a big demand for the school which shows every sign of continuing. The Headmaster has a long Waiting List. There are also additional places to be made available to LEAs under the new grant regulations. Some means of expansion is therefore necessary.

3 – The present arrangement of having Junior and Senior boys accommodated together in one building is open to serious objections.

4 – Brandeston Hall is a pleasant house in attractive surroundings and provides a ready means of expansion. The buildings can be adapted without great expense. The main building provides adequate boarding accommodation for about 80 boys and staff, together with some classroom space. There are huts and other buildings in the grounds, some of which might be acquired from the War Department for use as classrooms, gymnasium etc.

5 – Before the opportunity for purchasing Brandeston arose, the Governors had drawn up a comprehensive scheme of improvements and extensions to the present buildings, including a Junior House. They realise that with the present building restrictions it is unlikely that permission could be obtained to build a Junior House for some years – it would in any case be much more expensive than purchasing and adapting Brandeston Hall. They are advised that, should they decide in the years ahead, to build a Junior House nearer the College, they would not find it difficult to obtain a purchaser for the Brandeston Hall property.

6 – Although at present requisitioned and unlikely to be released in the immediate future, Brandeston Hall is the only property in the locality suitable for conversion into a school. The Governors consider that the opportunity to purchase should not, on any account, be missed.

It is proposed to transfer to BH all boys under 13-14. In this connection it is observed that the number of boys in the school of Primary School age, (5-10) is very small. No change would be made in the curriculum: boys would pursue a continuous course of study as at present. Junior Day Boys would attend school at Brandeston. Arrangements would be made for transport where necessary.

The Governors have carefully considered the financial position. It is proposed to raise a loan to cover the cost of the purchase of the property, the cost of conversion, and the purchase later of a small number of army huts, if these should be available. The total amount of the loan should not exceed £16,000.

GOVERNORS AND OFs INVOLVED

Governors at the time included: Chairman: **Sir George Elliston** (OF) MC MA DL JP, with **The Earl of Stradbroke** KCMG, CB, CVO, CBE, (President of the Corporation), **The Earl of Cranbrook**, **Viscount Dunwich**, Rev Canon HCO Lanchester MA, **Col EP Clarke** DSO TD JP, **A Rose** (OF) CIE, FRGS, JP, **MJ Rendall** CMG, LL D MA JP, **GR Pocklington**, **AHF Harwood**, **HP Gaze**

(OF) M Inst CE, **The Hon AA Vanneck** MC, JD Craig CBE, **The Ven Archdeacon TR Browne** MA, **James M Martin** (OF). The Headmaster was **RW Kirkman** MA.

Members of the Society closely involved in the appeal and negotiations were **Air Marshal Sir John D'Albiac**, President, (then working for the Ministry of Civil Aviation to reconstruct London Airport), **L Mark Liell**, Treasurer, **Major JC Sheldrake**, **JH Stransom** (President 1946), **A Howard-Smith**, **Major General RD Inskip** (then living in Brandeston)

APPEAL

As is still the case, the Society of Old Framlinghamians provides a significant proportion of the Governors. The Society was therefore well aware of what was planned. So how much would it cost to buy Brandeston Hall, and how would the purchase be funded? There already existed an Old Framlinghamian War Memorial Fund, intended to support the sons of OFs who had died in the war, and to provide a war memorial in the Chapel as well as to build a new Junior House. There was enough money to support the first two objectives, with surplus funds to divert to the third. The Appeal Fund was further promoted by means of a booklet written by **John Booth** (Author of 'The First Sixty Years' – a history of Framlingham College), and published and distributed in July 1947 alongside 'The Framlinghamian'). This Revised Appeal Booklet identified the merits of the new proposals and invited further donations to the fund – the total sum of £20,000 was specified. The College Governors already had a significant bank overdraft, so the prospect of purchasing Brandeston Hall would not be possible without additional funds.

Few Former Pupils' Societies have been as generous to their

FRAMLINGHAM COLLEGE
New Buildings and War Memorial
Report and Revised Appeal

Brandeston Hall
THE NEW
JUNIOR SCHOOL

alma mater over the years as the Society of Old Framlinghamians. It was imperative that something be done to accommodate the extra numbers of pupils. The Society was not found wanting.

The SOF and Governors put out a joint statement whereby it was agreed that the War Memorial Fund should be made over to the College to reduce the overdraft and to allow the purchase of the Hall to go ahead. The Society was true to its collective word. The War Memorial Appeal continued to attract donations for some years to come and was crucial in enabling the purchase to proceed.

PURCHASE OF THE HALL

Everything was now in place to permit the purchase of the Hall: the funding was available, the sale negotiations with the vendor were complete, the War Office had declared the building surplus to requirements and the Ministry of Education had declared that it was fit for educational purposes, and that the Governors' intentions were approved.

On August 28th 1947 a local paper announced the completion of the purchase and confirmed much of the above, including the launch of the above appeal and the confidence that sufficient funds would accrue to allow the Governors to proceed with the purchase.

The report notes:
"It is strange to hear of someone buying a magnificent house for a third of its former price. The Governors of Framlingham College, in Suffolk, have bought Brandeston Hall, a beautiful 16th century Manor house. They paid £12,000 for it. In 1842, Charles Austin, one of the most eminent lawyers of his time, paid £35000 for the hall and its adjoining 26 acres of park land. An additional £8,000 will be needed to convert Brandeston Hall into the Junior School of Framlingham College"

Other interesting newspaper extracts note:
"...the proposal to build on the College 'Front' is to be regarded as withdrawn", *also*: "in response to the appeal made to the Old Boys and other friends of the College in 1946, gifts from OFs have already provided for the cost of educational assistance for the sons of Old Boys who fell in the war and for that of the erection of a memorial in the College chapel, and that funds remain in hand, or are forthcoming under covenant to be applied to the cost of new buildings."

"There is a waiting list for admission to Framlingham of nearly 400 boys from London and the Eastern Counties, many of them from Suffolk or with local associations. The purchase of Brandeston Hall means that these boys will be received at far earlier dates than could be offered if it was necessary to await the completion of a large new building at a time when constructional works are fraught with vexatious difficulty and delay."

"The Governors and the Society of Old Framlinghamians now renew the appeal they made a year ago, and they are asking for a further £20,000. This is an ambitious target, they state, but Framlingham has many friends. The acquisition of Brandeston Hall means so much for the greater future of the College that it justifies a big effort to raise the balance of the purchase price and the cost of conversion and equipment in the near future."

The vendor was Major Charles Austin (retired). The negotiated sale price was £12,000, offset by War Office payments acknowledging dilapidation, and sale of surplus huts. This meant that the nett cost was £8,178. It was as late as 15th November 1948 that the Bursar acknowledged receipt of a cheque for £3,628.2.2 as compensation from the War Office in respect of said dilapidation (Interior, exterior, outbuildings, tennis courts, lawns, flat and adjacent outbuildings, renewal of electricity, plumbing). This figure had clearly been arrived at with some difficulty: the cost of making good of the lawns was conceded with reluctance, and reduced from the original claim. The claimants were advised to settle for what was on offer. Recourse to a tribunal was not recommended.

CONVERSION OF THE HALL AND THE FIRST PUPILS

The purchase completed, all that remained to be done was to convert the building to educational use.

The alterations: were set in hand by **Colonel Hooper**, 9 Museum Street, Ipswich, the architect acting for **Knapp-Fisher**. The lists of needs by way of furniture and equipment were prepared by the Bursar working with **Sir George Elliston**, Chairman of the Governors. Just one year remained before the arrival of the first pupils. The first Headmaster, **David Kittermaster** was appointed at the end of 1947, but the date of opening had to be deferred, so he spent the intervening time teaching at the Junior School at the College, as well as providing input for the design and layout of dormitories and classrooms for his new school.

This demanding task was completed, and the first boys duly crossed the threshold in September 1948. Many of them had already started their lives at Framlingham in the Junior House, bringing

with them a certain knowledge of College traditions and procedures... others joined the school for the first time. None was prepared for the excitement of being a pioneer in a brand new school, adapted to fit the framework of a splendid country mansion, still showing much evidence of recent military occupation, or indeed of being the first to explore the exciting and adventurous possibilities of the extensive grounds, with a river flowing through.

Under the avuncular guidance of David Kittermaster the first year passed and great excitement was felt at the anticipation of the formal opening of the school by Princess Alice of Athlone, grand-daughter of Queen Victoria. This would be the culmination and the ultimate recognition of what had been achieved.

JULY 2ND 1949

This was one of the most auspicious days in the history of the College and of Brandeston Hall. **Her Royal Highness Princess Alice of Athlone** together with her husband **The Earl of Athlone** firstly unveiled the War Memorial in the College Chapel to the Old Framlinghamians and one Master who had died in the 1939-45 War. A memorial service was held at noon, and the

Top: Ann Podd presenting a bouquet to Princess Alice, July 2nd 1949. Headmaster DD Kittermaster and Mrs Kittermaster, on left.
Above: Latin inscription over entrance door.

Memorial unveiled by the Earl. **Archdeacon TR Browne** then delivered the address in the course of which he said that he could recall many of those whose names were on the Memorial as happy schoolboys, enjoying to the full all the joys and activities of their school life. He expressed the hope that boys who came to this school would be proud of those Old Framlinghamians whose names were inscribed on both War Memorials.

After lunch the royal guests drove through Framlingham to Brandeston to be greeted by Mr and Mrs Kittermaster. A bouquet was presented by Ann Podd, after which the Head Boy, **MG Wright** asked Her Royal Highness to accept a replica of the tablet to be unveiled.

Before a large audience facing the North Porch of the Hall **Sir Frank Garrett** welcomed Princess Alice. He declared that this "historic house is not just a proud possession in itself – for Brandeston Hall is a very part of Framlingham – but is the sacred memorial to all the men of the school who gave their lives in two world wars." He further recalled that "this unique War Memorial is the munificent gift of that most generous body – the Society of Old Framlinghamians, who are ever ready to give beyond their means when their school is in need."

He then called upon one of the most famous of Old Framlinghamians, **Sir John D'Albiac**, President of the SOF. Sir John expressed his pride both at the occasion and in the Society.

Clockwise from right: DD Kittermaster, Princess Alice and Mrs Kittermaster during tea on the south terrace, with the distinctively trimmed yew bushes. Princess Alice delivers the opening day speech. Part of the audience on the Front.
Facing page: Princess Alice mingling with the guests.

It was a privilege for the Society to have secured this noble house and some acres of free England in memory of the fallen. He expressed the earnest hope that "when future generations enter Brandeston School, and see before them in letters of gold the famous words 'Their Swords are in your keeping', they will spare a thought for those brave men who made the supreme sacrifice."

Princess Alice then unveiled the tablet, and made a memorable speech. She understood that in the hearts of many taking part in the ceremony there would be memories of those "young lads who spent their early carefree years here before going forth into that fierce conflict for the preservation of our beloved country from which, for many there was no returning." She was sure that "Their memory will be enshrined within these beautiful walls as a beacon to light successive generations of small boys, such as they were."

She went on to recall memories of her grandfather, Prince Albert, the Prince Consort, in whose memory the College was founded, and praised his virtues as someone who was independent of thought, and who had, through his far-sighted projects, brought much benefit.

THE COMMEMORATION TABLETS

Finally Dr MJ Rendall, Governor and scholar, spoke of the three inscriptions, one of which had been brought to the attention of the guests in the Dining Hall at the College.

The first in stone foretold a great future for Brandeston Hall and recorded pride and happiness on that memorable occasion. The second exhorted future generations to remember those brave men who made the supreme sacrifice. The third (in the vulgar tongue – ie plain English!) commemorates the great generosity of the Society of Old Framlinghamians in presenting Brandeston Hall to their old school.

CONCLUSION OF THE VISIT

The Royal party then entered the Hall and moved to the South terrace, where tea was provided, to the accompaniment of music by the Band of the Royal Marines from HMS Ganges. After further

presentations, Her Royal Highness planted a tree in the Hall garden.

'*The Framlinghamian' reporter concludes*: "So ended a day which will live for ever in the memory of those who participated in it."

RECOLLECTIONS

David Kittermaster

There were some 1,500 guests. One remembers three incidents which endeared her to us all: Princess Alice and her husband actually shared a glass of sherry at the pre-lunch Reception; at tea, on the terrace, she tossed the dregs of her cup over her shoulder into one of the yew bushes, while the Headmaster's wife hovered rather helplessly with the silver slop basin; and when a retired College master slipped and crashed down the front stairs – highly polished for the Royal Visit – Princess Alice was standing talking to the Headmaster in the Black and White Hall, at the bottom of the stairs, and she never 'batted an eyelid', or even turned round, for fear of embarrassing the poor man! A day not easily forgotten.

Michael Wright – Head Boy

The highlight of the year was the Official Opening by Princess Alice and the Earl of Athlone on 2nd July 1949. Princess Alice unveiled a memorial tablet over the porch of the main door to declare the school open and I then presented the Princess with a framed copy of the tablet. I had rehearsed with Mr Kittermaster many times what I was going to say to the Princess and afterwards he told my father that he was more nervous about the presentation than I appeared to be. After the opening ceremony I served tea to the Royal Party on the terrace at the back of the hall.

Returning to the scene 60 years later to plant a lime tree brought this all back to me.

John Edwards

I recall vividly Speech Day, 1948, with Princess Alice, The Earl of Athlone and Dr Rendall, Master of Pembroke College, Cambridge, as guests of honour. Sitting in front of the school and having Dr Rendall give his address in Latin was a bit too much for my untutored mind, and is something I will never forget.

Tony Martin, recalls the day from the point of view of an 11 year old: All who were there remember the great Opening Ceremony attended by the Earl and Countess of Athlone. I remember how hot it was, sitting on the grass as Montague Rendall, who had been Headmaster at Winchester, read the inscription on the tablet over the front door. I remember my parents and others commenting that

John Rankin remembers that Speech Day when the memorial plaque was unveiled. It was a glorious occasion. We small boys were sat on the grass and I remember dappled patterns produced by sun and trees and the extreme colour of it all. I felt great happiness when we realised how magnificent this gift was from the Old Boys, and how appropriate. Those who gave their lives could not be

Above: Staff and pupils in the customary style school photo, 1948/49.

it would have been helpful if he had also read an English translation of the Latin so that the importance of the memorial was impressed upon us. As an impressionable 11 year old, it was Dr Rendall's scarlet scholastic gown that remains most memorably in my mind. No doubt, in this immediate post-war period, the suits were probably dull and the colours sober, but I do remember Mrs Kittermaster's pretty floral frock.

brought back but at least this would enrich many other people's lives for many years to come – as it was already enriching my own. What better way indeed of remembering their ultimate sacrifice?

Following up: It was noted in the SOF Council Minutes of October 11th 1948 that "It was resolved to present to the first pupil to cross the threshold of Brandeston Hall, on the opening day, Monday 20th

September 1948, a coloured wall plaque of the Crest of the School suitably inscribed. It was further resolved also to offer him, on leaving school, a Full Life Membership of this Society. It is notified and recorded that the name of this first pupil is **PMG Stewart**, of Hill House, East Bergholt, Suffolk."

It should be noted that **RJ Blythe** was a close second – he claims to have been first into the grounds, but, alas, was not the first to have stepped across the threshold.

The role of the Society is acknowledged in a letter dated 29th Oct 1948 from the Bursar, **EG Palmer**, to Air Marshal **Sir John D'Albiac** (President of the SOF):

"The opening of Brandeston Hall as a Junior House for the College is an important milestone in the history of Framlingham. The Governors are very conscious that without the active support of the Society of Old Framlinghamians this great scheme could not have been undertaken and they wish me to express to you, and through you to the Society, their deep gratitude of all that you have done."

Later in the year on 13th July 1949, and subsequent to the official opening ceremony, the Council Meeting of the Society of Old Framlinghamians passed two significant resolutions, congratulating those primarily responsible for the successful conclusion of the project.

The first expressed "to the corporation, the Board of Governors, the Headmaster and the Headmaster of the Junior School their sincere appreciation of the dignity and form of the service and ceremonies arranged for and carried out upon the occasion of the unveiling of the 1939-45 War Memorial in the School Chapel and the dedication of Brandeston Hall as a Junior

Above: "It is notified and recorded that the name of this first pupil is PMG Stewart (below), of Hill House, East Bergholt, Suffolk." It should be noted that RJ Blythe was a close second.

School to the memory of the Fallen in War, on the 2nd July 1949".

The second resolution expressed "to the War Memorial Committee their very deep appreciation and sincere thanks for the able manner in which they have carried out their duties. In particular they desire to emphasize the very great assistance rendered by **Major General RD Inskip**, as a member of this Committee, resident at Brandeston, in carrying out the difficult and complicated task of organisation involved in the ceremonies of the unveiling of the 1939-45 War Memorial and the Dedication of Brandeston Hall on 2nd July 1949."

Footnote: Princess Alice of Athlone was the sister of Prince Charles Edward, one of Queen Victoria's youngest grandchildren. He had seemed destined for life as a minor royal. But then his grandmother sent him, as an Eton schoolboy, to fill a vacancy as Duke of Saxe-Coburg in Germany. Although this made him the owner of 13 castles, it also meant that the Kaiser required him to fight for Germany on the Eastern Front in 1914.

In the post-war years, he backed Hitler as the nation's saviour from the Bolshevik menace. When the Nazis came to power he was made Head of the Red Cross, and an envoy to Britain. He died in 1954, a year after watching, in a cinema, the coronation of his cousin, Elizabeth.

His sister, Alice, by contrast, became one of the best loved royals, while Charles Edward was effectively written out of history. All because of Grandma Victoria's decision to ensure the continuation of the family name in Coburg. Her family had dominated 19th century Europe – the Kaiser, the Tsar and the Empress Victoria were all related. The Coburg family name was changed to Windsor to avoid embarrassment when England and Germany were in conflict. A Channel 4 television broadcast on 6th December 2007 resuscitated the memory of Charles Edward, and made viewers all the more conscious, perhaps, of the vagaries of history.

From left: The reticulate diamond pattern dark bricks provide decorative relief, typical of the brickwork of this period. The Hall in 1846, the year before the fire. An illustration of the south facade looking dangerously fragile, with temporary supports. The Greenhouse, part of a range of extensive out-buildings, c1946.

THE BUILDING - INTRODUCTION

The history of the Manor goes back a thousand years, but the Lords of the Manor had no seat in Brandeston until Andrew Revett built the Hall in the mid-16th century, in the reign of Edward VI, and some 25 years after the building of Hampton Court Palace. The building, despite the ravages of the great fire in 1847, but thanks to painstaking reconstruction, displays many of the architectural features of that time.

Suffolk boasts a number of these wonderful Tudor buildings, including Seckford Hall, Christchurch Mansion, and the Moat Hall at Parham. The dominant feature is the brickwork. East Anglia was the traditional home of brickwork. Eric Sandon's book on Suffolk Houses is a valuable source of information on this subject. Suffice it to say that Brandeston Hall displays many features of the brick-building art of the time, a fashion led, perhaps, by Thomas Wolsey and exemplified by his building of Hampton Court. At Brandeston Hall note the chimney stacks, and the walls with a reticulate (diamond-shaped) pattern traced on them (see above), adding interest and character to the surface. Suffolk was clearly very much in touch with national building fashions. Thomas Wolsey and Thomas Seckford, two of the best known Suffolk figures of that age, both pursued careers in the capital. Eric Sandon (p98) describes Wolsey as a 'fashion leader' – evidence remains in Wolsey's gate in Ipswich. It almost goes without saying that building in brick was the province of the wealthy. Inevitably the passage of some four and a half centuries, together with the many changes of ownership has, in common with many of the great houses of Suffolk, led to changes. Happily, thanks to Charles Austin's reconstruction after the great fire, the central building, as befits its listed status, has remained recognisably the same as the original.

The first view of the façade as one drives in between those imposing brick pillars is an experience to remember. Handsome wrought-iron gates, set between equally handsome brick walls lead in to the North front. Now that the stone work has been cleaned up and contrasts the more with the warm tudor-style brickwork and chimneys, the first impression is all the more striking.

HISTORY OF THE BUILDING

Andrew Revett came from Monewden. When the time came to build a house for himself, as Lord of the Manor, Andrew sought no better site than the Suffolk countryside where he was bred. As a country gentleman and government official he was clearly well aware of developing architectural styles of the mid-16th century. The Hall was built, demonstrating many of the features of the Tudor age. Members of the Revett family then lived in the Hall for three hundred years.

In 1842, some three hundred years after its construction, the Manor, including the Hall, was bought by Charles Austin. He lived in London until he retired from practice in 1848. So it was that he was not in residence at the time of the great fire. In his absence he had commissioned a costly scheme of alterations and repairs. Work had been in progress for some six months and many workmen were living in the Hall. The fire broke out in a room at the East end, in the early hours of 22nd April 1847, and destroyed much of the original part of the Hall. 'The Framlinghamian' of December 1949 quoted a report from the 'Ipswich Journal' of 24th April 1947:

'Destruction of Brandeston Hall: It is with regret we have to record this week the destruction of Brandeston Hall by fire. From the inquiries instituted it appears that the calamity took place under the following circumstances. For the last six months, the Hall had been undergoing a series of expensive alterations and repairs, involving the employment of many artisans upon the works. The architect under whose directions the works proceeded was Mr JM Clark of Ipswich; the contractor, Mr Tillett, of Grundisburgh. The Hall was placed under the care of Mr Tillett, the elder, and some workmen also slept in the building. Soon after 12 o'clock on Wednesday night (Wednesday 21st April 1847), Mr Tillett was awoke by a boy occupying the same room, which was filled with smoke, and in the course of a few minutes the apartment was in flames.

The fire soon raged with such violence that the boy jumped from a window in front, about 12 feet in height, and in his fall was

considerably hurt. In the meantime Mr Tillett rushed from the room and alarmed the other inmates, and several of the workmen having left their beds, it was soon ascertained that the fire had broken out in an apartment over the drawing room, at the East end (*this is erroneous – the fire in fact broke out at the West end*). The parties without delay procured a supply of water, but this was to no avail, the fire communicating with the utmost rapidity to an elaborate wood ceiling in the library below, and it seems from that moment all hopes of saving the edifice were lost. Messengers were forwarded to Framlingham and other places for engines, but ere their arrival all further efforts were in vain. The interior was one vast body of fire; the roof soon fell in, with portions of the gables, and before 3 o'clock Brandeston was in ruins. It is stated that the fire was purely accidental. It seems that in the course of the day a fire had been kept up in a register stove in the apartment under the room in which Mr Tillett slept. When this apartment was first entered, the floor in front of the stove was discovered burnt away to the extent of two or three feet: and it is supposed that the calamity was caused by a coal having shot from the stove when nobody was present, and fallen into a crevice between the hearth stone and the rafters. It is probable, we understand, that the outer walls of the two wings may stand, but it is very questionable whether the whole will not have to be taken down and rebuilt. We are unable to state whether the hall was insured but have learned that the contractor was insured to the amount of £1,500 in the Guardian Fire Office.'

A century and a half later this still makes for instructive reading. A reminder to schools that Fire Practices need to be taken seriously.

The extent of the damage was such that the task of rebuilding was a major undertaking. When Austin retired, the work had been in hand for six months. He devoted the last 27 years of his life to the rebuilding and beautifying of the mansion. The rebuilding was completed in 1856, with only the East Wing now considered original. Charles Austin faithfully reproduced the features that had perished in the flames. His agents were instructed to buy suitable materials of the same style and period as the original building,

wherever they were to be found. One of the carved mantelpieces came from the Great White Horse, in Ipswich, some of the oak wainscotting from the High House at Campsea Ashe, and tiles from the 14th century house of the Black Friars in Ipswich which had been his childhood home. The original brickwork is still clearly visible by the front door and around the east end where the Common Room now is. Much that was ancient was matched with some that was new, and Austin lived to see restored in his house the panelled walls and coffered ceilings which had delighted the owners of the Hall for the previous 300 years.

OFFER FOR SALE AND SURVEY NOTICES IN 1946

Mid-twentieth century estate agents knew how to use words to good effect. The following description of the building was alluring. The hall was clearly a property evoking the activities and life-style of a country gentleman:

"Charmingly situated Elizabethan Country Residence, a suite of well proportioned reception rooms, Gun room, cloak room etc, Game larder, Servants' Offices, including Housekeeper's Room, Servants Hall, Butler's Pantry etc. Hand-worked luggage lift to both floors. 8 servants' bedrooms, 1 bathroom, Linen Room and 2 housemaid's sinks. All the principal rooms are handsomely panelled in oak, and contain some very beautifully carved mantels and antique fireplaces; range of stabling, consisting of loose boxes, Harness Room, range of kennels with enclosed runs and exercising yard, also a water tower from artesian bore and water softening apparatus."

The grounds "are prettily timbered in park-like surroundings and tastefully laid out in terrace and lawns, and include Flower Garden, Kitchen and Fruit Gardens, Greenhouse (above), Cucumber House and half span range of vinery and peach house."

The original asking price was £15,000 to include about 28 acres. It was noted that "There are numerous army huts about the grounds in good condition."

The 'Old' Billiard Room 1898

Brandeston Hall

Clockwise from left:
The 'Old' Billiard room (now Reception); The South Room (now the Headmaster's Study); The Drawing Room in 1898; The Billiard Room in the same year; 19th century watercolour of the Library, artist unknown – bought at auction in 2007 – now in the Headmaster's study; The White Hall; and the South Room with Mantelpiece motto, 1898.

South Room mantelpiece with motto

Drawing Room

Clockwise from left:
The current building –
Ceiling depicting
Shakespeare
and other literary
luminaries; Charles
Austin/Harriet Ingleby
motif on the ceiling above
the main staircase; Tudor
chimneys in abundance;
Library ceiling (reputedly
repainted by Heinz
Bartels, a German
prisoner during WWII);
Charles Austin initials on
chimneys; the Main
Staircase.

THE MAIN ROOMS

Most of the elements of the description of the rooms are taken from the description given to the Governors of Framlingham College when they were proposing to purchase the building in 1947. The booklet was prepared by John Booth. Of course, the building has since had to evolve, to suit its purpose as a school, and a range of purpose-built buildings required for educational purposes have been added on, but the main building remains as impressive as ever.

Entrance Hall: The principal door opens into an Entrance Hall, paved with black and white marble. In the view of the late Simon Fuller this represents an ecclesiastical theme, reflecting the view out through the front door of All Saints Church. The Entrance Hall now has a display representing the heritage of both the Hall and the College. A picture of the official opening in 1949 hangs on the left hand wall, with the Munnings painting of the Flowerdew Charge further away from the main entrance. Between them is the wooden tablet recording the dedication of the Hall. This once hung in the Dining Hall. Between these two are framed citations of the three Framlingham VCs – Flowerdew, Hewitt and Agar. Also in the entrance can be seen the fine clock presented by the SOF in memory of former Headmaster, Ron Jones (1974-1980). Strikingly, the visitor is now confronted by a fine wooden carving of an owl, whose wise features may serve to remind us of the College motto 'Studio Sapientia Crescit'. The Entrance Hall is now an eloquent reminder to Brandestonians of their heritage.

The large some-time state rooms, leading into one another on the ground floor include **the Library, the Morning Room, the South Room, the Billiard Room, the Dining Room and the Drawing Room.** All of them are oak-panelled, and five of the rooms have carved oak mantelpieces. 16th century England believed that there was nothing better than oak panelling for dining room walls. Tudor Carpenters were noted for their skill. Some of the carved stone chimney arches are 19th century work and bear the initials C.A., for Charles Austin, and H.I. for his wife, whose maiden name was Harriet Ingleby.

The Dining Room and the Billiard Room (now the Reception Area and Head's Study) look South on to the terrace. The area which was once the dining room was converted into the school library, with fine glass doors presented to the school as a centenary present by The SOF and benefactor **Roy Denby** (OF). In 2008, to enhance the facilities for receiving parents and other visitors, the library moved to the Jones Room, once known as the Morning Room.

Several doors have carved on them the prayer: Dominus misereatur mei. These are reminders of the strength of professed religious belief in Victorian England. The influence of the church and its close ties with the middle classes was so much greater in that century than in our own times, and was unashamedly proclaimed.

The Library, (currently the Staff Common Room), a magnificent room which is one of the finest features of Brandeston, extends the full depth of the house from North to South. Its windows face in one direction towards the parish church, and in the other, over the park. The ceiling is painted in red, blue and gold, and is shown with roses and mullets (5-pointed stars). A German prisoner of war, Heinz Bartels, was responsible for repainting the ceiling during the Second World War. The arms of England, Scotland, Ireland and Wales shine amid a mass of rich ornament; in the mantelpiece, carved figures and foliage are associated with panels inlaid with designs in variously coloured woods.

It was in his Library that the Lord of the Manor would receive visitors who came to see him on county business or on matters connected with the estate. (See also the interests and literary friends of Charles Austin I in the Pre-1939 chapter). As one enters the Library via the narrow corridor from the Entrance Hall, a small door, to the right, leads into the sometime Mortuary. This part of the Hall is the oldest section of the building, dating back to its Tudor origins. A lobby, between the South West side of the Library and the Morning Room contains an original spiral staircase leading to the upper floors.

A 19th century watercolour bought at auction by Mrs Paula Woolnough seems to be an architect's impression of the library. The figure is not identifiable (see p38).

The Morning Room, had as its principle feature a frieze, painted on canvas, of hunting scenes in strange exotic forests. In one the wild boar standing at bay is the subject; in another, the stag hunt; angling is a third. These interesting decorations, evidence of the pursuits of country gentlemen, were of sentimental value to the vendor and passed into the possession of Major Charles Austin. Initially a classroom, the room then became the Staff Common Room before being allotted its current function, that of School Library.

The South Room, now the Headmaster's study, was evidently designed to be used also for dining. The ceiling is adorned with

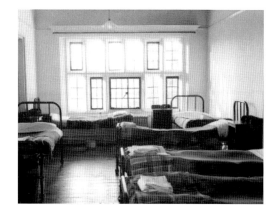

twenty four medallion portraits of historical personages, among them Geoffrey Chaucer, Edmund Spenser, William Shakespeare and John Milton. The damage to the ceiling is reputed to be the result of an overflowing tap during the time of requisition. The damaged figures cry out to be further restored – a worthwhile project for anyone interested in the restoration of this beautiful ceiling. The mantelpiece bears the words: *It is as it is.* On the wall one reads: *But through my cates** be mean,* (*archaic = foodstuffs; cf caterer), *Take them in good part, Better cheer may you have, But not with better heart.*

There is a blunt reminder to diners reminding them of man's duty to remember that God provides: *He that seteth down to mete and leteth grace pass, Seteth down like an oxe and riseth like an ass.* We cannot be sure about the pronunciation of this rhyming couplet!

The Drawing Room (now the Dining Room). The Drawing Room (over 800 square feet) was the largest room in the Hall and it was, according to the custom of the time, a room for the ladies – a withdrawing room. It is a vast room, panelled to the height of a man with square-patterned wainscot. The rose of England and the fleur-de-lys of France are repeated in the moulded plaster ceiling. Large though it was, it was not large enough to seat the whole school, so an extension was built in 1967. There are now several school Honours Boards in this room, recording the scholarships won by pupils over the years.

The Staircase, wooden, and of splendid proportions, rises up from the Entrance Hall. There is another fine painted ceiling above it: twelve of the coffers display the proud Tudor rose beneath a royal crown, and the other twelve have the initials 'C.A.' and 'H.I.' tied with a true-lover's knot. The inscription reads: 'Welcome the coming, speed the parting guest.' At the top of the stairway in 2008, an innovation: a tapestry depicting Leonardo da Vinci's 'The Last Supper'.

On the first floor there is another range of oak-

Above: The dormitories have become less spartan, and allow rather more scope for personalisation and comforts.

panelled rooms. The most important of them face South and have superb views of the grounds. In 1948 a flat was built here as a residence for the Headmaster, and the other rooms became dormitories. The 1947 description notes: "In two solars the fireplaces are lined with faience tiles, some painted in blue monochrome, others in purple. They are Dutch work of the 17th or early 18th century. Some of the most engaging of these are New Testament illustrations; others depict landscapes and the North Sea fishing fleet; in the rest the subjects are flower compositions and birds."

The Queen's Bedroom is on the first floor and used to have an exceptionally fine carved mantelpiece. There is no evidence of any Queen having sojourned here – but it sounds impressive. This became the largest dormitory, sleeping 12 boys. In 2008 it had become a fully equipped music room. The dormitories have become less spartan, and allow rather more scope for personalisation and comforts. Also on the first floor is the Kittermaster Boys' Games Room, recalling the name of the first Headmaster.

The 1948 booklet concludes: 'By skilful planning and reconstruction, and the necessary insertion of additional dormer windows, dormitories, with the necessary washing accommodation, have been provided on the second floor for 40 boys. The arrangement is, therefore, that the Headmaster, the resident Masters, the Matron and Assistant Matrons, and the 80 boarders are all accommodated in the Hall.

The permanent buildings erected by Charles Austin in the grounds immediately adjoining the Hall are being converted into five well-lit classrooms (the stable block). Temporary buildings of hut type (ex-army Nissen) in the grounds are used as additional classrooms, changing rooms (with hot and cold shower baths) and store-rooms.'

The status of the building is reflected in its present-day Grade II listed status. It is interesting to note that the Entrance Gateway to The Hall, together with the attached walling, is separately listed as Grade II, being of special architectural or historic interest.

The gardens, grounds, trees, shrubs and sports fields of Brandeston Hall are very special. Not only do they provide facilities for a full range of organised games, but they doubly offer delights to the eye and challenges to the adventurous of mind. From the visible neglect of the war years through to the more tended appearance of the 21st century, the grounds, bordered by woods, the river Deben and sundry streams or ditches, are one of the great attractions of the site. For those who spend their early schooldays there, they are part of the fabric of childhood. There can be few places better suited to the nurturing of young minds in the ways of the countryside, and to an appreciation of it. The rich agricultural history of the county of Suffolk goes hand in hand with the induction of its progeny into the ways of the land and countryside.

How many schools could boast of having had gardening lessons in their curriculum? How reassuring it is to record that in our environmentally-aware age such nature-friendly education is creeping tentatively back on to the educational agenda.

Above: A gardener manicures one of the terraces in the gardens to the west of the Hall in the 1920s. The Scrimgeours are said to have taken men off the dole to create these gardens.

A 1947 description of the 'Park' shows the attractiveness of the general prospect: "On the South side of the Hall two terraces and semi-circular flights of steps lead into the Park and towards the river Deben, which flows through it at some distance from the house. On the upper terrace is a fine magnolia tree; on the lower one are twelve ancient yew trees cut to a curious geometrical shape. The Park presents beautiful views of pasture, tree and stream which are characteristic of the landscape of East Anglia – scenery that has inspired some of the greatest of English painters. Near the Hall are pleasure grounds and flower and vegetable gardens and glass-houses, all planned on the generous scale of the Victorian era. In the tall trees North of the Hall is a rookery, one of the largest in the neighbourhood, and on sunny days in Spring the old red walls echo the cries of the birds. In the early months of 1947, when snow lay for eight weeks in the Park, they did not allow the bitter weather to deter them from their instructive task, and built two dozen nests in the highest branches of beech and pine." Many of those elements remain.

THE KITCHEN GARDEN

Like all great houses, the Hall had its own kitchen garden and orchard, together with gardeners, responsible for maintaining supplies of fruit and vegetables for the house. The kitchen garden of about an acre also had a range of glass houses, a vinery, black and white grapes, a peach house with the branches trained on wires under the roof. Cucumbers and tomatoes, among other things, were grown in the other houses. The red brick wall soaked up the sun, nurturing and ripening fruit trained along it. To this day there is fruit. The kitchen garden was kept going during the war, and this garden came with the purchase of the building. For some years it continued to be productive, providing healthy vegetables for early generations of Brandestonians. The kitchen garden supplied all the vegetables the school needed. It was where the tennis courts now are – covering about an acre. Beetroot, cabbages, leeks, salads, radishes and onions were grown for school consumption. There were also lots of apple trees, gooseberry bushes and a large bed of peas. **Mrs Kittermaster**, as Housekeeper, ordered what was needed for the week. Harvesting had to be carefully organised to have produce ready when needed. The garden was **Peter Arbon's** pride and joy – a lifetime's achievement. There was one School Inspection when the only thing which really impressed was the kitchen garden.

When the produce from the garden was no longer needed, Peter made 25 "trainee" gardens for the boys. **Mrs Podd** did the teaching. The produce was taken home. The boys learnt gardening. True to their rural roots, the boys did also help out in other unofficial capacities,

Above: Gardening classes. Learning about vegetables and 'Pride in the Patch'. **Below:** Trainee allotments.

sweeping up leaves, for instance. Their help was certainly needed as there was a shortage both of manpower and of machinery. Helpers were rewarded with carrots and apples. The gardens were lost in 1986 at the end of **Paddy Newbery's** time. As he and his wife were leaving, the diggers were in the walled garden creating the all-weather hockey/tennis area. Paddy suspects that the thinking was that the garden was not very profitable and the hard play-area was more urgently needed. It was ironic, given his own interest and involvement in hockey, that the development was being made just at the moment of his departure.

This was 'The good life' on the institutional level – Jamie Oliver, the cult chef who in the early 21st century tried to bring healthiness back into school meals, would doubtless have approved of the diet and the principle, even if some of the 'healthy' vegetables once had to be forced down unwilling gullets.

PETER ARBON

For many Brandestonians the gardens and the grounds will be permanently linked with the name of Peter Arbon, the source of so many of the anecdotes and memories gathered together in these pages. Peter was born in the village in 1927, left school at the age of 15, spent virtually the whole of his working life, some 48 years in all, maintaining the Brandeston grounds until his retirement, after which he continued to live in the village. His 80th birthday, celebrated on 14th January 2007 by villagers and former staff and pupils of Brandeston was a fitting tribute to a lifetime's dedication both to the village and the school.

Prep school Headmasters tend to be all-rounders, turning their hand to many things, including sports coaching and checking on the grounds. Groundsmen

Peter Arbon, head gardener 1956-1990, casts admiring glances at the brussels sprouts ready for picking.

like to be noticed. They also notice what is going on. For Peter Arbon the first Headmaster, DD Kittermaster, was very involved in all aspects of school life and was very much in charge. He was 'hands-on' everything from checking studs and towels to getting the pitches improved. He loved coaching cricket. Paddy Newbery was keen on hockey. Ron Jones started the golf. Nigel Johnson didn't interfere – and that probably was the most important thing for Peter. He was allowed to get on with his job.

Peter began by helping the Head Gardener, **Mr John Turner**, from Yoxford. After moving briefly to Aldeburgh, Peter returned in 1949 as Under Gardener, with Mr Turner still in charge. He was promoted to Head Gardener in 1956 and remained in that post until 1990 when he retired from full time work, but carried on part-time. On his retirement the Governors presented him with a chair and certificate plus carriage clock. Peter was not just a gardener. Above and beyond his love of the grounds, and his expertise in caring for them, he had a ready rapport with the young people in the school, and helped them to share in and appreciate his work. He was approachable, he understood young people, and they trusted him.

Peter remains a treasure chest of assorted memories, a selection of which follows:

– There were peacocks in the 60s. There were 5 or 6 peacocks, including Fred, the oldest, who was 14. They made too much noise and mess, defecating all over the terrace. They survived until 1988.

– The pupils were appreciative of the grounds. They even helped occasionally, if they could, and were mostly well mannered. Helping with tasks in the grounds was not beneath them.

– On Sundays, with only three exeats a term, most boys were around all day. No-one was allowed in the village. Dams and tree houses were built. No bikes were allowed until Richard Broad's time. Then they were allowed to go to Kettleburgh and the Post Office, but they had to sign in and out.

– Letters written by pupils from the school were checked out by the Headmaster. One boy was very hungry but didn't dare say so in an official letter, so he wrote a letter unofficially, and asked me to post it.

– Most of the villagers had work at The Hall sometime during their working lives. The owners of The Hall had moved out in 1910, and after that tenants hired the Hall on 7 year leases. The last tenant's family maintained the kitchen garden, employing labour to maintain it and sell the produce.

– One man was employed by the army during the war. He used to send his time sheet in every week. Every week was filled in with 'clipping the yew hedges and burning the trimmings'.

– Two big boilers were housed in the cellars, one for radiators, the other for hot water. The coke used to come by rail to Framlingham until the station closed in 1965. After that it came from Mansfield by road. They used to get through 70 tons of coke, plus anthracite for the aga, plus several tons of coal for all the open fires. The iron gratings are still there where the coke was discharged, the ash coming out of the same shute.

– Early days the carrier from Fram collected the laundry on Monday mornings, returning the same on Friday.

– On Sundays there was church at 10.00am. After that the boys were free and they spent their time making dams or huts made of

Left: Peacock parading.
Far left: Ground staff and team in 2008 – Ray and Tony Pike with Mike Rutterford promoting Norwich City colours.

sticks and grass. Some would make themselves useful by raking leaves – I always made sure they had plenty of fruit or carrots. I don't know how many were involved – the box was always empty.

– The kitchen garden was out of bounds until I took over, then they could get permission from the duty master to help.

– A popular pastime was sending off for farm machinery catalogues. On one occasion a lorry load of crop sprayers turned up. The boy who sent for them made sure they arrived during holiday time and didn't mention that he was at a boarding school. I looked at the driver's paper work – delivery address: Brandeston Hall – no mention of a school – he was not amused.

– The school inspectors, on one of their visits, were very impressed to think that the boys were having fresh garden produce every day.

– The domestic staff cycled in from the surrounding villages. All the Day Boys cycled in too.

MIKE RUTTERFORD

Peter Arbon is closely identified with the early years, but the traditions he established have been brought forward seamlessly to the present day. Indeed, there was a time when he and his successor, Mike Rutterford, briefly worked together, with Mike theoretically in charge. Peter did not instinctively respond to the modern concept of an 'hours' sheet, but doubtless put in many more informal hours than were measured. And for close on twenty years **Ray and Tony Pike** have been part of the team which has cared for the grounds and makes those grounds the envy of many a local school. Mike was born in Lakenheath, played cricket for the local village, and helped with the pitch. He spent three and a half years as groundsman at Emmanuel College, Cambridge, before moving to Framlingham in 1982. Mike, an unashamed Norwich City supporter, took over from

his brother, Colin, Head Groundsman and Cricket Professional at the College, conversely an enthusiastic Ipswich Town supporter. Yellow and green Norwich City posters now proliferate cheekily in the Groundsman's Office at the College. Mike assumes responsibility for both sites.

THE GAMES FIELDS

Framlingham College has enjoyed and still does enjoy a fine reputation as a games-playing school. That is not achieved without the appropriate facilities, expertise and loving attention from groundsmen. Imagine the young Brandeston fledglings arriving in 1948 and trying to develop their games skills on unkempt pasture land masquerading as games fields. The grounds had been very low priority while the army was occupying the Hall. As in every other area of activity in the late 1940s, people had to make do, and cope. It is a tribute to the devotion of those members of staff who did the coaching that those early teams still managed to emulate the proud records of achievement of their predecessors. Indeed, those immediate post-war generations went on to Framlingham to achieve many notable successes.

The top two pitches had been ploughed up during the war to grow potatoes. They were very wet, and the water was eventually drained off into the Deben. They had a horse to plough and harrow and rake the playing fields. There was no equipment. They couldn't afford a roller, so they had to bring one in from Framlingham. The College gang-mowers were sent down once a week to keep the grass in check. There was no tractor, so when David Kittermaster raised the matter at a Governors' Meeting the Earl of Stradbroke said he had just the thing and donated an old Austin 16 to do the job. It served several years until the clutch burnt out. It never got above second gear, and had to stop every ten minutes or so to take on petrol and water. A coupé, it was less than comfortable, and anyone riding in the back had an bumpy ride. Potters, at the end of the 50s, had second hand tractors at around £50. Eventually the

College bought a new tractor, so Brandeston got the old one.

In an age when many schools have been criticised for contributing to the national obesity problem by selling off sports grounds, Brandeston has gone from strength to strength. The pitches and facilities are a far cry from what was originally offered in the late 40s. There are seven full-size pitches – sometimes divided up for mini-games. It is recounted how, in one year, when the school had two very fast hockey wingers, the pitches were widened in order to maximise this advantage. In the event, not a match was won. There are two cricket pitches, together with a couple of "where-do-you-want-'em" pitches. The hard tennis courts, constructed in 1985, made a great difference. All groundsmen take great pride in their pitches. Staff who venture on to the wrong patch or who use them when unfit incur righteous wrath. Mike recalls the late **Simon Fuller** who misguidedly started a scrummaging practice on the Colts cricket square. Mike's language is not recorded, but was sturdy enough for the scrummagers to leave instantly. Early generations of Brandestonians will remember that the land leading from the terrace down to the river was pastureland. This is now all properly cared for and mown. Indeed attempts were made to construct a cricket pitch here but it was not flat enough.

The Golf Course started off as a six-green course, initiated by **Ron Jones**, who superintended the design and early lay-out. Three additional tees made it a nine-hole course. **Bill Latimer-Jones**, Assistant Bursar, took on golf coaching for a while, notably after Ron Jones' enforced retirement. The Suffolk groundsman network swung into action when further design plans were drawn up, with Peter calling in his cousin, **Lynn Arbon**, then working at Woodbridge Golf Club, to help develop the course. Brandeston now offers a fine nine-hole course, presenting various challenges. There is a small pond by the course which was dug out for the Science Department for aquatic studies, and it now serves a dual function, doubling up as a water hazard. It is linked to the river by a ditch built some 10 years ago. In the course of construction bunkers had to be dug out. This was not uneventful: on one occasion smoke started billowing behind the tractor – an old phosphorus bomb had been disturbed.

On another occasion in 2008 the Headmaster's son, searching for his ball in thick undergrowth struck a World War II bullet (see War-time – aftermath).

There are golf House Matches, and School Matches are occasionally played against the likes of Orwell Park and Old Buckenham Hall. The Cretingham professional – from the Debenside course less than a mile away, gives lessons. It is recorded that there have been two holes-in-one. **Colin Rutterford** registered the first, and Bob Williams knocked in the second some weeks later. There must have been others, as that was some 20 years ago.

Not all shots are as accurate as that: when a rough patch was cleared, a treasure trove of some 200 lost golf balls was found. It is similarly remembered how a former Master, **Stephen Player**, had his jaw broken as he unwisely found himself behind the backswing of an aspiring young female golfer.

The Brandeston pond (*above*) of the early years was a central feature, and a place of mystery. It had been the repository of all sorts of military cast-offs, including phosphorous bombs. Many memories revolve around the pond. It used to hold many fish. Some time in the early 50s hundreds of fish were found floating on the surface, victims either of dormant phosphorous bombs, or of airlessness, or of nitrates coming in off the fields. The ducks, pochard and pintail disappeared – they were incompatible with on-site dogs, or maybe allergic to the contents of their habitat.

One story, recounted by **Bob Clayton** not only tells us something of the role of the pond, but also something about ad hoc disciplinary procedures of the early days:

One of the least popular boys in the school had for some reason or other upset one of the older and larger of the old guard of boys who had previously been at the college. For his punishment the boy was hurled bodily into the pond. The matter was reported to the Headmaster (**David Kittermaster**) who dealt with the matter at Assembly on the following day by dryly pointing out to us all, and knowing that the boy in question was a well known troublemaker, that a school rule had been broken and that it was against the school rules to throw rubbish into the pond.

The pond was finally dredged by Mr Pike, Senior, in the mid-80s. His two sons still work at the Hall. More of the old phosphorous bombs were brought out. They had clearly been dumped there as the army moved out. Until recently venturous spirits were warned off by a sign proclaiming 'Danger – Deep Water'. As 'Health and Safety' concerns impacted upon the scene, in the early years of the 21st century, the pond had to be fenced off.

The 1987 hurricane – Trees. The aftermath of the hurricane belongs to folklore. From a groundsman's perspective there is the memory of some 30 trees blown over, hours of cutting up the trunks and branches – Peter Arbon had to fetch his own chain-saw, as there was none other on site. The road was blocked. One tree – a whitebeam, caused particular problems – the saw choked on a nail 20 feet up – the military had obviously nailed communication lines high up in the tree, and left the nails in when taking down the lines. Another tree with a history was a poplar tree which had been used traditionally by young Maths students to measure heights geometrically. The tree came down – they measured it – and the theoretical height was borne out by actual measurement. After the devastation caused by Dutch elm disease, a little copse of disease-resistant trees was planted. At the time of the building of the Rowley Hall one of the three was dug up, another was knocked over by machinery, leaving just one survivor.

BEYOND THE CALL OF DUTY

Groundsmen, particularly in Junior Schools, often see much more of the informal side of the pupils, and witness some of their misdemeanours.

Basil Brush was a lime tree. The top had crashed down during a gale leaving 30ft of trunk with massive suckers coming out about 10 feet. A great place for exploring. One lunch-time in the 60s 4 boys rushed into the garden to tell Peter that a young lad called **David Pritchard** was stranded up at the top and was very frightened. Peter had to get a 30 ft extension ladder and help him down, backwards.

On another occasion a young boy, suffering from severe home-sickness was spotted by Peter Arbon near the old blacksmiths, bolting into a wheat-field. Adopting the kindly approach, he put an arm round him, trying to stem the floods of tears and was escorting him back to the school in an avuncular sort of way, when the pair came across the Headmaster. He grabbed the absconder unceremoniously, muttered something on the lines of "Little Bugger" and took him back to school. Kindly groundsmen can have

an important role beyond their duties. And probably the Head knew something that Peter didn't. Whoever it was, all is now probably forgiven.

Mike remembers another young man who managed to get himself up to the waist in mud by the river. A rope had to be used to pull him out, leaving his wellies in the mud. He was hosed down – and later discovered back at the scene, constructing a path of boards, venturing out in an attempt to retrieve his wellies, and clearly worried that trouble was in store if he lost them.

AN APPRECIATION

Groundsmen and gardeners are part of the history of Brandeston. The grounds and pitches and gardens make them an integral part of Brandeston's story. The equipment is now fit-for-purpose: gang mowers, roller, greens mower, wicket mower –all that you would expect. But there is still the need for knowledge of soil, seasons and know-how. In Mike Rutterford's self-deprecating words there is still scope for "Bullshit to baffle brains" – and the passed-on groundsmanship of men rooted in Suffolk agricultural lore ensures quality of product. They are "of the stock."

Mike sees things in the 21st century as "better than ever". They have their own machinery, but also share machinery with the College. The flexibility of those who do the work is vital. You employ groundsmen, but find yourself with a carpenter and a welder on the side. No demarcation problems. Pride in the job, flexibility and versatility –these are the qualities that promote success in the job. And the job must surely have its own attractions, given that Brandeston has had but three Head Groundsmen in close on 70 years.

TREES WE HAVE LOVED (Contributed by Bob Williams)

When asked what the out-standing memories were, of their BH days, it is probably no surprise that the trigger-fast response of so many pupils of pre-late' 80s vintage is often... 'It has to be climbing Basil Brush.'

Such nostalgia takes us all back to the considerably freer and easier, although never negligent, days before the suffocating hand of Health and Safety started to spread into every corner of our daily lives. Tree-climbing is now very much a thing of the past, together with conker and snowball fights. Indeed, poor old 'BB' perished, together with 35 other very fine trees around the Brandeston estate, on the night of the Great Hurricane of 1987, but during its mature life cycle this elegant lime gave enormous pleasure, not to mention a panoramic view of whatever else was going on at the time, to generations of youngsters.

Incidentally, it is not widely known that a number of the larger oaks lost in October '87 were shipped off to Hampton Court, for use by skilled craftsmen in the restoration work there, following the serious fire of 1986.

Fierce storms were not the only threat to the Brandeston trees. I can clearly recall the occasion that **Miles Hitcham** 'fell' into one of the rather special Yew Pyramids on the Terrace. Peter Arbon, who tended these yews with particular affection was not best pleased. Neither was Ron Jones. The incident sorely tested Ron's recently enlightened stance on the place for corporal punishment within the school. The yew in question took a great deal longer (ten years) to recover than Hitcham's person! Peter confided in me recently that it wasn't the first occasion that the yews had come under threat. A not dissimilar incident, during the period of Forces' occupation during the early 1940s, involved an army Captain returning from a liquid supper at the Queen's Head, becoming increasingly irate with one of these yews at not being able to find the flap on what he firmly believed was his bell tent!

Other trees that are no longer with us and with resonance to particular generations include a trio of beech trees to the north side of the Changing Rooms, surgically removed in 1951 then, some twenty years later, the Californian Redwood that stood smack in the middle of what is now the Colts Rugby/1st Rounders pitch on the meadow. Also lost in the 1970s was the two hundred year old elm (with an impressive 23 foot girth and a measured height of 103 feet), which, once felled as deemed dangerous, gave the Stump Lawn its name – with the stump itself eventually making way for the testing short 8th hole (Rutterford's Revenge) on the developing golf course. Another old elm, situated on the westerly section of the front lawn, very nearly made national headlines on July 1st, 1949. A mere twenty-four hours before Princess Alice was to undertake the official opening of the school, and without warning, a substantial lower limb broke off, crushing a number of chairs which were already in place to accommodate the great and the good of Suffolk! The tree itself survived into the mid-60s when it was, finally, condemned. Another, more recent, casualty was the other ancient ash down by the river; a great favourite with the young who found its Tolkienesque roots a great place to sit and gossip. It was also a unique location for our less formal, annual Tutor Group photographs. In August 2005 it suddenly shed fifty percent of its bulk in dramatic style, temporarily wrecking the 7th green of the golf course. Those of us who were able to view the scene in the immediate aftermath silently offered up a prayer of thanks that its collapse had not occurred six weeks earlier, again with very possibly, tragic consequences.

Special trees were, of course, planted on various commemorative occasions. Princess Alice's Oak, which came from **Lord Stradbroke's** Henham Estate, and was planted by HRH as part of the day's ceremonial on July 2nd, 1949, suffered the indignity of having its main central growth stem eaten by one of OF **David Risk's** horses who, at the time, enjoyed grazing rights on the meadow. Hence its rather strange subsequent growth pattern. In the late 1980s **Princess Diana** and former BH Head of School, **Karen Buttenshaw** both had a sapling planted, in their respective memory, on the Front Lawn: a Subbhirtella Autumnalis winter-flowering cherry for Karen and a cedar for the Princess. The Late **Lord Belstead**, together with **Emily Morgan**, the youngest pupil on the school roll, did the honours – again on the meadow – with a tree for the Golden Jubilee in 1998, a copper beech, under which a time capsule with assorted 20th Century memorabilia was buried.

Other arboreal gifts include at the southern end of the Shrubbery Walk, three elms (sadly only one survives) given by the **Lochhead family** in the early 1990s (**Seonaid, Malcolm and Fiona**); four red horse chestnuts along the eastern boundary of the meadow, presented by the **Freer family (Alexandra and Antonia)**; an elm – Sapporo Autumn Gold – funded by the girls of Alice Hall, and planted on the front lawn, in memory of **Eleanor and George Smith's mother, Alexandra**, who sadly died of Breast Cancer in 2005. Also in 2005, the departing Australian Gap Year Students, **Stephanie Henry and Danica Vress**, left a little bit of 'Aus' behind in the shape of an entirely appropriate eucalyptus, also to be seen on the front lawn.

The row of fine oaks along the western approach, from Cretingham, continue to mature into a very fine stand of trees. The cricket bat willows, first planted in the 1960s by an OF, by name of **Watts** on the then unused piece of ground on the north bank of the river, have been harvested twice and a third planting is now well established. They have proved to be money-spinners, of benefit both to the bat-makers and to the school.

The 60th anniversary of the school was also appropriately commemorated when, in September 2008, a lime tree, donated by the Society of Old Framlinghamians, was planted by Messrs **Michael Wright** (first Head Boy) and **Peter Stewart** (first boy to cross the threshold in 1948).

Credit for the on-going care of the tree stock over a good many years, and the visionary re-planting associated with it, must go to the late **Harry Townshend**, from the Governing Body, with Peter Arbon and now Mike Rutterford and his team operating at the sharp end. We owe them all a debt of gratitude.

Top: The Croquet Ground 1898. **Middle row from left:** The Princess Alice Oak sapling and 60 years later (in front of Rowley Hall); Princess Diana's Tree. **Bottom row:** Ridge-tent shaped Yews; Michael Wright and Peter Stewart plant the 60th birthday Lime tree – gift of the SOF. **Footnote:** *Charles Austin I is reputed to have been inadvertently responsible for the naming of the Monkey Puzzle tree.*

Croquet Ground. 1898

PART 2
A BRANDESTON EDUCATION

To Educate: Origin: late Middle English: from Latin verb 'educare', related to 'educere' – to lead out

Right: Eyes down for PNY Craig's latin lesson – in an old stable block classroom

THE CLASSROOM

W ell yes, the concept of schooling does revolve around the classroom and formal teaching. Even though a Brandeston education is so much more than what happens in the classroom, we should nevertheless spend time considering how this more formal aspect of education has evolved over the years. The changes have been dramatic.

A Brandeston education does not evolve in isolation from the rest of the country. The location may be unique, but developments in curriculum, syllabuses, educational technology, examinations, teaching methods and educational attitudes are nationwide, indeed difficult to avoid. Independence does not absolve a school from conforming to a whole range of government requirements. The numbers of readers who empathise with the efficacy of the chalk-and-talk 1950s methods as demonstrated in the TV Programme "That'll teach 'em" may well be outweighed by the numbers now in sympathy with more progressive child-centred methods. Across the country the dusty black chalk board has been replaced by the inter-active white board; slide rules and log tables have given way to calculators; carpentry shops have become Design and Technology centres; Art has become multi-media; languages are no longer taught as if they were classical languages –the primary aim is to communicate; the teaching of science has had to keep pace with the great leaps forward in scientific knowledge. Anyone who had been cocooned away in a 1940s Brandeston classroom would be astounded at the transformation. Conversely, modern pupils would probably implode emotionally if they had to confront the formal rigour of 60 years ago. The purpose of this chapter is not to make value judgements, but to trace elements in the development of education over the past 60 years and to show how Brandeston responded.

ACCOMMODATION

In the late 40s lessons were taught in the old converted stable block, in rooms inside the main building, and in a variety of Nissen huts. **David Kittermaster** had the difficult task of laying the foundations of a new community. In 1974, seven years on from retirement, he contributed to a short history of the school that **Bob Williams** had been asked to put together for 'News and Views', the Journal of the Society of Assistants Teaching in Preparatory Schools.

DDK's reminiscences follow:

…Starting a new school must always produce problems – and we had plenty of those. We were in fact due to open in January 1948, but things were far from ready. Even the revised deadline for September of that year began to look a little unrealistic. A week before the boys were due to arrive there wasn't a stick of furniture in the building and it was a race against time to install the necessary beds, lockers, tables, benches, desks, etc. Seventy-five boarders and twenty-five day boys – about half of each category actually being transferred from the Junior House at the College – eventually arrived to begin a new career in a fine building, set in some twenty-six acres of ground, in a particularly attractive part of Suffolk.

At this early stage many of the facilities and amenities accepted as essential for a school were still lacking. Two small class-rooms had been created in the old stables (now the Flat 1 and Alice Hall Common Room area), but the majority of the teaching had to be done in the large ground-floor rooms of the main building (now the Staff Common Room, and Television/Hobbies Room areas). This inevitably meant that there was no space for a proper Library, very little play space for leisure hours, an inadequate Staff Room and an Assembly Hall permanently cluttered with desks! Several of the unsightly Nissen huts, a relic of the wartime occupation of the building as Army Divisional Headquarters, were put to good use as supplementary class-rooms: a Science 'Laboratory' and an Art Room. Others were pressed into use as a Tuck Shop, a Model Room and a Cricket Pavilion.

This was the utility image of Brandeston Hall in its infancy However, in the course of time, difficulties large and small were ironed out and structural improvements made life so much easier for all. Gradually the school grew into a thoroughly well-equipped

From left: Mrs Podd checks pupils' work; the 'modern' extension to the old Stables on a warm summer's day – classroom buildings in the 'chalk and blackboard' period.
Right: Today's relaxed dress code and informal teaching.

unit. In 1952 the Governors decided to increase the numbers of boys to enable the school to accept 8/9 year olds. Previously there was a lower limit of 10, while at the higher end of the scale most of the boys were 14+ at the time of their transfer to the College. With the arrival of the 8/9 year-olds the numbers increased to 130, of whom 100 were boarders, and the age of transfer to Framlingham was reduced to 13, thus conforming to the more familiar Preparatory School age range.

Major alterations to the skyline included a Gymnasium, which doubled as an Assembly Hall, in 1957; a new Changing Room – on the site of the old Army NAAFI canteen – in 1962; the draining of the Playing Fields in 1964 and, the major item of capital expenditure, a new purpose-built Classroom Block, physically joined to the Hall itself, via the Long Corridor, finally completed in 1967.

The Jubilee Block (with Art Studio and Music/Drama/Assembly Room was opened on 16th June 1978 by Lord Stradbroke, and later converted to Pre-Prep needs). A Junior Classroom Block was built and, of course, the opening of the Rowley Hall in 1997 offered greatly enhanced facilities. The Queens Room Music Centre on the first floor greatly helped the teaching of music, and the opening of Foundation House further extended the teaching facilities, with all necessary differentiation according to the needs of the various age groups.

Nigel Johnson *acknowledges the significant changes of the last 20 years:*

It was under Gwen Randall that Brandeston really prospered in terms of new and magnificent capital developments. Between 1990-95 the growth in numbers had impacted upon the teaching life at Brandeston; we were quite simply pushed for space. In 1995 I was asked to put forward a development plan that would see Brandeston achieve a new Sports Hall and, at the same time, offer a new and exciting Design and Technology Centre. The opening of the Rowley Hall in 1997 was a marvellous and exciting development, the more so since Gwen Randall agreed that it must not be simply a square box but should complement and add to the

marvellous façade of the stepped Terrace and the Hall itself. The design, created by the Messrs Hollins of Framlingham, achieved everything that we could have hoped for with a wonderful space that was used to the full to support a whole range of activities including drama, sport and music. However, it was the linked decision to change the use of the old Gymnasium to a new DT suite that was a key initiative with its mezzanine design floor and lower workshop facility. It was a teaching area that no other Prep School in Suffolk could match! The re-development of the Library in 1999, funded by the OFs, was the final piece of the jigsaw and saw Brandeston achieve facilities that any school would be proud to possess. These governorial decisions were a demonstration of a huge confidence in the Prep School and the part that it would play in the overall well-being of the College.

CURRICULUM

Over the past 60 years much has been added. Probably the most notable loss has been that of Latin, but Latin made a comeback in the 90s, albeit under a different guise, as a 'Lunch Club' (**Catherine Gassmann**). The demise of Latin led to a greatly increased profile for Science at the senior end of the school, with a triple offering of Chemistry/Physics/Biology. The sciences had been particularly disadvantaged in terms both of lesson allocation and of laboratory facilities in the early days of the school.

As in most schools, there has been no settled view on what constitutes the optimum length of a lesson. Much depends on concentration spans, which in turn may be linked to ability levels and the time of day. The requirements of the various subjects vary. Some like short sharp bursts. Others like a more settled double lesson. How many lessons are needed to fit in an ever-expanding curriculum? How much time and how many half-days should be devoted to games? Discussion will doubtless rage on, and the wheel will be invented many times over. Inspectors will continue to have an input. Fashions will change.

Of course new subjects have been introduced as the role of schools has been increasingly seen as important in the education of pupils beyond the core subjects. PHSE aims to develop understanding of personal, health and social issues. Prep school pupils are now given a taste of languages beyond the standard and traditional French lessons, thereby encouraging a broader linguistic awareness.

As fewer linguistic demands are made on pupils at senior school level, so do our educational experts, by way of compensation, increasingly propound the view that pupils are more linguistically receptive in the early years.

One of the big issues in recent years has been that of Saturday lessons. It has long been considered important to keep boarders fully occupied, and that is done through the seven-day ethos. However, with an ever higher proportion of day pupils, Saturday school has come under increasing pressure.

By 2009 only Years 7 and 8 attended Saturday school, and that by way of a transition to senior school patterns of work.

Government initiatives, the near-exponential growth of knowledge, the demands of the work-place, the challenges of modern life, concerns of parents – all will continue to produce pressure on an evolving curriculum.

Above: The opening of the Jubilee Block in 1978 by Lord Stradbroke, with Headmasters Laurie Rimmer and Ron Jones, and Roger Paul – Chairman of Governors. Below: A period photo showing the new building.

EXAMS

In the late 40s there was an entrance exam to the College, which ran in parallel to the 11+ intake who were sponsored by Local Education Authorities. Such 11+ entrants could then also take the College Scholarship exam. For many years it was assumed that Brandeston pupils would move on to the College – that indeed was the concept behind having a Junior House. It had long been taken as understood that Framlingham, and by association, Brandeston, did not attach exclusive importance to academic entrance exams, but that all-round potential was sufficient, and that perfectly worthwhile citizens could be forged from young people who might struggle academically. College Heads have had varying views about this. Sometimes it has been felt that the academic status of the College would be boosted by a more overtly demanding entrance examination. At other times the view has prevailed that the College should have a broad intake, and that its greatest achievement over the years has been its ability to provide value-added education for students of all abilities.

A significant change occurred in Nigel Johnson's time, when it was decided to move from the College Entrance Exam to the Common Entrance Exam. This meant that Brandeston pupils could be prepared for entry to any independent school. While maintaining the close link to the College, it also conferred a degree of independence on Brandeston in that it could take on pupils who were not necessarily destined to move on to the Senior School. The majority do, however, still move on to the College.

AGE RANGE

In 1948 the Junior House catered only for the 10-13 age group, and all were boys. In 1952 the range was extended downwards to 8 and 9 year-olds. In 1976/7 it was agreed that Brandeston and Framlingham should be co-educational establishments. Many boys' independent schools already accepted girls in the sixth form, but both Framlingham and Brandeston took the bold decision to go completely co-educational. The pre-Prep was added, and finally Foundation House, thereby offering a primary education spanning the 10 years from 3-13, boys and girls, all on the same site, but separately accommodated. This is the Brandeston of 2009, a school now almost two thirds the size of its parent, and a microcosmic reflection of it.

SCHOOL DRESS

In the 1940s (boys only!) the only school-wear was the grey herring-bone uniform, to be worn all day. Casual wear was unheard of: the grey suit was discarded to be replaced only by sports clothes or pyjamas at bedtime. As society has become less formal, so too have school uniforms. Suits, particularly for young boys are no longer considered compatible with their age and energetic behaviour, not even in a formal classroom situation. Maroon blazers were Summer-wear, with matching maroon caps, both emblazoned with the school crest. The current light blue polo shirts and crested navy over-garments are much more comfortable and fit for purpose.

Girls: Again an evolution from the 70s through to present day. Initially they wore the same blazers as the boys with white shirts and tie and grey skirts – with the option of a "ghastly" green pullover. (Gingham dresses for the Summer Term). Thereafter there were a variety of changes (seemingly initiated by each succeeding Master's wife!): Open neck white blouses in Summer.. Rather smart grey blazers for girls only... Plaid Kilts were introduced (by **Judi Johnson**) and so onwards to the present day with both boys and girls wearing the same light blue polo tops and crested navy blue pullovers, with the girls having attractive tartan skirts. School clothes are definitely more comfortable, more attractive – and all due allowance is made for those times when young people prefer to relax and be casual. Formal occasions do still call for dressing up: white shirts and ties are worn by both boys and girls and the fleece is the outer layer rather than a blazer.

Above: Extending the age range downwards. The Headmaster, Martin Myers-Allen and staff with some of the youngest pupils.

SANCTIONS AND REWARDS

60 years ago sanctions ruled. Punishments were more evident than rewards. Corporal punishment lurked, and was accepted as a natural hazard by those contemplating misbehaviour.

David Summers, *now living in Australia, offered his reflexions on late-1940s discipline:* "I was not a good or well-behaved student, but, although I tried

the patience of many in authority I did learn life skills which have sustained me throughout my life. Tolerance was one I learned from Mr Kittermaster. He could 'slipper' me one day, and be out giving me extra bowling coaching for the 1st XI the next."

A good performance in the fortnightly orders, the approval of teachers, plus an encouraging report and the outside possibility of winning a prize on Speech Day were incentive enough to try hard and do well. The repetitive writing out of Lines was a common sanction through to the mid-70s or, perhaps copying out the first Chapter of Genesis.

The Plus and Minus System was effectively a rolled-up conduct-and-work weekly total and it instantly reflected positive or negative all-round performance. A very poor performance resulted in a traditional Detention. The 'conduct' aspect was eventually dropped early in Nigel Johnson's time, and since then +/- has only reflected progress in academic and related subjects. A 'Ringed' Plus or Minus reflects extremes of achievement/abject lack of effort... sloppiness). Nigel Johnson also instigated a Head's Detention (in a pupil's weekend free time) for major transgressions or cumulative anti-social behaviour.

Above: Mr 'Doody' Day imparting skills in chisel sharpening during a carpentry lesson c1949.

The approach to discipline in 2009 can be summed up in the philosophy that where possible teachers try to reward children for doing the right thing rather than punishing for wrong-doing. *The rewards include:*

1. Plusses for good work and Bronze, Silver and Gold Awards – Gold also gets a £5 voucher. Platinum Cup for pupils with most plusses in each year group

2. Merits in Reception to Year 5 for good behaviour – various rewards and badges and certificates.

3. Good Citizenship Cups and £5 voucher awarded termly to Years 6, 7 and 8 – chosen by staff.

Sanctions range from 'a quiet word', to removal of free time, minuses for poor work, one hour detentions, all-day Sunday 'Master's detentions – and then, horror of horrors, suspension through to exclusion.

The above all apply, of course, both inside and outside the classroom. Does it all work? Are children better behaved or better motivated as a result of evolving attitudes? Now there is a debate in itself.

ACCESS TO KNOWLEDGE

This has expanded exponentially over 60 years. In the 1940/50s Prep School the human voice, plus chalk, and text books with minimal illustrations were the only resource – teachers were almost the sole repository of knowledge.

In 1948 there was no television, certainly no television programmes made specially for schools, no videos, no cassettes, no tape recorders. There were schools' radio programmes but little hope of recording them: the lesson had to coincide with the broadcast. There were no photocopiers, no handouts. Good note-taking was a pre-requisite for a good student. Plus concentration. And good hand-writing, as there was no word-processing facility to disguise bad hand-writing, and no spell checker either.

The world of almost total knowledge is now accessible via libraries and the internet. 60 years ago libraries were poorly stocked, often with dusty, musty, unattractive-looking, outdated books. Knowledge itself was not attractively packaged. The stimulus to interest was the human factor, generated either by the enthusiasm of the teacher or by fear and respect instilled by him/her. Things have indeed changed. Access to the internet puts the world of information at a student's finger-tips, and it is all visually enhanced by illustration. Libraries stock attractively presented volumes designed to appeal to young children, rather than dowdy volumes, considered to be edifying. The décor is a welcoming one.

In the first decade of the 21st century there are few areas of knowledge that are inaccessible to the enthusiastic student.

INSPECTIONS/ASSESSMENT

Education in the immediate post-war period seems almost amateur when set alongside more recent government-led developments in the field of education: regular external inspections, not only of teaching but also of pastoral arrangements, regular pupil assessments, on-going teacher appraisal, observed lessons, target-setting, league tables. 60 years ago there were few Heads of Department meetings as no-one

seemed to be aware of the concept of Departments – just a range of teachers teaching a range of basic subjects in their own individual ways. It is unlikely that there was much subject liaison between Brandeston and the College. Maybe the 1940s were subject to more rigorous scrutiny than pupils at that time imagined, but the memory can only record fortnightly orders, end-of-term reports, all in diverse, more or less legible hand-writing, with eccentric potential, and no noticeable external interference. It is a matter of personal opinion as to the extent which things have improved as a consequence of such initiatives.

PARENTAL INVOLVEMENT

Changes in this respect have been massive. 60 years ago parents delivered their offspring to the school, trusting the professionals to get on with the business of educating and disciplining. It would have seemed impertinent, and an intrusion to have interfered with the process. Teachers were, for many parents, rather intimidating. To question their judgement would have been unthinkable. Parental involvement was welcomed with the annual Fathers' cricket match – see picture of **Rodney Crabtree** and his father – but little else.

Education today is much more of a partnership between schools and parents. Parents like to be directly involved. Communications are more frequent. Part of the family's social life is tied in with school activities. Parent-Teacher Associations abound, even though a balance has to be struck between parental involvement and unwarranted parental interference. At Brandeston there are now regular Parents Meetings – these emanated in the mid '80s from the vision of **Nick Stafford** – (See Chapter on Parents' perspective). For a school like Brandeston which prides itself on its happy family atmosphere such changes can only have been beneficial. The years between 3-13 are the years in the course of which young children are gradually weaned away from total family dependence to the point where they are flexing their fledgling wings. Parents and teachers between them manage that transition.

Above: Rodney Crabtree and his father, an Essex cricketer, tossing a coin in the 1951 Fathers' cricket match.

A PLACE FOR THE ARTS

Suffolk has not always been viewed as a county of culture. In the mid-twentieth century there were few art exhibitions, few concerts, no great opportunities for theatre. Culture rather passed by the population at large. The same applied to many schools. There were musical and dramatic productions, enthusiastically undertaken by a determined minority, but generally schools concentrated on traditional classroom subjects and sport. In assessing the changes of the last fifty years, consider three factors:

Firstly the impact made by Benjamin Britten, the Aldeburgh Festival and the development of Snape Maltings. The ripple effects have spread far beyond the county. Similarly The Wolsey Theatre, both initially, and in its reincarnation as the New Wolsey, together

Above: This photo was taken in the Brandeston Hall grounds when the very first IAPS course was in residence. It shows (from left) Richard Broad, Headmaster; Arthur Harrison, Founding Chairman of IAPS Orchestra; Lord Britten, (its first Patron); and Robin Wilson (see p100), for 15 years Administrator of IAPS Music Courses.

with open air productions, and peripatetic theatre companies have brought theatre to a wider Suffolk audience. Cultural experiences are now much more readily and more widely accessible than they were.

Secondly we must note the ways in which schools have evolved, particularly in their ambitions to produce all-round excellence, and to provide opportunities for children to shine across an increasingly broad curriculum. Music, theatre and art now play a far greater role than they did. It is expected that a good school will not only provide these opportunities, but also achieve a level of performance capable of persuading parents that their offspring are involved in something more than a brave but slightly embarrassing attempt at amateur entertainment.

Finally we must remember how independent schools have

Below: Rachel Kittermaster at a music rehearsal.
Right: A 21st century rehearsal.

benefited from the fact that most of them are now mixed. All-male orchestras, and all-male theatre productions were restricted in what they could perform. Male pupils would understandably shrink from taking on female roles. Singing was usually limited to rumbustious renderings of house songs. Membership of the chapel choir was for a few brave masculine souls. The bringing in of female artistic talents has resulted in an impressive extension of repertoire and improvement in performances. We cannot now imagine artistic life without them.

1. MUSICAL MOMENTS – research by Bob Williams

All three factors have contributed to the development of music and theatre at Brandeston. Perhaps one of the most important developments was the advent of the IAPS (Independent Association of Preparatory Schools) Snape Concerts at Snape Maltings Concert Hall. It was agreed that each July, these young musicians, from across the UK should be accommodated at Brandeston Hall for a full week while they were preparing for the concerts. Benjamin Britten visited the school as Patron of the concerts.

The Trust came to Brandeston for 20 years. Orchestra numbers then reached such a size that there was no longer a single rehearsal room large enough to accommodate them. Those residential courses made an impact. Participants did not just rehearse. There were visits to Saxtead Mill, Framlingham Castle, and picnic teas on Aldeburgh Beach. Those days were not without memorable anecdotes. Back at the Hall, one bemused townee visitor, on asking a Brandeston master "Where is the swimming pool, sir?" was advised to "Turn left past the peacocks." Another Brandeston Master, on hearing the popping of champagne corks on the final night was heard to

expostulate: "I knew they would shoot those damn kids before the week was out."

The IAPS orchestra stayed at Brandeston from 1972 to 1991, and then relocated to St Felix, after the 21st Anniversary Concert had been held in London at the Barbican. The link was of considerable significance for Brandeston music.

MUSIC OVER THE YEARS

Directors of Music over the years have all made their mark in different ways. What follows is a summary attempt to chart the development of musicians and performances over the 60 years of Brandeston's existence as a school.

Music is taught to whole classes and to individuals. The author remembers sitting on an uncomfortable bench and being introduced by **Eric Copperwheat** to the robust strains of Wagner's 'The Ride of the Valkyries'. Looking back, it would be easy to dismiss whole-class music lessons as making a limited impact, particularly if they are curriculum's attempt to add a little bit of unexamined cultural polish to the compulsory core subjects. Brandeston music, as with many schools, was, in the early days, polarised between the special occasions, the concerts which impacted on the whole school, and the performances of individuals with special talents and interests. In the 40s and 50s music-making was a relatively esoteric interest, often lamentably under-appreciated by the school at large. **Rachel Kittermaster** and **Marjorie Gillett** from the College, were sensitive teachers to those prepared to learn. **Geoffrey Bland** was one of those who remembers his music-making with affection, and endorses some of the points above:

I remember my time at Brandeston (from 1949 to 1951) with some affection. I was encouraged to pursue my more artistic interests. It was there that I continued my early piano lessons as well as learning to play the recorder and starting the cello. Mr. and Mrs. Kittermaster were central to this and I do not recall any teasing or unpleasant remarks from other boys, although I do remember feeling embarrassment at their reactions to Mr. Kittermaster's attempts to interest them in Tchaikovsky. Thanks to an uncle who had introduced me to "classical" music many years before, I already loved it and wanted to listen to it - but they seemed to feel that it was unmanly and did their best to disrupt all the music periods.

The Kittermasters made it possible for me to go to my very first live orchestral concert. Mrs. Kittermaster played the flute in the local amateur orchestra and we were invited to go along to one of the orchestra's annual concerts in Ipswich. Even now I can remember that the soloist on that occasion was the pianist Peter Katin and the guest conductor was a very young Colin Davis. We sat just behind the conductor's rostrum and I well remember his exaggerated wincing at some of the deliberate discords in the Malcolm Arnold dances that the orchestra played. Anyway, the whole thing was an absolute revelation to me. In the days before hi-fi I had had no idea that an orchestra could sound so sumptuous. I have never forgotten the experience and I shall be forever grateful for it.

Music was a minority interest in those days. This was partly the fault of the syllabus and of music teachers generally for whom the only music worthy of academic attention was classical music. Only in more recent times has the broader appeal of music – from rock and pop bands to songs from the shows and music from the movies – been acknowledged and encouraged in schools. Crossing over between the genres has become common place and the ability of music to capture the attention of young people and to channel their energies is recognised in the broadening of the musical syllabus, as in the wider participation of pupils. Nor does the choice have to be made between sport and music. It is not only possible to do both, but actively encouraged as part of an all-round education.

We referred above to the influence of Snape, Aldeburgh and Benjamin Britten on the perception of Suffolk Music, and on the provision of cultural opportunities within the county. Both Framlingham and Brandeston benefited from that connection. Participation brought not only wider recognition of the possibilities of music but also wider involvement of pupils.

A choral tradition was established early when the Brandeston Choir combined with the College Choir to deliver a joint Carol Service at St Michael's, Framlingham, on December 12th, 1948. **Alan Hall** was pivotal in this. From the earliest years he, and then

Eric Copperwheat, looked after the musical interests of both the College and Brandeston Hall. Performances within the community, more often than not a joint undertaking with the College Choir, have always served to keep the school within the public eye. Brandeston youngsters thus had the opportunity to perform in some imposing venues across East Anglia; the first such mentioned in records appears to be a Festival Evensong in Bury St Edmunds Cathedral, in 1953.

In 1958 Benjamin Britten's 'Noye's Fludde', the Chester Miracle Play, was premiered in Orford Church. At the composer's request, Framlingham College supplied and trained the recorder players and four "property men." In 1970 the College and Brandeston combined to re-stage this work under the direction of **Bob Gillett**. The recorders were trained by **Marjorie Gillett**. Costumes were made by parents of boys both at the College and at Brandeston.

Brandeston, under the supervision of **Bob Williams**, also produced the animal masks. Bob recalls his welcome to the school in the Summer Term 1970 from **Graham Ireland**, (working with Bob Gillett on the production): "By the way, you won't mind making 50 animal masks for our production of Noye's Fludde in two months time, will you?" Bob proceeded to spend most evenings, for weeks, churning them out, and still has colour slides of members of the cast wearing them, taken in situ on the terrace. Such are the extra-curricular demands made on ever-willing Heads of the Art Department. **Penny Jarvis** was Wardrobe Mistress for the production.

Roger Radice was appointed Brandeston Hall Director of Music in 1959 to be followed, in 1963, by **Graham Ireland** who enjoyed a particularly fruitful relationship with the then College Director, **Deryck Cox**. Graham very quickly made his mark. In his very first year a blockbuster performance of Bach's 'St John Passion', in St Michael's, (the first big joint Framlingham College/Brandeston Hall choral production) received acclaim. ...'A moving and exacting work with Brandeston choristers producing a confident treble line'. That same year, six senior choristers were invited to join the College Choir, for the landmark College Centenary Concert, in the new Athlone Hall. Back at Brandeston, the introduction of instrumental accompaniment to the hymns at Morning Assembly was very much welcomed. By 1968 this orchestral group could even boast a euphonium! The Cox/Ireland years continued to deliver well performed choral works: 'The Messiah', Fauré's 'Requiem' (1965 and 1969, including a performance in Swaffham Parish Church), another 'St John Passion' (Framlingham College/Brandeston Hall and St Felix Combined Choirs), 'St Nicolas' (Brandeston Hall providing the

Left: Robed chapel choir with Malcolm Russell, Director of Music 1971-1978.
Below: Mellow tints of brickwork and stringed instruments. 1995 – with Martyn Lane, Director of Music, centre.

Left: A disciplined early years singing lesson (sound track sadly unavailable). **Right:** Rob Rogers in the hi-tech music room 2008.

Gallery Choir, at St. Michael's), Bach's 'Christmas Oratorio', 'Noyes's Fludde' as referred to above and Haydn's 'Creation'.

Malcolm Russell, Director of Music 1971-1978, operated both a Chapel and a School Choir. In his first year Britten's 'Golden Vanity' was performed at Brandeston Hall and the Chapel Choir were kept busy, singing with the College choristers at both the Aldeburgh and Wangford Festivals, in Ely Cathedral, and in three performances of Honegger's symphonic psalm 'King David', – at St Michael's, Bury Cathedral and Blythburgh. The following year saw the combined voices of four schools (Framlingham College/Brandeston Hall/St Felix and Thomas Mills) come together for another 'St John Passion'. In 1974, an exciting new work, by Tony Hewitt-Jones – 'Edmund, King and Martyr', was performed in Bury Cathedral with Peter Pears and Merlyn Channon. Over the remainder of the decade there followed another couple of Framlingham College/Brandeston Hall 'Messiahs' and Purcell's 'King Arthur'. Malcolm adds the comment: *I suspect that my forays into progressive music education, "Musique concrète", may have shocked parents on several occasions with some avant-garde offerings – the most shattering being Harrison Birtwhistle's " Mark of the Goat" coupled with Tony Lawrence's take on the Tolpuddle Martyrs!*

The **John Green** (appointed Framlingham College Director of Music in 1980)/**Andrew Bushell** years were again noted for the variety of music-making and the dual furrow ploughed by the combined choirs: An Evensong at Peterborough Cathedral, a memorable 'Last Night of the Proms', in the Athlone Hall, the Brandeston Chapel Choir's performance of Britten's 'Missa Brevis' and a rendering of the 'Messiah', with the added ingredient of the extra female voices from Felixstowe College. John recalls the rather

poignant occasion on Good Friday, 2005, when the Brandeston Hall Choir sang the Ripieno part in Bach's 'St. Matthew Passion' at Snape Maltings, the very last occasion that Peter Pears attended a concert there. He died three days later. Participation in the Prep Schools' Orchestra Festival at Uppingham, in 1989, was another 'first'. The breadth achieved over this period was aptly underlined at John's final Brandeston End of Term Concert, Christmas 1990, when the programme featured 1st and 2nd School Orchestra, a Wind Band, Recorder Consort, String Duets/Trios and the full Chapel Choir. Through the '80s and '90s, credit for the emergence of an increasingly confident Wind Band lay, initially, with **Andrew Cronin** and, thereafter, with **Ian Bauers**. Also in a supporting role was the tireless **Laurie Griffiths** who devoted nearly two decades to nurturing the 'green shoots' of talent among the ranks of those doing battle with stringed instruments.

The early '90s saw Brandeston under the tutelage of **Martyn Lane** aided, in their specialities, by **John le Grove** (himself a former Brandeston Hall pupil) and Ian Bauers. 'Noye's Fludde' was performed in the College Chapel with **Michael Vipond** as the more than convincing voice of God! John's Recorder Consort performed, with distinction, in the Suffolk Music Festival and Ian masterminded two very successful Prep Schools' 'Wind Days' at the College, working under the baton of Calum Gray and members of his Band of the 1st Battalion, the Princess of Wales Regiment.

From 1995 the tireless endeavours of the **Rob Rogers** (first incarnation)/**le Grove/Bauers** triumvirate continued to bring out the best in Brandeston Hall youngsters in all musical disciplines:

A contribution to Mozart's 'Requiem Mass' and 'Carmina Burana' and, in 1997, a celebration concert with orchestras, bands

Left: Martyn Lane and the chapel choir 1992/93.
Above: Recorder group 1966.

and choirs, in the spanking new Rowley Hall, featured no less than 130 musicians from Brandeston and Framlingham. That same year saw no fewer than eight Recital Evenings in the Queen's Room. While all were greatly saddened by the departure of Rob Rogers, in 2000, news of the return of the prodigal, in September 2007, this time to take sovereign charge of musical affairs at Brandeston Hall, was heralded with 'sounding trumpets' – and the rest! Rob produced the items performed by the Brandeston singers at the Old Framlinghamians' Suffolk Supper on September 20th 2008, celebrating Brandeston's 60th birthday.

Others holding Departmental responsibility, albeit rather briefly, at interim points between 1978 and 2005 have been **Malcolm Foster**, **Caroline Atherton**, **Alison Reed** and **Claire Gower**.

The parallel paths of Music and Drama have been a strong feature of the Brandeston Hall cultural scene since the 1960 **Dennis Earley/Roger Radice** production of 'The Pirates of Penzance'. Major musical presentations are listed in the Drama review. Suffice to say that Framlingham College/Brandeston Hall Directors of Music, together with their sectional assistants, have always pulled out all the stops in ensuring the success of each and every one.

Not to be forgotten, over the years, is the veritable army of peripatetic teachers who have put in countless hours on individual tuition. Former pupils from the earliest days, who benefited from **Marjorie Gillett's** patient instruction on piano and recorder, will be astonished to learn that she was still teaching Brandeston Hall youngsters in 1990, although by then, only by private arrangement at home. Similarly, many pupils reached a high standard on the piano, recorder and flute under the tutelage of **Rachel Kittermaster**. In more recent times **David Strauss** deserves a long-service medal for his thirty years of patient instruction on the piano.

While the base of the musical pyramid has, for most of sixty years, been broad there have, of course, been outstanding individual performers, both instrumentalist and chorister. In June 1958, **David List's** inclusion (at the tender age of 12) in the Orchestra, for the World Premiere of Benjamin Britten's 'Noye's Fludde' was something of a coup.

Marjorie Gillett's renowned College Recorder group were also involved in their first, Aldeburgh Festival performance, at Orford and again, with David, in Southwark Cathedral, in the November of that year. A steady trickle of musically talented youngsters have earned themselves a place on the annual IAPS Training Orchestra Course but **Peter MacFarlane** was, in July 1977, the first Brandeston Hall pupil to audition successfully for a place on the IAPS National Symphony Orchestra Course: a week's residential summer course concluding, by tradition, with a public concert at Snape Maltings. Peter now plays the fiddle for an American group called 'Atlantic Crossing' who have, so far issued four albums of largely traditional New England music.

Following in Peter's footsteps have been **Tim Griffiths**, in 1986, **Ben Potter**, on bassoon, in 1993 and 1994, **Lisa Cooper**, also in 1993 and **Jeanine Thorpe** who also had two years, 1999 and 2000, in the Symphony Orchestra, as a 1st Violin. Ben, in his time at Brandeston Hall, also played for the Colchester Youth Chamber Orchestra and, in September 1994, won a place at the Guildhall School of Music. Lisa, who took up the French Horn at the age of 10, also played with the National Youth Orchestra of Great Britain and her subsequent professional career has seen her playing with three different orchestras in Germany, most importantly, as

Right: September 2007 – Chantal Clelland, Laura Wright and Christina Johnson at the 30th anniversary supper, celebrating the admisson of girls to Brandeston and Framlingham.
Below: Charlie Simpson at Brandeston in the '90s, later became lead guitarist with the boy band 'Busted'.

principal horn with the Nurnberg Symphonie. Jeanine, who must rank as the most outstanding instrumentalist to have passed through Brandeston Hall in its sixty year history; gave a stunning series of performances over a number of termly school concerts, always very well received by an appreciative audience. She subsequently became the youngest ever musician to perform a solo in St Martins in the Field, Trafalgar Square, and is engaged in carving out a professional career. Honourable mention should also go to flautist **Roberta Organ** who was offered a place on the IAPS Easter Band Course in 2000 and to another strings exponent, **Dide Siemmond**, who left Brandeston Hall on a Music Scholarship, to Woodbridge. She too, is also establishing a name for herself as a concert soloist around East Anglia. As the 2007-08 Academic Year draws to a close it is heartening to learn that the base of the pyramid is yet broader. Under Rob Rogers' new period of tenure, 57% of pupils are currently receiving instruction on at least one instrument.

On the choral front names that might resonate are **Malcolm Thomas**, thanked in July 1965 for his… 'many solos sung in Church'; **Charles Blackmore** singing the part of the boy Nicolas, at St Michael's, in 1968; **Simon Brunger** who, by the time he left as Head Chorister in 1969, had devoted thirteen terms to the choir; **Ian Ellerby**, in the role of Amahl in Menotti's 'Amahl and the Night Visitors'(an augmented production at the College); **Andrew Twite**, invited to perform as the boy soloist in the 1986 Aldeburgh Festival production of 'Albert Herring'; in 1997 **Matthew Sheeran** was another invitee to sing the treble role in 'St Nicolas', with the Phoenix Singers, in St Michael's, repeating this, in Orford, twelve months later. He then took the role of Sem in the Aldeburgh Millennium Production of 'Noye's Fludde', performed in St Peter

and St Paul, Aldeburgh. Not forgetting the kudos earned by **Dominic Ross** in successfully carrying off the demanding part of the boy Oliver in Tony Lawrence's musical production of the same name in 1999. The 'big players' of recent years though, have to be **Chantal Clelland**, at Brandeston Hall in the late 1990s and possessing a seriously good voice – and **Laura Wright**. Laura, who came to Brandeston Hall in the early years of this new century, went on to develop her singing at the College and was acclaimed BBC Radio 2 Chorister of the Year in 2005. She somehow managed to juggle her considerable school commitments at Framlingham (She was Head of School in 2007-08) with an established performing/recording career as a member of the Classical Group 'All Angels'. In September, 2007 both girls, together with **Christina Johnson**, contributed to a superb evening of musical and dramatic entertainment at the College, to celebrate the 30th anniversary of the admission of girls to Framlingham and Brandeston.

An important footnote, stressing diversification amongst Brandeston's fledgling musicians, is to mention **Charlie Simpson**. At Brandeston Hall in the '90s, he 'made it big' in the world of Popular Music, as lead guitar with the boy band 'Busted'... and is still in the (rather more specialist) limelight with his current group 'Fightstar'.

In summary let us recall the words of John Tavener in a recent television interview. He described Music as both a mysterious language and a wonderful channel of communication. A long succession of Directors of Music and other dedicated music staff at Brandeston would most certainly agree with that. And there are many Brandestonians who have benefited from the talents and enthusiasm of these teachers, developing their own talents, carrying them forward to the wider world, and continuing to derive pleasure from playing and listening to music.

2. SIXTY YEARS OF DRAMA – research by Bob Williams

A full list of dramatic productions at Brandeston would give some idea of their range and scope over the years. The mind boggles at the number of teacher-hours, rehearsal hours, costume-making hours, stage-management hours involved – to say nothing of panics, first night nerves, forgotten lines, parental pride, exhaustion, exhilaration, and ultimately, the sense of achievement instilled into so many over the years.

Dennis Earley's 'Pirates of Penzance' in 1960 was the first large-scale production on a whole-school basis. Until then house and form plays had been the norm. Major dramatic Productions since then have included Shakespeare, various musicals, Gilbert and Sullivan, stage versions of children's classics and home-written productions. Titles have ranged from 'The Pirates of Penzance', 'Trial by Jury', 'Toad of Toad Hall', 'Beowolf', 'Alice in Wonderland', 'Hansel and Gretel', 'Peter Pan', 'Contest for a Kingdom', 'The Thwarting of Baron Bolligrew', 'The Hobbit', 'Jungle Book', 'The Wizard of Oz', 'Joseph and his amazing Technicolour Dreamcoat', 'The Dream of Chief Crazy Horse', 'The Tempest', 'Macbeth', 'The Pied Piper of Hamelin' and 'Charlie and the Chocolate Factory' – to make just a few mentions from an extensive repertoire.

Producers over the years have included **Denis Earley, Roger Radice, Philip Tushingham, Ian West, John Haslam, John Richards, Will Garnett, Tony Lawrence, Michael Vipond, Janet Blatchly, Dominique Thomas, Eileen Barclay, Jim Bidwell, John Green, Nigel Cox, Stephen Player, Alison Millington, Nick Prowse, Ruth Barnes, Gill Roberts, Chris Parker, Claire Goodin, Mary Proctor and Fiona Brooks.**

Music Directors have included **Roger Radice, Graham Ireland, Malcolm Russell, Malcolm Foster, Andrew Bushell, Alison Reed, Ian Bauers, Colin Virr, Claire Gower and Rob Rogers.**

Performing venues have included the Old Gymnasium, the Rowley Hall, All Saints Church, under canvas, al fresco and the original Athlone Hall, at Framlingham.

Brandeston pupils have also been invited to provide a chorus line of young voices, in the Athlone Hall for major College productions: 'Noye's Fludde' (1970 and 1992) 'Joseph and his Amazing Technicolour Dreamcoat' (1981 and 1994), 'Smike' (1982), 'Oliver' (1986 and 1997) and 'Annie' (1990).

We can but offer a passing mention of key contributors over the years. Dennis Earley was obviously a definitive figure in the 1950s and '60s. Both he and **John Richards**, in the early '70s, demonstrated their obvious enthusiasm for the development of school drama in

that they actually wrote a number of plays for this age group. World Premieres at Brandeston, indeed! Dennis Earley's 'No Shaking on The Home Front', written initially as a Form Play, was performed in 1958 at the then annual Festival of School Plays hosted by the American School at USAF Bentwaters. **Nigel Cox**, in the late 80s and more recently **Stephen Player** were also gifted in the art of production/direction. Interestingly enough, both were responsible for memorable productions of 'Peter Pan', performed ten years apart. Nigel's 1989 production (as a musical) tested the capacity of the old Gymnasium/Assembly Hall to the very limit while Steve, in 2000, very boldly decided that, with the Athlone Hall at his disposal, the cast should, quite literally have the floor. The audience were on stage and under the balcony, with a magnificent pirate ship and a multi-storey 'Neverland' bridging the gap 'stage left and stage right'. In 1989 audiences greatly enjoyed **Caroline Donoghue** as Peter and **Karen Cooper** as Wendy with **Mike Vipond**, himself a drama 'nut' – also with a string of Brandeston productions to his credit, doubling as a splendid and sinister Captain Hook and Mr Darling. In 2000 Steve used no less than sixty youngsters with **Piers Colby** playing Peter, **Colette Hamilton** Wendy and Drama Scholar of the Year, **Josh Price**, certainly living up to his billing as a fearsome Hook. Again, a grave injustice not to mention a string of impressive starring roles by other budding thespians, over the decades, but lack of space prohibits this.

TONY LAWRENCE – Services to Drama at Brandeston Hall and the College over four decades

It was singularly fortunate that **Tony Lawrence**, the now long-serving Pastoral Deputy Head at Framlingham, chose to accept an appointment, back in 1974, as Head of English at Brandeston Hall. His exploits in the field of drama production at the College are legendary. Never one to shrink from taking on the challenge of a difficult play ('Equus' 2001 and 'Hamlet' 2003) and his choreography of so many memorable block-buster musicals, on wonderfully inventive stage sets, live long in the memory. 'Cabaret', 'Oliver', 'Jesus Christ Superstar', 'Joseph'… and the spectacular 'Les Miserables.', to celebrate the re-launching of the magnificent Headmaster Porter Theatre in December, 2006, to name but a few. What those on the youthful side of thirty may not appreciate is the fact that he cut his producer's teeth on some memorable dramatic presentations with the very much younger Brandeston age-group. One such play which made a very real impact at the time was 'The

Clockwise from right:
Dennis Earley's 1958
production of 'No Shaking
on the Home Front'
performed at the USAF
Bentwaters Schools Drama
Festival;
'Contest for a Kingdom'
1973, seated in front row
from left, André
Rosenberg, Michael
Stewart and Jeremy Wade;
'The Thwarting of Baron
Bolligrew' – Tony
Lawrence's 1977
production;
'Noye's Fludde' (Speech
Day 1970) – The BH cast
of masked animals, in the
old gallery of the Athlone
Hall, awaiting their cue;
The 1971 cast of John
Richard's production of
'The Thwarting of Baron
Bolligrew' – Guy Jenkinson
as the Baron (5th from
left, middle row), Ian
Willett as the Lord Mayor
(6th from left, middle row)
and James Denny as the
Storyteller 2nd from left,
front row).

Clockwise from left: Charles O'Neill playing 'Henry V' (2007); Florence Elson as Juliet in the Summer Shakespeare Spectacular (2007); 'Dracula – the Musical' (2008); Nigel Cox's 'Beowulf' with David Tickler and Floris Pietzch.

Dream of Chief Crazy Horse', performed in March 1978. Bob Williams unearthed a rather yellowing typewritten review that he was asked to provide, at very short notice, by the Editor of The Framlinghamian who was anxious to go to Press with the Spring Term edition of the magazine!

'The Dream of Chief Crazy Horse'...
'To write a clear-headed critique of any play within twenty minutes of its final performance is perhaps not ideal, but, the printer waits for no man, so I make no apologies for what may seem like a piece written while its author is still on Cloud 9!

The play, by David Pownall, has a powerful theme, although it does suffer from a certain weakness in the basic script. It has a story-line which has, often with gross inaccuracies, been the mainstay of Hollywood for half a century. Here we were seeing the truth played out as the vivid dream of a long-deceased indigenous Indian chief.

The events portrayed on stage as a series of sketches were essentially the watershed moments in the history of the Inca, Aztec and North American Indian. These dramatic thumbnail sketches gave fair scope for some sixty boys and girls to act out 10,000 years of American history. Of the many supporting roles those that particularly caught the eye were **Richard Busby**, portraying a suitably bustling Cortes; **Toby Davies**' amusing French Real Estate Agent, doing his best to sell Louisiana at a knock-down price because of the inconvenient presence of the Natchez and Choctaws as squatters (on what they believed to be their own land); **Mark Newson** and **Patrick Ripley** as the most righteously indignant of the numerous highly painted Indian chiefs, with **Angus Hancock** making an equally strong yet regal impact as the grossly wronged Sitting Bull. **Jonathan Sears** made an understandably sad buffalo while **Jules Arthur** and **Guy King** struck a glittering note as Montezuma and Atualpa, both managing to convey the inevitability of their impending fate.

The play of course hinged on the roles of Chief Crazy Horse – **Jeremy Morris** and General George Crook – **Thomas Carpenter** who, for one and a quarter hours, act as narrators and interpreters of the action. Both grew in stature with each performance and, for Tuesday's finale reached the sort of peak that one rarely sees in Prep School Drama. Tom again demonstrated that he can, apparently effortlessly, sustain a chosen accent for the duration of a performance while Jeremy, dressed in the most magnificent buffalo-hide outfit, turned in the performance of his young lifetime. Not merely word-perfect but, with exactly the right blend of pride, pathos and despair,

he succeeded in convincing us that Crazy Horse was in our midst as a very real person. He would seem set to follow his grandfather into a Stage career.

A great many people put in the hours to make this very colourful production possible. The Wardrobe and Make-up personnel carried a particularly heavy load and the results were spectacular. Finally, without a Producer there would be no play. Tony Lawrence painstakingly built some rather ordinary bits into an impressive whole and, in the process, succeeded in turning what seemed, on a first reading, a rather static play into a fluid and pleasurable experience. He insists that he is no choreographer. I would disagree. After the first performance chants of "hena waci" and the sounds of tribal dancing were heard around the dormitories late into the night; a sure sign that this play had captured the imagination of its young audience.'

Thirty years on, it activates memories of a wonderful evening, which left those fortunate enough to be present, marvelling at the standard of stage-work that 11-13 year-olds can achieve. It also serves as a timely reminder of the considerable reputation that the College, and its Junior School, have long enjoyed with stage productions. For that, since the mid '70s, much of the credit must go to **Tony Lawrence**.

Since 2004 there have been a number of Year Six Shakespearean evenings of Dance/Drama, often 'en plein air', staged in the final weeks of the Summer Term. Production was initially in the hands of **Mary Proctor**; thereafter **Chris Parker** and **Claire Goodin**.

The 2007 production took place on and around the terrace. Chris Parker produced an outdoor Shakespeare performance, not one play, but a series of tableaux and speeches from different plays, played by various actors at various points around the terrace area. The best of Shakespeare was made accessible – not dumbed down, but enjoyed in the original, both by performers and spectators, in a beautiful setting on a Summer's evening, In an age when Shakespeare is often perceived as too demanding, it was wonderful to see and hear producer and actors taking on a challenge, and emerging triumphant. Learning Shakespearean language by heart, and declaiming it, understanding it, and acting it out at such a tender age? Yes, a triumph, and instructive to those who would eradicate Shakespeare from the curriculum on the grounds of difficulty.

The dramatic arts are in good shape at Brandeston, reputations further enhanced by the 2008 production, of 'Dracula, the Musical', another World Premiere, written and conceived on site. Let the shows go on, and may young talent continue to thrive and develop.

3. AN ART ROOM FOCUS

From the very start, in 1948, responsibility for imparting both graphic skills and an appreciation of artistic heritage was in the hands of **Alan 'Oink' Manthorp**; this was an extension of his primary role at the College. Art classes took place in an old Nissen hut.

Mansell Beard took on the Manthorp mantle in 1962. From 1967 he had the distinction of working in Brandeston's first, purpose-built Art Room, a fine, well-lit room at the western extremity of the first floor of the new Teaching Block There was still but a single period of Art timetabled for all pupils. **Richard Broad** decided that this did not do justice to either pupils or the spanking new Art Room, so the weekly 'double' was introduced that persists to this day. It was during his Headship that the framed prints in the dining hall were replaced by boys' own works and this was also the period when the Annual Art and Craft Exhibitions became a regular feature in the year's calendar of events.

The Teaching Block facility served the needs of the pupils well until 1978, when the construction of the Jubilee Block allowed for a much improved specialist area, again at first floor level. This was designed as an Art Studio and separate Pottery with a glazed dividing wall. **Bob Williams,** appointed in 1970 as successor to Mansell, had the pleasure of working approximately half his weekly timetable in both these Art Studios. The move to the current nerve centre of artistic happenings, a conversion of the two former Year 5 classrooms at the western extremity of the old gym, coincided with his retirement in 2001, since which time **Tim Walsh,**

Top: Bruce Pearson – at Brandeston in the early '60s – with the print presented to the School.
Above: Bob Williams – 31 years teaching at Brandeston Hall – Art being one of his subjects.

briefly from 2001-03 and, thereafter, **Chris Lenton** have presided as Heads of Department. The advent of Art/CDT Scholarships, in 1990 gave both gravitas to, and impetus within, the Department.

The outstanding 'product' over the first couple of decades has to be **Bruce Pearson**, at Brandeston in the early '60s. Indeed, to this day, the school has yet to see his equal.

In my (**Bob Williams**) *humble opinion, his output as a professional artist (let alone as ecologist, author, photographer and film-maker) puts him firmly on a par with The College's other, rather better-known OF painter of an earlier generation,* **Alfred Munnings***; in fact, superior in his interpretation of birdlife – although I know that Bruce would happily concede that he doesn't match Munnings where horse-flesh is concerned!*

Bob's reminiscences continue: Over my particular 31 year sojourn I had the satisfaction of being able to work with an enormous variety of fledgling talent. Harking back to the '70s, names that immediately spring to mind are **Simon Cowell** – remembered for his fine ceramics – **Simon Pemberton, Michael Green, Simon Turner, Andrew Thornton** – his flair for ornithological subject matter suggested another budding **Bruce Pearson**, and **Darren McLagan** – now a busy and successful cabinet maker/designer. **Paul Broad**, despite the fact that he left us early, showed the promise that took him all the way to the Slade and is now Head of Faculty of Creative Arts at the Grange School, Warmley, and was the winner of the Wild and Wild Prize, at the South Bank Picture Show, at the Royal Festival Hall, in 1998.

Charles Machin-Goodall, even at age 12, was readily soaking up elements of Art History and, whenever our paths cross, still enthuses about the best of the Norwich School! **Philip Allwood** was another in whom important seeds must have taken root. It was he who gave credence to the belief that a small oil 'self-portrait' found in a dark corner of a Cotswold cottage in 2007, might well be a Rembrandt. In his professional capacity as an auctioneer, he then knocked it down for a cool £2.2M, the highest sum ever paid for a painting at auction outside London. (To Philip's chagrin, a number of experts did indeed later confirm that it was a work by the great master and valued it at a cool £20M!)

And, of course, the name **Jonathan 'Soapy' Campbell** has a permanent place in the pages of Brandeston Hall Art Room history, for triggering the 'Humphrey Revolution' that endured for generations. Those who experienced it are unlikely to forget it – and, hopefully, the fun it engendered!

High profile pupils of the '80s included two multi-talented pupils who produced some memorable graphic cartoon work - **Giles Smallcombe** and **Graeme Jones** - whose subsequent career has led her into theatre set design. All-rounders **John Coates** and **Robin Dunlop**, now a successful free-lance designer, also made their mark and there were wonderfully creative ceramics from **Guy Chalkley, Mark Young** and **Michael Dempsey**. Over the closing years of the decade **Helen Robinson** and **Suzy McEwan** were head-to-head in producing quality artwork through their Years 6-8. Suzy was, in fact, the very first recipient of a designated Art Scholarship on moving to the College.

Through the '90s annual exhibitions featured the work of a further tranche of talented youngsters: **James Reeve** was another who had both a cartoonist's eye for a humorous situation and a drawing ability well in advance of his years. **Emily Sato** and

Top: Philip Allwood – astute auctioneer, grounded in the Brandeston Art Room. **Above:** 'And this is Susannah, our Head Girl' – by Graeme Jones.

Beatriz LaMadrid - from Japan and Spain, respectively; both had a wonderful feel for any given graphic materials as, indeed, did **Sarah Johnson, Rosemary Moore-Moffatt, Sarah Gallagher, Kimberley Hamilton** and **Nick Cundy. Hazel Flack** had a well-developed sense of design which in later years led her to focus on the production of exciting 3-D pieces in papier mâché. **Alex Alabaster**, whose father was a local sculptor of note and **James Parkinson** were both Art Room devotees who particularly enjoyed working in 3-dimensions.

Into the new century, 2001 proved a vintage year with the likes of **Ben Hayes, Thomas Colville**, following in the footsteps of his almost equally talented brother **Richard,** and **Rosie Lawrence**, a gifted practitioner in all media, setting the seal on their years of productivity in the Brandeston Art Room and providing a stamp of real quality to the annual exhibition. **Tim Walsh** would be delighted to learn that **Edward Sheeran** has recently registered an A* (100%!) in his GCSE Art.

A school Art Room can provide a refreshing escape from things 'strictly academic'; some can also be accused of being isolationist. Hopefully, not so at Brandeston Hall. In spite of being somewhat out on a limb there are regular visits to important galleries and exhibitions – we have even exhibited our own work in some: The Crome Gallery, Norwich, an IAPS show in the Cathedral and a SATIPS exhibition at Austin Reeds in Regent Street, London!

Locally, we tried to ensure that senior pupils could see the best of what was on offer at Christchurch Mansion, Ipswich and, often linked to London Day, The National Gallery and both Tates Britain and Modern were built into the itinerary, as was, in 1999, the Monet blockbuster at the Royal Academy.

A couple of visits, in 2000/1 to the Henry Moore Foundation, at Much Hadham also proved inspirational. A visit to the Dali Gallery, on the South Bank, in 2007 made a predictable impact on Year 8.

4. POETRY PLEASE

Developing native language skills, a love of good books and a strong encouragement to push one's own personal creative writing boundaries, whether in prose or verse, has always been given a high profile within the English Department. An Annual Book Week, targeting all ages, has been a feature of the Autumn Term for a good many years. This has often included the involvement of a guest author which always makes for greater impact. **Kevin Crossley-Holland** (in 1987) and **Gervase Phinn** (2001) left a particularly deep impression. Unconnected with Book Week, but equally memorable, was **David Kossoff's** visit in 1988. The Christmas Term edition of the 'Framlinghamian' carried **Nigel Cox's** report on a quite remarkable experience:

"Think of absolutely nothing"… It was an unusual instruction for the school to receive at the end of a busy week of lessons, but we closed our eyes and emptied our minds as David Kossoff talked staff and pupils alike back to the very beginning of time. The hush in the crowded room was a testimony to his skill as Mr Kossoff settled back into an armchair and held his audience spellbound with his re-telling of part of the Book of Genesis and the tale of Tobias and the Angel from the Apocrypha. The humour with which Mr Kossoff handled his material and his absolute control over the children made for a memorable morning. We were allowed the occasional wriggle and even were encouraged to shout our names for Tobias' dog but a raised hand restored total calm and order. In the period before lunch everyone who wanted to was able to buy a copy of Mr Kossoff's "Bible Stories" and so great was the demand that another box-load of signed copies had to be

Christmas Joy

The audience, chilled from the frosty night
Fumbled into the stuffy hall.
Silver stars clung;
Tinsel was drooped around the crammed room.
They sat, not knowing what to expect
From a group of children wearing old curtains
And tinsel round their heads.
The hall grew warmer,
A light beamed on to a home-made crib.
A cloth was draped over Jesus' worn face.
Backstage everyone was excited.
Except me.
Hot and clammy, I sat in a corner... ...
Waiting for my turn.
I was pushed on to the stage
And blinded.
My angel's costume was crumpled;
My face was numb.
I could see the Headmaster
Lounging in his plastic chair.
He gave a smile,
Urging me to speak.
One eye gave a friendly wink.
It was Christmas.

Helen Robinson

Above: Helen Robinson with her poem at Cadbury's National Poetry Competition in 1990.

delivered at a later date! These books have formed the backbone of the boarders' night-time reading ever since.

The morning was memorable for everyone who experienced it. The children were impressed by Mr Kossoff's charisma and were thrilled to have met a famous personality, whilst, for the staff, who sometimes despair of having to compete with the television, it was a unique demonstration of the appeal of live entertainment and the power of the spoken word'.

The English Department manage to persuade the young to work, in verse format, in an un-selfconscious and seemingly effortless manner. Back in 1989, a day spent with **Paul Berry** (the very first 'Writer in Residence' linked to the Autumn Book Week) at the long-deserted USAF bomber base at Thorpe Abbotts, resulted in an astonishing folio of published work ('The Stars are Falling') by **Mike Vipond's** Year 7 pupils. The standard of work achieved is underlined by the fact that, in 1988 at age 13, **David Tickler** and **James Jennings** had entries accepted for the Observer National Children's Poetry Competition. Again, in 1990, **Helen Robinson** and **Emma Davies** were successful (from a submitted entry of 50,000!) in having poems selected for the Cadbury's National Poetry Competition, for inclusion both in the touring exhibition and the printed anthology: 'Cadbury's Eighth Book of Children's Poetry'.

Helen's poem will have to serve as just one example of the quality of work produced over the years by budding Brandeston poets. There is a freshness about the language used by children which more than compensates for their relative lack of experience of life. Or perhaps it is that very innocence which imbues their work with freshness.

SPORT – A VIEW FROM THE GRANDSTAND

Brandeston has a rich sporting history. Its sporting heritage could almost fill a book by itself. What follows in this book is a general overview. We have tried to pick out individual and team highlights, but, inevitably much has had to be omitted. We have had to limit ourselves to a number of so-called major sports, omitting such sports as boxing, swimming, boys' tennis, rounders, equestrian sports, triathlon, sailing, table tennis, golf and billiards. A supplement is available, on request from the author, which covers these additional sports. In this present book we do our best to distil out the Brandeston sporting ethos, the ways in which sport has evolved over the past 60 years, and the key achievements of its teams and pupils over that time.

PHILOSOPHY – SPORT IN EDUCATION

Neither Framlingham College nor Brandeston Hall has ever subscribed to the theory that competitive sport inflicts terminal psychological damage to those who fail to win. Brandeston has, throughout its history, believed in the challenges of competition, both collectively, for its teams, and for its individuals. Sport, with its triumphs and disasters, its hopes and its disappointments, is part of an educational preparation for the ups and downs of life. It can develop confidence in the emerging but brittle, adolescent physical and psychological self, bringing a sense of achievement, not necessarily limited to winning. Happily, for those who, in varying degrees, dislike sport, there is now a wide choice of alternatives, a whole range of activities offering an education parallel to that of the classroom. In an age obsessed with healthy eating, and the avoidance of obesity, sport has an important role to play, not only in encouraging health and fitness, but also in encouraging such habits for life. It goes almost without saying that sport generates friendships.

COMPETITION AND ACHIEVEMENT

Brandeston has traditionally pitched its sports teams into a wider competitive arena. Not only are there matches against school teams within reasonable travelling distance, but increasingly, teams participate in county, regional and national competitions. The school regularly takes part in Hockey, Netball and Tennis Tournaments and Athletic meetings. Over the 60 years of Brandeston's history there have been many notable successes both of teams and of individuals, at all levels of competition. Former pupils have gone on to represent county, region and country.

COACHES

Coaching has become more professional over the years. In the mid-20th century virtually everyone involved in the life of a boarding school, including the Headmaster, was expected to help with sport. Most afternoons were devoted to sport, and sport was not a time-tabled part of the curriculum. It was more by way of relaxation after classes. The coaches, teachers all, were largely amateurs, often enthusiastic practitioners of the various sports, but rarely with any qualification for coaching them beyond their own experience, enthusiasm and enjoyment of the game. That in no way diminished the quality either of the input or of the results. Indeed **Richard Overend** recalls that it was the sight of David Kittermaster conducting a slip-fielding practice which led to his father deciding that Brandeston was the school for him.

In more recent years appointments have increasingly been made which put appropriately qualified PE staff in charge of organising sports, even if part of their remit still lies in directing the more amateur energies of their colleagues. **Carlos Reynell**, the first Director of Sport, has been in this position for 10 Years, succeeding **David Brook** who briefly took over from **Robin Sampson**, now Second Master. Courses are organised for coaches, not least to ensure that health and safety issues in sport are not overlooked. Sport is now more formally part of the curriculum. Expectations are higher. Demanding standards are set, not only for those aspiring to representative honours, but also by the challenges of inter-school rivalries. Schools do their best to extract maximum publicity advantage from success in the sporting arena. It is part of their sales pitch. It makes for good sound bites on Speech Day. Coaches are under pressure, not only to achieve results, but also, happily, to continue to ensure appropriate standards of behaviour, not always observable in professional sportsmen and women. That is the dual role of the teacher-coach.

One of the great frustrations of school sports coaches is that they have to hand over their teams to someone else. Success is short-lived, and dependent on the quality of each annual intake. Over the years, however, the quality of young sportsmen and women moving mostly on to Framlingham College has been extremely high, and the College is fortunate indeed to have such a

themselves complain very often about this.

To endorse the wider horizons of Brandeston's sporting ambitions, and looking ahead to the London Olympics of 2012, we should recall the Olympic fund-raising efforts of the school in 1984 when they participated in the all-England run and were rewarded for their efforts by a visit from **John H Stracey**, the boxer.

SPORT IN THE CURRICULUM

In the early years of the school, which was then all-boys with a limited age range of 10-13, sport was just an assumed afternoon activity. Now that a 10 year age span has to be catered for, with both boys and girls, sport has to be more tightly scheduled and it has a more formal place in the curriculum. Not all age groups can play the same major sports in the same term – the use of facilities would not allow this. What follows is a brief summary of games played at Brandeston over a period of 60 years – very much a deepening, broadening and extension of the sporting programme available.

BOYS' GAMES

Rugby: For the greater part of Brandeston's first quarter century, Association Football was the flagship winter sport. The difficulties of putting together a sufficiently cohesive Rugby XV, over the final three weeks of the Autumn Term and the first month or so of The Easter Term, with all the attendant weather problems that the 'pre-global warming' winter months often brought, placed limitations on the development of the sport. A short fixture list, against local Prep Schools which followed the same pattern, left Brandeston with narrow horizons. The report, in the school magazine for the Spring Term,1970, that...'*the 1st XV have, at last, managed to play its first match in three years*' may well have been the final straw. Thus, as from September 1972, the concept of one term each for senior Rugby and Hockey (Autumn and Spring, respectively) was tried for a couple of seasons. It was not until November 1980 that soccer finally bowed out at U13 level.

Thus, in the early years, there was not a great deal to shout about, in terms of competitive results. The philosophy was to pass boys on to the College who were coached in the basics of the game

'nursery', giving so many young and talented people the coaching foundations necessary to progress further.

Equally important is the instillation of that initial enthusiasm. It is a mark of the impact made by sports coaches that considerable numbers of young people remember their coaches better than they remember their classroom teachers. Conversely, from the teaching/coaching point of view, it is a wonderful way of getting to know young protégés 'in the round'.

OPPONENTS

In the early days of the school, fixtures were limited to schools easily accessible by coach. Away matches were particularly difficult as travellers were prone to travel sickness in ancient vehicles on bendy roads. Major opponents included St Edmund's School, Kesgrave, recently converted into a Milsoms Hotel and Restaurant establishment, Eversley, just outside Southwold, and now part of St Felix School, Culford, Orwell Park and Greshams. With better roads, better communications and the spreading of county, regional and national competitions, teams and individuals have had to travel ever further. Regular opponents now include Orwell Park, Barnardiston Hall, Old Buckenham Hall, Holmwood House, The Abbey School Woodbridge, Felsted, Littlegarth, Amberfield, Taverham Hall, Culford, Greshams, Norwich School, Thomas Mills and Town Close.

Not only are there more opponents, but one has to fit in Cup competitions, and also realise that sport is just one part of a crowded curriculum which has to reconcile the conflicting claims of enthusiastic Directors of Music and Directors of Drama, to say nothing of those who regret the incursions made into the classroom curriculum by the timings of sports events. Not that the pupils

and could handle a rugby ball with confidence and, even better, run with it at speed!

John Capon's 1951-52 team, completing a 5-fixture season unbeaten, was considered outstanding. Their capacity for hard and resolute tackling was confirmed in the season's statistics of only 8 pts 'against'/124 'for'.

The 1981/2 season with its 100% record of 7/7 for a very determined team, under the captaincy of **Mark Ledwards**, brought much joy to coach **Mike Vipond's** heart! **Marcos Mayhew's** team of 1990-91 proved to be another particularly effective unit, losing only 2/14, featuring as it did a rare win over Felsted. The late 90s saw Brandeston teams playing some memorable rugby. The 1996-97 XV, under **Simon Stacpoole's** canny captaincy, proved an unstoppable juggernaut, winning a straight 12/12 and, in the process, notched up the first-ever defeat of Gresham's, at U13 level. The 43-3 winning margin, on a foreign field, is forever etched deep in the team coach's memory. **Richard Daykin**, usually the most laid back of individuals rather 'lost it' that particular afternoon – and **Nigel Johnson** was fulsome in his praise for all concerned. A key member of the '96 team was **Chris Read**, at number 8, who went to captain a highly successful College XV and earn himself an England U.18 Trial in 2001-02.

Two seasons later it was the turn of **Charles Davidson's** XV to compete and entertain. This they did in style (442 pts 'for' to 100 'against') in a 14-match season. **Mark Stacpoole**, the openside flanker, and **Sam Mitchell**, at outside centre, notched up fifty tries between them. Ampleforth, St.Olave's (Yorkshire), Gt Houghton (Northants) and Witham Hall (Lincs) are among the schools that have entertained the school on 1st XV and Colts tours in recent

Top: Early rugby team – CJ Capon, captain.
Above: Rugby team 1996 with Simon Stacpoole as Captain. Chris Read – middle row, far right.

years. Rugby Sevens (Spring Term) was reintroduced for top rugby players in 2006. We finally acknowledge recent achievements of some emerging stars of the 21st Century. During the 2006 season 1st XV Captain, **Ryan Clarke**, was invited to join Northampton Saints Player Development Academy. Over the course of 2007/8 Sports Scholars **William Owen**, **Matthew Warren** and **Jack Scott** were named for the Leicester Tigers England Elite Player Development Group with a further invitation extended to these three boys, together with **Jack Pearson** (also a Sports Scholar), all members of the 2007-08 XV, to participate in a first ever Barbarians Preparatory Schools match, hosted at Harrow. This promotion provided an opportunity for talented players from across the South of England, to participate in a celebration of schoolboy rugby. One has the firm impression that, with the 60th season completed, rugby football at Brandeston Hall is in very good order.

Association Football: History records that the very first school match contested, in any discipline, was with the round leather ball: Away to Felixstowe Old House. Having established a tidy 2-0 lead Brandeston Hall apparently had to settle for a 2-2 Draw! **Michael Wright's** soccer XI was even more successful on its Home debut: a 4-0 win over St Felix, with **Bernard Woolley** scoring all four goals. Michael, operating at Centre Half (as was the then designation) was 'clearly the best player in the side'.

By the start of the 1950-51 season a full fixture programme was in place and a record of only two defeats in 16 matches played (by

1st and U.12 XIs) was the cause for some satisfaction. **Brian Parker** was considered to be 'easily the best footballer seen this term, either at this school or any other, being equally influential in both attack and defence'. The 1952-53 1st XI achieved even greater heights. **Andrew Wright**... 'a doughty defender' led his team to an unblemished 10/10 match record which included a 13-0 Away win at Orwell Park, no less! **Michael Spencer**, with an aggregate 43 goals to his credit, together with the Captain's 'they shall not pass' approach at the back were largely responsible for what must surely be the best 'stats' ever) for a Brandeston Hall premier soccer team. (79 scored/9 conceded).

We entered the 60s in good order with **Peter White's** 1961-62 XI completing a seven match season unbeaten largely on account of **David Smith's** haul of 24 goals out of a total of 34. By the following season, David was himself 1st team captain and described as having... 'a cannonball shot and highly dangerous with his head'. A combination of his nose for goal, and **Arthur Thomson's** agility between the posts, produced figures of 41 'Goals For' to 2 'Goals Against' in an eight match unbeaten sequence. The School XI of 1967-68 is best remembered for the performance of a youthful **David Carr**.
Playing for the 1st team at the age of 10, he more than justified his place in the team - 'his intelligence and forethought on the field of play is remarkable; you have only to watch his eyes to see how he constantly reads the game'. By the 1969-70 season David was a veteran of the team, although **Simon Bloomfield** was 1st XI captain. 58 Goals For to 8 Goals Against was impressive, although the figures were somewhat inflated by the 16-0 Home win over Nowton Court! Only Orwell Park stood between an unbeaten

Top: Guy Goddard – mascot at Carrow Road. **Centre:** Justin Osborne, Jonathan Gooderham and Jules Arthur have their hands on Ipswich Town's 1978 FA Cup, with Simon Whittley and David Handley.
Above: 1977 Colts Soccer – Simon Newson (Capt).

season for both soccer and cricket XIs.

The soccer fixture list came under threat from the perceived need to improve both rugby and hockey standards in line with the best interests of the College.

Thus **David Hunter's** team of 1970-71 were the last to offer a full fixture list until the winter of 1974-75 at which point senior Soccer was re-introduced for a further half a dozen seasons. The 'phoenix arose' rather effectively in the Autumn of 1974 when a well balanced side, employing very effective, old fashioned wing-play and captained by **Tim Smart** (played 8, won 7 with one match drawn), went on record as the last Brandeston Hall 1st XI to complete a season undefeated. The satisfaction of 61 Goals For to 5 Goals Against still burns bright in the memory of team coaches **Tony Lawrence** and **Bob Williams**! Such heights were never reached again, but it was **Stephen Mansfield**, a consummate 'mid-field general', who had the honour of captaining the XI in its final, 1980-81 season and, indeed, contributing to the 6-3 score-line, to see off Orwell Park – always resilient opponents, in the very last official contest, on home soil.

Thereafter soccer had to come to terms with a gradual retrenchment. For another seven years the Colts continued to engage in a full programme of XI-a-side fixtures over the first half of the Autumn Term then, they too, were drawn into the 'one term rugby/one hockey' structure. From 1988 until the early '90s it was left to an U10 'A' and 'B' VII to do battle with round ball. By 1994 it was just the U9s who were engaged in a mini-soccer programme – and who provided good spectator value with their 'total football'. **Henry Johnstone's** tidy little 1997-98 unit was the only one to bring home the silverware

from both the Orwell Park (7-a-side) and Moreton Hall (5-a-side) Tournaments in the same season but, undoubtedly, the most talented of these junior squads was the 1996-97 team, unbeaten throughout (but unable to contest the Moreton event) including, as it did **Tom Usher**, **Ben Davies**, **Ali Cameron**, **Graham Sweetman** and **John Wybar**; names that continued to resonate in the Brandeston and Framlingham sporting lexicon for the ensuing nine years.

Some of the best entertainment over the 'soccer years' was undoubtedly served up at the 6-a-side Tournament, an integral part of the East Anglian Prep Schools Festival of Sport, hosted by Holmwood House, annually, for 29 years from 1971. From a start list of twenty-four senior teams Brandeston Hall battled through to the Semi-Finals on more than half-a dozen occasions but sadly never quite making the Final. The closest was in the Semi-Finals of 1974 and 1979, decided only on the dreaded 'penalties'; King's, Ely getting the better of **Tim Smart's** VI in 1974 and, in 1979, **Simon Newson's** excellent VI losing out having taken Forest School (perennial winners of the event) right to the wire with a 1-1 scoreline. Honourable mention should also go to **Jeremy Kemp** who played for three consecutive years for the 'A' VI and as team captain in 1973 (another S-F exit). A marvellous day's competition invariably ended with a few tears, such was the level of commitment!

Remarkable indeed is the number of Brandestonians who have been chosen as mascots for East Anglian football clubs, mostly, of course, being firmly rooted in Suffolk, for Ipswich Town, with one deviant trotting out of the tunnel at Carrow Road. The photo is in black and white, so readers of Portman Road inclination will not be visually assailed by canary colours!

So we see that Association Football was enthusiastically played, with formal fixtures, for many years. But it is difficult to maintain a standard of excellence in a relatively small school in two major sports in any one term. It was a little sad to see how, in 2002, Association Football finally disappeared from the coaching and fixtures programme.

Left: The first ever Brandeston Hall Hockey XI, 1949. Note the stick shape.
Right: Norman Porter, in his role as Woodbridge School U13 coach, receives a shield from Brandeston Hall's Robin Sampson in recognition of his services to Hockey, spanning a remarkable 55 years.

Hockey: Of all our major sports it is hockey that can claim to have undergone the greatest transformation since 1948; rule changes, stick design and, of course, the proliferation of all-weather surfaces have turned it into a very different game. Nevertheless, over the last twenty or so years, hockey is perhaps the sport where Brandeston Hall has enjoyed the largest numerical representation at 'county' level (Cross-country devotees might beg to differ!) and, in the case of the elite, selection for the Eastern Counties.

Allocated just the final five weeks of the Spring Term one can imagine the difficulties that the coaching staff had to contend with over the early years. Even as late as 1974 (1st XI captain – **Jeremy Wade**) the team coach was lamenting 'the problems of ball control, on account of long grass and a bumpy ground'. Although there is little recorded in print by way of outstanding team success until the 80s, the seeds of much promise for the future must have been evident in watching the likes of **Michael Wright** (1948-49), **Norman Mayhew** (1948-50 England trialist) and **Norman Porter** (1950-53 and, in due course, 12 caps for Scotland) in action for the 1st XI. The XI of 1961-62, quite remarkably, included in its constituency two young men who also went on to make their mark in the game at the highest level: **Peter White** (Capped for England U21's and the Senior Indoor team) and **James Crosbie** (51 caps for Scotland in the 70s). However, it would appear than **Richard Campbell's** XI of 1967-68 were the first to register an unbeaten season, albeit with just 5 matches played.

Under the guidance of **Paddy Newbury** and **Brian Rosen**, together with the acquisition, in 1982-83, of 'twin assets' in the shape of a new, highly qualified Head Groundsman and our own tarmac All-weather surface, literally, made it a whole new ball game. Horizons began to extend – the Aldenham Hockey Festival and, since 1986 regular participants at the prestigious East Anglian Prep Schools Festival at Gresham's. In the mid-80s **Charles Taylor** and **Jonathan Newton** were imperial but we had to wait until 1987-88 to

celebrate another unbeaten side (**Andrew Selby's** XI), over a fixture list of 8 matches... and coming away from the March '88 Gresham's Festival as runners-up in both Indoor and Outdoor Tournaments (to the host team in each case). **Robin Sampson's** arrival in 1987 injected a further stimulus and the increasing use of the Framlingham Sports Hall and eventually Borretts, gave the best possible training conditions. Hockey is now a game played on Astro by all who take the game seriously thus Borretts is where all 1st team home matches have been played in recent years. Those Brandestonians fortunate enough to attend GB Hockey Olympian, Sean Kerly's coaching clinic on the newly opened facility, in 1991, are unlikely to forget the day. The XI of 1990-91 suffered only two (0-1) reverses in an 11 match season and, under **Floris Pietzch's** captaincy, showed outstanding form at the Bedford, Mercian and Greshams Tournaments, losing only to Greshams (in the Indoor Final) over a 22 match sequence. Key to this level of performance was the man guarding the net. Robin Sampson:...'A better 'keeper than **Ian Lancaster** I have yet to see, in this age group'. The 1992-93 XI also enjoyed an unbeaten run at the Greshams 'Outdoors' with captain, **David Lambert** a titan in mid-field.

In 1999 hockey received a further enormous boost with the appointment of **Carlos Reynell** as Director of Sport. A gifted coach with enormous enthusiasm for the game, he has spent many hours with youngsters of all abilities and the results speak for themselves: An unbeaten U.9 mini-hockey season in 1997-98, seeing no fewer than eleven Brandeston Hall boys and girls earning county selection in the 2003-04 season and his 2004-05 Colts team, under the captaincy of **Tommy Hobson**, end their season as both the Suffolk and East of England Champions.

Pride of place over the six decades of senior hockey at Brandeston Hall must go to **Robin Sampson's** 2001-02 team who returned from Millfield with the coveted trophy confirming them as National Prep Schools Mini-hockey Champions. Captained by **Toby Tibbenham**, who has gone on to captain the Eastern

Counties U.15 team and to earn a place in the England U.16 squad (although, sadly, not capped), this talented squad comprised of **Andy Leung**, **Oliver Woodgate**, **Peter Wu**, **Oliver Cutting**, **Nick Lawson**, **Jack Westcott**, **Kit Hardy** and Eastern Counties U.14 goalkeeper **Tom Baldwin**. The almost equally talented team of 2002-03, led by **Oliver Woodgate**, took the Suffolk title, were losing finalists in the East of England Championships and made a brave attempt to persuade history to repeat itself at the national IAPS Tournament but, in the event, had to settle for runners-up spot. This outstanding spell continued through the following season with **Sean Collins'** XI undefeated, with **Sean** and **Josh Cutting** also in the Suffolk team crowned as East of England Inter-County Champions that year.

Another young man who continues to make his mark is **Jonathan Proud**. After only two years at Brandeston Hall and having never previously held a hockey stick, he was a member of the aforementioned 2002-03 1st XI. Taking up a place at Solihull School, following a family move to the Midlands, his remarkable progress within the sport earned him a regular place in the England U16 team of 2006-07 and subsequently with the U18 National Squad.

Bringing the story right up to date, it was pleasing to see Brandeston Hall acquit themselves well in another new regional event – the inaugural IAPS U.13 South of England Mini-hockey Tournament, held at Tonbridge School in March 2008, where the boys ran out as winners of the 'Plate' competition.

Cricket: 'The Summer Game' has always enjoyed a high profile at Brandeston Hall although the days when every boy was compelled to put in three solid afternoons of cricket, to the exclusion of other sporting alternatives, have long since gone. The flagship teams (1st XI and Colts 'A') have, over the greater part of the sixty years, benefited from the input of some outstanding coaches – **David Kittermaster**, **Robin Williams**, **Robin Sampson** and **Carlos Reynell** amongst others. David was, of course, potty about cricket and must have

Left: David Kittermaster, dedicated cricket coach.
Right: Lanky Larter, 6' 7", fast bowler needing a bigger bed – and large size boots.

derived enormous pleasure from overseeing emerging talent from the likes of **Michael Wright**, his first 1st XI Captain (...'a very effective left arm round bowler'), **John Edwards**, 1949 (...'will be a devastating left arm bowler when he has more control over length and direction!') and **Rodney Crabtree** who, as captain of a very promising XI, suffering just one ('unexplained'!) defeat, at Culford, registered outstanding averages of 32.5 with the bat and 4.6 for his bowling. Of the legendary **David Larter** (subsequently Northants and England), in the Summer of 1953, DDK was constructively critical in his assessment – 'If Larter can learn to control his length and direction he should develop into a good bowler'...

notwithstanding that David took 5 for 7 in the home match v. RHS. Nothing less than perfection would satisfy this particular coach! Records show that he had to wait until 1963 to celebrate the achievement of an unbeaten XI. Under the captaincy of **Nicholas Burtt** Brandeston Hall won all thirteen matches contested, the secret apparently lying in 'power-batting and good catching in the field'. **Timothy Borrett's** batting average of 29.8 and 47 wickets for 190, off a mere 106 overs, provided the spring-board for a memorable season. Under **David Carr's** captaincy, the 1970 XI suffered just one defeat, to Orwell Park. The 1971 season was notable for the fact that **Michael Stewart** had to be promoted, from the Colts to the 1st XI (where he then spent two and a half seasons); the problem being...*'The value of Stewart's extraordinary pace bowling was all too often offset by the wicket keeper's inability to hold the ball!'* 5 of 6 U11 matches that summer were lost, almost entirely due to the excessive total of '4 bye' boundaries conceded! The summer of 1980 again threw up a 1st XI of note; **David Handley's** team suffered but one defeat, again to the old enemy, Orwell Park. The 1982 XI, a somewhat erratic team, was captained by a young man, **Ian Graham**, who went on to play senior cricket for Suffolk, in the Minor Counties League. In 1984 we celebrated another unbeaten season (winning 11 of a particularly demanding 15 matches), with **Anthony Bull** as captain and **Simon Giller** awarded the Weston Bat and Ball for topping both batting and bowling averages. **Richard Dyde's** 1990 XI repeated the achievement (10 matches completed) with Richard registering 100 n/o v. Moreton Hall. The XI of 1999 also finished unbeaten (but over a reduced series of 8 matches) with **Mark Stacpoole** imperious: 30

2nd Innings	ENGLAND BOWLING		5th Test.	
Bowler	Overs	Mdns.	Runs	Wkts.
Coldwell	23	4	60	1
Larter	21.1	0	88	4
Knight	11	3	33	1
Illingworth	21	9	54	1
Allen	27	14	52	1
Dexter	6	1	16	0
Barrington	2	0	10	0

BBC tv

Above: David Larter's bowling figures at the Oval, 5th Test 1962 (2nd innings) – 1st innings 5 wickets.

wickets taken and 350 runs scored. The new century has, thus far, thrown up a number of happenings of archival merit: Two 3-figure scores in consecutive seasons - **Oscar Paul's** very confident 122 n/o, for the 1st XI, v Barnardiston Hall in 2004 and, in 2005, **William Squirrell's** unbeaten 109 in response to a target of 165 set by Orwell Park. The ensuing 8 wicket victory was certainly one to savour and the icing on the cake of an excellent season under **Harry Wrinch's** captaincy. Our sixtieth season on the greensward saw two young men again carry their bats in securing centuries: **Kristian Williman**, who plays for Norfolk (and whose grandfather **Paul** was at Brandeston Hall in the early '50s but was more at home with a rugby ball!), and **Jack Scott**, both with a score of 102 n/o.

The 1990s saw tours to Stamford, Ampleforth and St Olave's, York. In 1996 Brandeston Hall were delighted to play host to Bishop Bavin School, from the Republic of South Africa. The Brandeston Hall Annual Cricket Festival was launched in 1999 and provided a suitably thrilling inaugural climax with a win for Beeston Hall, with a 'run out' on the very last ball! About to celebrate its tenth anniversary, it remains a popular event in the East Anglian summer sporting calendar.

The vagaries of our great summer game are often exaggerated at Prep School level. **John Pemberton** tells of a Saturday afternoon, in the dim and distant past, when he and **David Kittermaster** accompanied the 1st XI on an 'Away' fixture at Nowton Court. Nowton knocked up a moderate 60 odd runs. In reply, at 0 for 8 Brandeston Hall were staring at a complete whitewash... yet, eventually lost by just 1 run! Sadly there is no surviving record of DDK's post-match 'de-brief'! **David Grace** has even more astonishing figures that live with him to this day. He recalls travelling to Moreton Hall with Colts' Soccer and Colts' Cricket teams within the same academic year and actually scoring more goals to win the football match (9) than runs accumulated (8 all out) with the cricket bat!

Athletics: Most boys require little encouragement in seeing how they stand in the citius, altius and fortius ratings. Personal incentive targets (House Standards, the AAA Star Award Scheme, first introduced in 1970, and the 'Reynell' Graded Standard Scheme) have ensured that the pursuit of the best of which each youngster is capable of – the treasured 'Personal Best' – has assumed equal importance to the achievements of the naturally talented. These are graded gold, silver and bronze and count for certificates and house points. In this way the school satisfies appetites for competition and achievement, as well as full participation.

Pupils are given a chance to develop skills in the full range of athletics sports. It also holds a popular pre-season athletics master-class with ex-GB decathlete **Darren Hatton**.

Sports Day has always been central to the calendar. Every child from Year 3-8 must compete in 3 events, more if they are taking part in 'open' events.

Every effort is made to introduce the technically difficult skills of Javelin, Discus and Shot as young as Year 5. Sports Day is inclusive: every one takes part. The races are graded so that top athletes compete against other top athletes, in the same way as weaker athletes compete against other weaker athletes.

For the first twenty-four years Sports Day was **John Pemberton's** baby. Responsibility then passed, briefly, to **Henry Goodman**. From the mid-70's, until 2001 **Bob Williams** was the supremo and the mantle currently rests comfortably on **Carlos Reynell's** shoulders.

Outstanding athleticism, in the early years, came in the shape of **Bernard Woolley** (a comfortable winner of the 1950 Senior Victor Ludorum title with 5/6 'Open' events to his name); **Michael McGuire** (Senior Victor Ludorum with a 13.1/63.8 double for the 100/440 yds – pretty good for the '50s); **Neil Utting's** 1960 sharp new 'Open' 100 yards Record of 12.4, further trimmed, in 1966, to a very impressive 11.8 by Senior V.L. winner **David Wells**. The 1967 Sports Day was somewhat dominated by the **Ellerby family**... brothers **Robert** (Senior V.L.) and **John**, with a top three placing (including four wins) in seven events between them, while their 'infant' siblings **Marion** and **Ian** placed 1st and 2nd in the Annual Young Visitors' Race! However, the record, from the earlier days, that never failed to raise a chorus of admiration, as the list of current School Records went on display, was: Senior Cricket Ball – **JDF Larter** – 207'6", 1953. **David Larter's** place in the Brandeston

sporting annals is well recorded and it was 44 years before his prodigious throw was bettered – by **Alastair Liddell**, (64.70m) in 1997 – although it is only fair to point out that, for a good many years now, the Shot Putt has, for seniors, been considered the more appropriate event for athletic competition. Alastair's record attempt was a specially staged event; remarkable nevertheless.

The first venture beyond the school gates in search of external competition came in the summer of 1970, at the inaugural IAPS Eastern Area Championships, at St Faith's, Cambridge. A wet day (on grass) made life difficult for sprinters and hurdlers but did nothing to deter **Jonathan Payne** with the Cricket Ball: His 57.60 secured our first 'Area' win and set an U12 Championship Record which was to stand for many years. In 1972 the event moved to the more appropriate environment of Oundle School, which boasted an 'Olympic' shale track. And there it remained for nearly 25 years. The concept of a national event for Preparatory Schools grew out of a not entirely representative

Above left: Michael McGuire, with an assortment of trophies in cluding the McGuire Cup for Hurdles. **Right**: Ben Davies coming off the last bend, Birmingham, National IAPS Championships 2001, (bronze medal), also setting a new school record.

gathering which was hosted, initially, at Denstone College, Uttoxeter (**Martin Murrell** therefore has the kudos of being our very first IAPS champion: Senior Shot – 1976) but it was not until the event was moved to London, in 1977, and promoted under AAA rules, with appropriately qualified officials, that it was deemed to be a fully fledged IAPS National Championship.

Of course metrication had brought with it the challenge of re-writing the record books or, more correctly, establishing new marks for track events. Names, from the '70s busily engaged upon such a task, were the likes of **Richard Larter** (new senior figures for 400, 800 and 1,500m on Sports Day, 1974), **Paul Hicks**, Team Captain for 1976-77, setting a Senior 100m record of 12.2 in the U14 Final at the IAPS National Championships, at Parliament Hill Fields, and a year later, in the same event, **Jonathan Wren's** astonishing 4min. 42.2 for just 4th place in the 1,500m Final!... both still on the record books 31 years later. In the field, a couple of vintage years from **John Morfoot** with the Javelin saw him win the IAPS Area Championships in both 1975 (U13) and 1976 (U14), setting Area and National Prep

Left: National Prep Schools' Triathlon team winners, Charterhouse, July 1979. Simon Turner and Chris Goodale flanking team captain, Mark Calvert, seen holding the 'Satipsathlon' shield. Mark had the distinction of setting the fastest 1,500m time of the day (4min 54.4).
Right: 2002 IAPS Eastern Area Netball Champions, with Sally Thomson.
Far right: U13 Netball 1990, unbeaten in all school matches.

School Records on both occasions, although, sadly, not able to move on to make it gold at the National. John's U14 record was to stand for 17 years, eventually falling to another talented Brandeston Hall athlete, **Justin Anstes**. The two **Jonathans – Campbell and Gooderham** both wreaked a degree of havoc with the record book in the late '70s (**Jonathan Gooderham**, together with **Richard Johnson**, in the early '80s, earned themselves a 'National' Long and High Jump medal, respectively) while the majestic running of **Christopher Woodruff**, with the rarely detached shadow of **Charles Taylor** in tow, has to be the abiding memory of the 1980s. A string of records and titles across the age groups culminated with Chris producing the performance of his young life, at Aldershot in July 1986, to win the U14 National IAPS title (in yet another School Record) by a whisker – tenacity personified! At the same Championships, Charles produced the finest 1,500m of his career, just 0.1 of a second shy of **Jonathan Wren's** 1978 record, also only good enough for 4th place!

The early '90s brought the 400m, the 'man-killer' event, into sharp focus with **David Lambert** and **Toby Hockley** providing some notable duels. David's 55.6, won the Suffolk Schools' U15 title, at Northgate, taking the event into new territory at Prep School level. Sadly he incurred an injury which, in spite of intensive physiotherapy, put paid to any realistic chance of a win at the National in the July of 1993; a brave 57.6 earned him 4th place. Outstanding technicians, in difficult field events, whose natural talent earned them both trophies and titles in the '70s and '80s were **Michael Pegg, David Wilson** and **Mark Young** in the Triple Jump, **Tosin Oguntayo** in the Long Jump and **Marcos Mayhew** with the Shot. In the '90s **Nick Andrews** earned himself a 50% share in **Richard Johnson's** 1983 U14 High Jump Record of 1.50m and Charlie Higgins (ineligible, for record purposes) actually cleared the bar at 1.52m in front of a crowd of disbelieving but admiring youngsters. The final act of Bob Williams' coaching career, in July 2001, was to witness his stop-watch reading 2m 13.7 as **Ben Davies** crossed the finishing line, in the U14 800m Final, at the National

Prep Schools Athletics Championships, at the Alexander Stadium, Birmingham. In trimming Woodruff's 'unbeatable' record Ben's name has to be coupled with that of Chris as the two finest male middle-distance runners in Brandeston Hall history. Whereas Chris had struck national gold with his time of 2m 14.9, in 1986, Ben had to settle for a bronze medal. Such is the relentless march of progress at this level!

Subsequent to Bob's retirement in 2001, coaching responsibility fell on Carlos, who somehow finds the time to combine front-line cricket and hockey team and Suffolk County coaching/managerial roles with enormous input into both the athletics and winter cross-country scene. He has overseen **William Burke's** success with the Shot (A gold medal – and a new National U12 Record – at the IAPS Championships in 2002) adding a bronze, over 100m, in 2003. Again, over this period, the track performances of **John Bird** were exciting to behold.

The timing of the Year 8 Adventure Week does no favours for senior athletes. They are called upon to produce their best at the Area Championships, Devon, or for the only other qualifying event for the 'National' within hours of arriving back from a very physical week. As a result numerical representation/ results record, at the National Championships has fallen short of its potential.

GIRLS' GAMES

With the advent of girls in 1977 an additional dimension was added to the sporting curriculum, and the demands on playing facilities became more complex. The girls' major sport in the Michaelmas Term has been Hockey, with Netball having pride of place in the Spring Term followed by Rounders and Tennis in the Summer Term.

Hockey: From the early days, in the late '70s, fielding a team where the minimum requirement is eleven quality players, was not easy. It took a few years for numbers to build up sufficiently to the point where Brandeston Hall could compete 'on a level playing field', as

current jargon would have it, but a welcome success for **Lucy Graham's** 1982-83 XI, in an inter-area tournament, at St Felix, served notice that Brandeston girls' games were finally on the map. Although there does not appear to have yet been a girls 1st XI who have recorded an entirely unbeaten season, there have been some very fine female hockey players demonstrating their skills on both grass and astro. Robin Sampson's perceptive analysis of the 1999-2000 season that... 'in the big games, the XI played well but lacked the self-belief that would have turned a solid season into a very good one' had a familiar ring to it.

Kara Kendall's squad of 2000-01 must register as one the most effective XIs in the school's history. Winning 11 out of 14 matches and runners-up in the Suffolk Mini-hockey Tournament (conceding just one goal in the entire competition!) underlined the quality of both defence and attack. With **Lauren Manzur** in goal and outfield players of the stature of **Carina Sage**, **Alexandra Reid**, **Poppy Long**, **Rosanna Walker**, **Katie Arnold** and **Grace Hutson** there was a nucleus of players who, one could confidently predict, would rapidly make their mark at Framlingham. Indeed Grace was promoted to the College 1st XI in her first term in Y9.

Bringing the story up to date, **Emily Wilford** has certainly made her mark over her one brief year at Brandeston: 5 hat-tricks for the 1st XI in 2006-07 and selection for the Suffolk U.15 squad.

Netball: 1986-87 saw an unusually competitive group of small, U10 girls gel into a very effective unit and progress through four successive seasons unbeaten in school matches. In addition, the girls reached the quarter-finals of the National IAPS Tournament, at Crystal Palace, as both an U11 and an U12 VII. In their final year, as U13s, the 'all stars' were captained by **Emma Davies**, playing at centre, **Fiona Lochhead**, **Victoria Ward** and **Harriet Sale** rock-solid in defence with **Helen Robinson**, **Caroline Donoghue** and **Naomi Horton** providing an attacking unit with real penetration.

Rather overshadowed by the roller-coaster U12s of 1988-89 were the U11 and U13s, of that same year who also registered an

unbeaten season. Again, in the Spring of 1996, **Grace Harries'** tenacious little U11 squad proved a real crowd-puller with another 'clean sheet'. It was always a fair bet that the 'class of 2000-01' were going to impress on the netball court. With team captain **Grace Hutson** leading the spearhead of attack and with the defenders rarely under any sort of pressure, a remarkable trawl of 244 goals gave team coach **Sally Thomson** considerable satisfaction; a pleasure that was further enhanced in seeing the team win the Felsted Tournament where the only reverse to Felsted (4-5), in the preliminary pool was more than matched by denying the hosts, in the final itself, by 8 goals to 5. Team member **Carina Sage** (GD) had the added distinction, that season, of an inclusion in the Suffolk U13 squad. The U13 team squad photograph for 2002-03 is 'all smiles' with good reason. Team captain **Fleur Colvile** is seen proudly displaying the trophy awarded to the senior winners of the IAPS Eastern Area Championship.

In 2006-07 the U13 girls, captained by **Charlotte Lawson**, were again supreme at the Felsted Tournament while it was the (undefeated) U12s turn to claim the title at the IAPS Eastern Area Championships. This effective squad of girls continued their imperial progress on through the 2007-08 season when, as the senior VII, and captained by **Victoria Jenkins** they ensured that they remained unbeaten, in a school match within the fixture list, since their very first match as Under 9s, in January 2005. A fine record.

Tennis: Within three years of the first, small, intake in 1977, Brandeston Hall was able to field a mixed school team where the girls could more than hold their own. In July, 1980, **Nicola King** and **Sian Pritchard** served notice that tennis, for girls, was going to be a serious business by winning the School Open Doubles Championship. The U13 league promoted by the Suffolk Schools LTA was, in those days, essentially a boys' competition, with girls allowed to make the team 'on merit'! Such was the strength of girls' tennis in the early '80s that the boys barely got a look in, and the sport rapidly assumed a parallel status, with rounders, as a major

summer activity. At about the same time the Prudential 'Grass Roots' coaching scheme, using the expertise of **Pam Rogers**, was introduced at Brandeston. In 1981 the talented trio of **Nicola** (a nationally-rated player and three years a member of the senior team), **Louise Rogers**, a county player at U14 (with a string of Suffolk titles to follow in later years), and **Sian** formed the nucleus of a fine foursome. In 1982 it was **Louise** and **Carolyne Butler** who were at the heart of an unbeaten season for the girls – and mopped up, between them, all four senior school trophies.

By 1987 the names of **Katie Bull** (another player with an extensive Suffolk CV as an adult) and **Kirsty King** were very much to the fore. They were the School Open Doubles winners and, together with squad members **Amanda Wright**, **Emma Dean and Jaqueline Hale**, won the Suffolk U13 team title. The following year **Katie**, **Kirsty**, **Amanda** and **Jaqueline** progressed even further, to make the regional final of the National Midland Bank Championship (East of England), losing to a very strong Queenswood team who, subsequently, took the national title.

Of all the outstanding young female tennis players who have passed through Brandeston Hall it is, once again, the name of **Grace Hutson** that would just about top the list. Showing promise at a very early age, in 1998 she won the Suffolk Closed Cup for U10s. Engaged in a series of Adidas-sponsored tournaments across the country, she progressed rapidly to achieve an LTA ranking of 5.2, the highest in the UK by a player in the U11 category. Aged 11 she won the Suffolk Closed U12 Championship and both the Frinton and Felixstowe Tournament Singles and Doubles titles. Playing No.1 for the county, tournament wins continued to accrue through her remaining years at Brandeston and her LTA rating by 2001 was an impressive 4.1.

A young lady rapidly doing her best to emulate Grace is **Lydia Green**. Lydia enjoyed an excellent 2007 season: Suffolk U12 Champion, involved in a series of Nike International 'Classics', at both U12 and U14, across France and resulting from her record of success in this series, an invitation to compete in the French Junior

Open (U12) Tournament, in Bressure. This led to the Suffolk LTA's 'Most Successful U.19 Player of the Year' award and an end-of-season national age group ranking at 30 and, in 2008 has again earned the plaudits in winning the county U.14 'The Road to Wimbledon' title, named Suffolk U18 Player of the Year, competing in the National Finals, at Wimbledon.

Tennis features strongly for both boys and girls throughout the year. At the time of writing there are strong hopes of establishing Brandeston as a centre of tennis excellence, complete with tennis dome. The school's past record stands as testimony to the strength of its claim to be just such a centre.

Athletics: In July, 1978, at the end of an historic first twelve months of co-education, it was the name of **Angela Creasy** that was emblazoned on the Senior Girls Victrix Ludorum trophy. Thereafter Athletics rapidly gained 'street cred.' Through the early '80s it was **Seonaid Lochhead**, **Laura Milne**, **Nicky Edwards** (a particularly elegant sprinter and the first recipient of an Athletics Colour award of any sort) and **Roberta Scott** who gradually fashioned a very respectable list of school records. Roberta, a member of Ipswich Harriers, had the makings of a good heptathlete.

In the summer of 1986 the girls were granted an IAPS Area Championship in their own right, hosted in the early days by King's, Ely. This eventually morphed into a joint boys'/girls' single day event at Corby and then Bedford. This was a real incentive for an improvement in standards. **Felicity le Fanu** dramatically revised the record books for the short sprints and long jump and, in 1988, was the first Brandeston Hall girl to gain a place in a final at the National IAPS Championships – a deserved bronze medal in the U12 Girls 200m. The bar was raised again, in the early '90s, with some remarkable performances from **Frances Brightey** (100/200m and Long Jump) and **Eleanor Atkinson** in the middle-distance events. Frances qualified for the National Prep Schools Championships on a number of occasions. Her best placing – another bronze, in 1992, in the U13G 200m. 1993 – proved a vintage

Left: Winners of the IAPS Area 9 Cross-Country Championships, held at Framlingham College, March 1992. Team Captain James Young holds the Overall Championship 'Orwell Shield'. Chris Goodfellow (back row 4th from rt), James Hale (far rt), Scott Cole (kneeling 2nd from rt) and Michael Shears (kneeling 5th from rt) provided a clean sweep of individual titles. A remarkable day's competition also saw 3/4 age-group team race trophies come Brandeston's way.

year with six girls (in 7 events) winning through to the IAPS Championships and, by 1995, the first 'National' Prep Schools Champion was **Ros Cooke** in the U14 Girls Shot Putt in the Alexandra Stadium, Birmingham. Through the mid '90s **Abigail Player**, another very sound technician, gradually wrestled various age-group high jump records away from **Naomi Horton** (and registered three top 6 finishes at the IAPS Championships).

The summer of 1997 would have a strong claim to be the best-ever season of girls' athletics. Over the years, the intensity of 'domestic' competition that was engendered by the Annual Inter-House Sports is hard to match. The Senior Girls 100m Final of 1997 would have a strong claim to be the best race yet seen at Brandeston Hall. It took an extended huddle (timekeepers and place judges) to ascertain that the first three girls over the line all registered a time of 13.5s. For **Angela Jackson** (1st) this constituted a new U14 school record, for **Kim Hamilton** (2nd) a new U13 record, leaving **Chantalle Day** merely as the third fastest Brandeston Hall girl in history! Nevertheless, it was Chantalle who finally stole the limelight. The talented girls' squad had, between them, turned in a string of fine performances at the Holmwood House Invitational, Langley Schools Meeting and in the Area IAPS Championships, with four of them making it through to the National IAPS Championships, in Stoke-on-Trent. Chantalle came away with a gold medal, twice breaking her own school record, with a final, prodigious leap of 4.77m in the U13 Girls Long Jump.

1998-2001 were the **Grace Hutson** years. Her 'national' haul of two silver and a bronze medal (1999-2001) remains unequalled by any Brandeston Hall athlete. All earned, with great tenacity, over 800m on the tartan surface of the Alexandra Stadium with Grace, on each occasion, setting new Brandeston Hall age-group figures. Her final year, 2001, was memorable for her triple re-write of both 800m and 1,500m records for U14s, winning, in Suffolk colours, the East of England Inter-Counties Junior Girls (U15!) 1,500m title (in an astonishing 4mins.56.6) and again dipping under 5minutes, as the only athlete thus far, to compete in the All England Schools Championships, in Exeter.

Not content to sit in her shadow, **Susannah Reid** has been in hot pursuit of both Grace's records and titles, earning herself a silver medal (and new School Record figures) in the U13 Girls 1,500m event in the 2008 National IAPS Championships, in Birmingham.

Other sports: The range of once so-called minor sports has increased, offering wider opportunities to youngsters. If you are not a natural all-rounder, and table-tennis or swimming is where the gods determine that you plough your personal furrow then that is, proudly, where you give your all. The concept of minor sports has been replaced by the idea of activities, many of which now feature on the formal Physical Education curriculum and include: dance, gymnastics, basketball, health-related fitness, adventurous activities. Unfortunately, as noted above, some of this material has had to be omitted, but is available in a supplement, on request, from the author. We could, however, not exclude cross-country – a sport in which Brandestonians have gained considerable success.

Cross-country is a sport taken rather seriously. Some from the early '70s will recall running in the Herts Open Junior C.C. League in Welwyn, and an equally long journey, in the '80s, to compete regularly in the Haileybury Prep Schools event (with that fearsome hill 1,200m from the finish). Runners ventured even further afield in 1999 for their one and only crack at the highly regarded Abberley Hall Relays, in Worcester (U11 3rd place team medals with **Ben Davies** 2nd fastest of the day) and, in the early 2000s the Suffolk Series Sunday League provided extra competitive experience.

Haileybury, in the years when there wasn't a clash of dates with County hockey happenings, proved a happy hunting ground: Senior and Junior Team champions in 1985 and 1986 and Senior event winners again in 1989 and 1990 with individual winners in the shape of **Matthew Osborne** and **Richard Dening-Smitherman**, in 1985 with **Chris Woodruff** taking the Senior title (and a magnificent Wedgwood plate) in 1986.

North Suffolk Schools Trials at Chantry and County Championships

at both Holbrook and Framlingham have, over the years, yielded an impressive role of honour and a number of champions in the Minor Boys and Minor Girls category. The crowning glory has to be **Grace Hutson's** East of England Schools' Inter-Counties Minor Girls' title in 1999. An accident at the start of the 2000 event robbed her of the chance of retaining that title. Nevertheless, this outstanding performance, together with four Suffolk Championships (2 Minor Girls and 2 Junior Girls... one of these having moved on to Framlingham) and a bronze medal in the 2000 National Prep Schools C.C. Championships, at Malvern, adds up to a remarkable record.

What a final year for Grace it might have been in 2001, had it not been for the 'Foot and Mouth' embargo...

Grace would certainly have a rival for 'top girl' in the diminutive **Eleanor Atkinson**. In March, 1992 the team travelled to Marlborough to contest the inaugural National Prep Schools C.C. Championships. In appalling conditions, Eleanor (then a Year 7 pupil) showed a clean pair of heels to the entire field, proudly leading home a Brandeston Hall sextet of **Shireen Cantrell**, **Alison Wildig**, **Melanie Tuckwell**, **Hazel Flack** and **Frances Brightey** for the gold medals. Eleanor returned twelve months later and, barely recovered from a bout of influenza, took a creditable bronze medal.

The IAPS Area 9 Annual C.C. Championship was spawned from what was becoming a regular gathering of a handful of local Prep Schools, at Orwell Park. From 1977 **Ian Angus** and his enthusiastic staff extended this with an invitation across East Anglia, embracing the area defined by Chigwell, Bedford and Norwich. Thus the Anglian Prep Schools Championship, for the

Orwell Shield, (incidentally fashioned by **Brian Rosen** from a fine piece of teak!) was born. Bedford and Orwell Park dominated the first three championships but then, in 1980, Brandeston commenced a winning streak that endured for thirteen years, (in 1981 beating a stunned Millfield Junior team, invited as a guest team from Somerset, by just 13 points) broken only by the intervention of a devastating 'flu bug in 1988 (relegated to 2nd place, behind a Woodbridge team coached by a determined **Margaret Kennon**, during her brief defection!) and the Arctic weather in 1991 (no event). After this extended 'day in the sun', for the remainder of the '90s, Brandeston Hall had to settle for second best against the likes of Brentwood, Forest, The King's School (Ely) and Orwell Park.

This virtual stranglehold, on the trophy, from 1980-1992, also featured a host of individual titles, with a number in course record times to add to the gloss. Those who perpetuated this purple patch were: 1980: U10 **Richard Johnson**; 1981: U11 **Guy Chalkley**; 1983: U12 **James Coe**; 1984: U11 **Chris Woodruff**; 1985: U12 **Chris Woodruff** and U13 **Matthew Osborne**; 1986: U10 **Philip Cantrell** and U13 **Chris Woodruff** (by one second from **Charles Taylor** – a classic duel in the last race of the day); 1987: U11 **Philip Cantrell**; 1988: U10 **James Young** and U12 **Philip Cantrell**; 1989: U10 **James Young** and U11 **Marcos Mayhew**; 1990: U10 **James Hale** and U11 **James Young**; 1992: U13 **Chris Goodfellow** (to add to his superb 3rd place in the NPSCC Championships, at Marlborough), U12: **James Hale**, U11 **Scott Cole** and U10 **Michael Shears**. The only title Brandeston Hall failed to annex, on an extraordinary afternoon, was the U10 team race (2nd!); 1998: U10 **Ben Davies**. All stunning performances to fondly reflect upon.

Above left: IAPS Stowe putters winners 1995, Philip Bligh, Luke Miller and Nick Golding, with Stephen Player. **Right:** Kirsty, John and David Wybar

In 1986 Brandeston had taken over the promotion of the event, at Framlingham. With start and finish, in those days, on the Front, and a course (for U12 and U13) that took competitors behind Robinson's Wood, to the Castle and back along the Mere, to face a water-splash and an uphill finish; this was a real test of character. Year on year, Brandeston Hall staff, with the invaluable help of **Hugh Kennon**, ensured the continued popularity of an event that has, on occasions, attracted a field in excess of 30 schools. In the mid '90s **Bob Williams** stood down as Championship Organiser, a responsibility taken on initially by **Graham Wigley** and, more recently by various Directors of Sport at Framlingham.

The hands-on enthusiasm of **Carlos Reynell** ensures that 'Brandeston Hall and Cross-country' remain synonymous with success in the new century, a period in which both **John Bird** and **Susannah Reid** have carved a particularly illustrious furrow within the county and further afield. The College continues to front a very professional promotion of the Area 9 Championships. The introduction of separate age group events for Girls (for the Kennon Shield) was widely welcomed. The Boys now compete for the Wigley Shield with the overall champions (combined boys'/girls' score) receiving the Williams Shield.

Vintage performances for Brandeston Hall over this period have seen the winning of the Williams Shield in 2004 and 2008, the Kennon Shield in 2004 with cancellation (severe weather) in both 2005 and 2007 undoubtedly costing dear. Individual champions have been – 2002: U10 **John Bird**; 2003: U10G **Harriet Starling** and U11 **John Bird**; 2004: U11Girls **Harriet Starling**, U12 **John Bird** and U13G **Rhiannon Wakefield**; 2006: U10 Girls **Susannah Reid**;

2008: U12 Girls **Susannah Reid** and U13 Girls **Lydia Green**.

... and rather appropriate that, as we celebrate this important anniversary in the school's history, the Overall Championship Shield should again be sitting in the Brandeston Hall trophy cabinet – six decades on from the first recorded competitive 'C.C.' event for Brandeston boys – **Bernard Woolley's** win in the 1948-49 Inter-House Championship!

TOURS AND TOURNAMENTS

One of the major sporting developments in recent years has been the number of tours undertaken by schools, thereby extending the range of opponents, developing a greater sense of team spirit and enabling coaches to have extended contact with their young charges.

Brandeston has undertaken a number of sports tours in recent years. The boys have travelled to Yorkshire, Surrey and Kent to play rugby and for the last 4 years have embarked on tours to Leicestershire and Lincolnshire. The Girls too have spread their wings, with a Netball tour in Kent, and the 1st XI hockey have been to Norfolk and Northants. Even younger teams enjoy touring experience: the under 11 hockey girls' and boys' teams have travelled widely, including visits to Norfolk, Hertfordshire and Bristol. Cricket and tennis teams have also displayed their talents on a wider stage. Apparently when the boys U11 team went to the National Hockey Finals at Beeston in 2005 they visited Trent Bridge and their guide took them to look at the changing rooms and told a story about **David Larter**. They

Above: A youthful John Pemberton, early 1950s, on Sports Day.

BRANDESTON HALL SWIMMING POOL

were told that David was so tall – he stood 6'7" in very large boots – that he had to have a special bed made for him when he played for England there in 1965.

Touring is nowadays very much part of Brandeston's sporting way of life. A far cry from the 50s and 60s, when even a day fixture outside Suffolk was something of an adventure.

Another major development has been the hosting of tournaments. In the course of the year Brandeston hosts several tournaments. An October tournament which caters for U11 Girls Hockey , U9 Netball and U9 Boys hockey attracts some 400 children. In December a rugby tournament helps to maintain links with Diss RFC and Southwold RFC. The value of Brandeston's involvement can be gauged by the fact that these clubs have provided six of the school's current sports scholars. Sports scholarships were introduced in 2006 and are having a massive impact.

In January seven of the top Under 11 Boys Hockey Club teams are hosted at Framlingham. In March there is an Under 9 Hockey (Girls) and Under 9 Rugby Tournament. In the Summer there is a 1st IV Tennis and 1st XI Cricket Festival.

Throughout the year Brandeston attracts teams to its tournaments, flexing its sporting muscles against a wide range of opponents, and, at the same time, showing off the school to the many young aspiring sportsmen and women who attend, together, of course, with their parents. Again this demonstrates the extent to which the sporting calendar has evolved in the course of the school's 60 year history.

It was perhaps the Brandeston International Rugby Sevens Tournament in March 2007 which

best exemplifies the educational value of sport. Under the auspices of the children's charity 'Touraid' 30 young rugby players from disadvantaged backgrounds in Romania, Bulgaria and the Ukraine, together with teams from Brandeston and Diss RFC, came together over a weekend, not just to play rugby, but to experience English culture and customs. The youngsters enjoyed a coaching session given by players from London Irish and Harlequins. Organised by **Carlos Reynell** and **Bruce Wilson**, the visitors were hosted by Brandeston families.

Nigel Woolnough, The Master, who had previously been Head of a school in the Ukraine said: "As the boys trooped off the pitch, muddied and weary, arms on one another's shoulders, I realised I couldn't distinguish between the boys of the four countries. It was truly a moment of friendship and wonderful bonding."

This surely exemplifies the wider educational value of sport – having the chance 'to tour for a week and learn for a lifetime'. Four cultures were brought together, linked by a common thread – their interest in rugby. The host school may have narrowly won the tournament, but that faded into relative insignificance alongside the wider impact of the occasion.

Ryan Clark, the Brandeston Captain, concluded by saying... "This tournament has really opened my eyes to what rugby means to me. I had not appreciated how lucky we are in England, and how rugby can provide a real chance for so many children all over the world. I have found the whole experience of meeting, playing against and learning about life in Eastern Europe fantastic." Brandeston embraced the spirit of Touraid, and all were winners.

Above left: The Swimming Pool in 1971.
Right: Successful Brandeston International
Rugby Sevens Charity Tournament, March 2007.

SENIOR AND JUNIOR SPORTSPERSONS OF THE YEAR

Most years, or close sequence of years, tend to throw up a young sportsman / woman who, by general assent, is blessed with an ability and an all-round record of achievement which places them at the pinnacle of the sporting pyramid. To identify budding superstars over the first forty years of the school's existence, particularly at this distance in time, is a dangerous game! However, those who cut the mustard, over a range of sports, would most certainly have included the following:

In the late '40s the names of **Michael Wright** (captain of all three major sports in the school's first year) and **Bernard Woolley** would certainly have fitted into this category. In the '50s **Rodney Crabtree**, **Michael Spencer**, **Norman Porter**, **David Larter** and **Michael McGuire** were making the headlines. In the '60s **David Smith** was the dominant force over a two-year period while **Bruce Pearson** (for his speed on land and in the water) and **Tony Knight** also had star billing.

Over the greater part of the three-year period '67-'70 **David Carr** had an outstanding record and, over the remainder of the '70s, **Jeremy Kemp**, **Simon Ferguson**, **Tim Smart**, **Iain Birrell**, **Julian Pollard**, **Jonathan Wren** and **Mark Calvert** were all a joy to behold when dominating play. The early '80s gave us **Jonathan Gooderham**, **Neil Stanhope** and a particularly strong showing of skilful and competitive girls - **Jaqueline Hale**, **Kirsty King** and **Amanda Wright**.

1986 was the year when the Senior Sportsperson of the Year was first given specific recognition with the award of the Oguntayo Cup (**Gbenga**, **Kayode** and **Tosin Oguntayo** had all been outstanding athletes, in their own right, during their Brandeston Hall years). The first recipient was **Charles Taylor**. In 1989 the Stracey Cup, the gift of **Samantha Stracey's** parents, made its appearance thus enabling us to recognise, independently, both Sportsman and Sportswoman of the Year. The Under 11s had to wait until 2001 for a tangible form of recognition of their achievements: the Rimmer Cup, the gift of **William Rimmer's** parents, for the Junior Sportsman of the Year and the Gaskin Bowl for the outstanding Junior Girl.

As many former pupils will be aware, an appeal launched in 2002, in memory of former SOF Secretary (and one of the first cohort of 1948 Brandeston Hall pupils) **Neville Bromage**, has generated a scholarship fund which supports, on their transfer to Framlingham, a boy or girl adjudged to be the budding sportsperson of the year. With Neville among the first cohort of 1948 joiners it was a poignant occasion when **Lydia Green**, received her award on Speech Day, 2008, the very day that Brandeston Hall completed sixty years 'in business'.

But sport is not only about winning. Everyone who plays sport will understand that winning and losing can be equally instructive. There have been seasons when Brandeston has boasted undefeated sides, and these are rightly celebrated. But that cannot happen all the time. Sometimes the pleasure has to come from participation and from doing one's best, while recognising that the opposition performs better. Players often learn more in defeat, both about themselves and about their shortcomings, than they do in victory. It is all part of education. It is certainly part of a Brandeston education.

POST-MATCH DE-BRIEF

The opportunity to represent the school at major sports is not elitist. In a school of 200-250 pupils (boys and girls) not many escape selection. Indeed, on Wednesday, 15th March 1997, 122 of 223 eligible pupils turned out for a school team, across all levels – a statistic to be proud of.

So yes, some of the fondest memories of Brandeston will be of sporting occasions, sporting achievements, friends made both on and off the playing fields. Not the playing fields of Eton, but playing fields which have taught so many values, seen so much enjoyment and witnessed so many achievements. Sport is something that Brandeston has traditionally done well. The school is rightly proud of its sporting history and of the many and various achievements of its pupils on sports fields. Sport always has been seen, and still is, as an important part of that rounded education which the best schools strive to provide.

Senior Sportsperson of the Year		
1986	Charles Taylor	
1987	Andrew Brightman	
1988	Katie Bull	

Senior Sportsman of the Year		Senior Sportswoman
1989	James Roberts	Antonia Key
1990	Richard Dyde	Fiona Lochhead
1991	Mark Rodwell	Sally Musgrave
1992	Chris Goodfellow	Alison Wildig
1993	David Lambert	Kelly Blemings/ Elizabeth Knight
1994	James Jackson	Sarah Compton-Dando
1995	Edward Simpson	Philippa Knight
1996	Guy Fleming	Eleni Read
1997	Simon Stacpoole	Abigail Player
1998	Ian McLaren	Kirsty Wybar
1999	Mark Stacpoole	Katie Millett
2000	William Rimmer	Colette Hamilton
2001	Ben Davies	Grace Hutson
2002	Nick Lawson	Sinead Collins
2003	Tom Baldwin	Laura Wright
2004	Sean Collins	Caroline Reid
2005	John Bird	Sarah Findlay
2006	William Squirrell	Anna deGrave
2007	Ryan Clarke	Charlotte Lawson
2008	William Owen	Lydia Green

Junior Sportsman of the Year		Junior Sportswoman
2001	Oliver Woodgate	Katie Beighton
2002	Sean Collins	Felicity Cobbold
2003	James Legg	Rebecca Saunders
2004	William Squirrell	Anna deGrave
2005	Tommy Hobson	Eleanor Smith
2006	Oliver Webb	Milly Hopkinson/ Jasmine Lawson
2007	Thomas Ridley	Susannah Reid
2008	George Coulson	Amanda Birch/ Saffron Wilford

LOOKING OUTWARDS – SPREADING OUR WINGS

Classroom subjects, music, drama, sport – these are mostly on-site activities. Brandeston Hall is a secure educational environment, and one in which it would be easy to become cocooned within an educational comfort zone. But that would be a stunted education – certainly not an education for life and for the outside world. Education at Brandeston has to take account of a wider context, and create a wider awareness of an increasingly challenging world. Visits – ever more difficult in a Health and Safety-conscious world – are complex undertakings, but Brandeston pupils have, over the years, been exposed to a rich variety of off-site experiences. Conversely events and special occasions are organised on-site which serve to remind young children of the world beyond their own necessarily limited horizons. From the first tentative excursion across the Channel – a school party led by Messrs Hewitt, Pemberton & Copperwheat to Paris, in April 1956, to the current assumption that both an Easter Skiing Week and a Skern Lodge Summer Activities Week will automatically appear in the school calendar, there has always been much to whet the appetite for travel. Brandeston youngsters are fortunate indeed to have had the opportunity to sample so much of it so early in their lives. Staff too, are part of a wider educational context. This section concludes with a look at the wider world of Prep Schools.

Above: One of the first Brandeston trips to London in the late 1980s, included a visit to the Tower of London.

EARLY VISITS

John Pemberton recalls that there were few visits in the early days. Life was challenging enough on site, and Europe was still in the aftermath of war. Then along came a teacher by the name of **Hewitt** who was a linguist and who got trips moving. There was a trip to Amsterdam, followed another visit to Belgium/Holland. In 1956 it was Paris. The party stayed near Versailles. Big cities and small boys are a dangerous mix – a young man by name of Hurst (his father was a big hitter in the parents' cricket team!) got lost – someone miscounted – almost a capital offence in the 21st century - John was dispatched to find him, and duly discovered him in a large Department store. There were three schools accommodated in one huge dormitory, one of them was a French lycée. They were heard making evil anti-Anglo-Saxon plans, thinking no-one could understand, but Hewitt, a proper linguist, did understand so he laid into the miscreants verbally and their plans were thwarted. John remembers the visit as being "vaguely cultural". In 1962 a party visited the North Dutch coast, including a trip to Bruges. John still recalls the mirth-inducing name of Op der Hooter, presumably translated with all due felicity into "Up the Hooter". They visited Nordwijk, apparently famous for its meatballs. From such beginnings...

LONDON DAYS – BY BOB WILLIAMS

It was only a matter of months after his arrival that **Nigel Johnson** decided that we ought to pilot a visit to London for the whole school – and felt that I should be the 'muggins' to take responsibility for organising it! The fact that the first venture, in October 1986, was voted a success was something of a mixed blessing... It became an annual responsibility for the next fifteen years!

In truth, it did quickly prove a very worth-while venture as we put together a programme for the day especially tailored to each year group. Any child with us for the full five, or even six year period pretty well 'did' London.

Extracts from the Brandeston Hall magazine coverage of 'London Day' October 1993 give something of the flavour of the day:

'The third Thursday in October traditionally sees a convoy of five Soames coaches heading south, down the A12, through the early morning mist. Will the Newbury Park drop be on schedule? Will our Central Line train grind to a halt at a critical moment? (Suspect package at Liverpool Street... signalling problems at Oxford Circus?) Anxious party leaders attempting to count heads that won't keep still! All familiar ingredients of our annual 'London Day'. In the event all deadlines are met and mild concerns prove groundless.

Year 3/4 hit the Natural History Museum and are, in turn, incredulous at the size of the Blue Whale, intrigued at the opportunities presented by the 'hands on' displays in the Human Body Exhibition and terrified by the extraordinarily realistic moving Dinosaurs and giant Megabugs.

Year 5 peel off to Regent's Park, to share an early lunch with the geese and ducks before moving on to sample the delights on offer at Mme Tussauds and the Planetarium. The visual and olfactory experience of the 'Spirit of London' ride is eagerly anticipated.

Year 6 aim for the very heart of the capital, Piccadilly, to check out the tallest, fattest and fastest at the Guinness World of Records, making quite certain that they don't miss out on the 'practical' by sampling the largest gobstoppers in England (from the Big Sweet Shop)! Then it's the Tower of London and its treasures with the day reaching an appropriate conclusion at Tower Hill Pageant, another intriguing 'ride-on' experience recounting the entire history of the Port of London.

Year 7, in keeping with recent custom, take to the Thames as the focus of their day. The Westminster-Greenwich waterbus gives us the opportunity to view many of the city's landmarks. Three old sea-dogs give us a fascinating guided tour of the Cutty Sark, vividly bringing to life the heyday of the great Tea Clipper. A quick sprint up the hill to the Observatory enables us to stand astride the Meridian and, perhaps, more fully comprehend the significance of longitude and latitude. Back down to the National Maritime Museum specifically to look at some of the fascinating memorabilia connected with Captain Cook and Nelson and an opportunity to view the cleverly devised new gallery devoted to 'British Sea Power in the 20th Century'. Fifty-one pairs of weary legs finally drag themselves aboard the red, white and blue train at Island Gardens for a journey through the futuristic Docklands landscape, the new 'High Tech' home for our newspaper industry.

Top: Year 7 on the Cutty Sark, Greenwich.
Above: Bressingham Steam Museum, near Diss.

First stop for Year 8 is the London Dungeon, with its somewhat macabre slant on history. Following the traditional city tour, with London Tour Guides, who always provide a first-rate service, we devote the greater part of the afternoon to the Museum of the Moving Image. This is an opportunity to see, first hand, something of the evolutionary development of cinema and television; an appropriate reminder of the astonishing input necessary to bring us to today's level of sophistication. The icing on the cake of an absorbing day is a visit to the evening performance of the record-breaking 'Les Miserables' at the Cambridge Theatre. Truly spectacular.

I think we always felt it important that, where possible, it should be a 'doing' as much as a 'seeing' day as these random quotes exemplify:

Sam Cobbold Year 3, at the Natural History Museum: 'There was an earthquake at the end of the room where we wobbled with it'.

Polly Griffiths Year 4, at the Science Museum: 'My favourite bit of London Day was 'Launch Pad' because you could see how everything worked, not by looking, but by touching everything'.

Rebecca Mills Year 8: 'The Museum of the Moving Image was great fun and interesting too, especially when you were recorded, on video, doing an ITV News report'. But there was the occasional downside as expressed by **Alex Condon** Year 8: 'I really enjoyed 'Grease'; the only bad thing was sitting next to Mr Baker and he started singing'!

The highlights for me, personally, which continue to stand the test of time? Probably gazing at that tiny piece of Moon Rock so beautifully displayed at the Natural History Museum – and, of course, (for the 'nth' time!) hearing the closing chorus reach its crescendo in the final tableau of 'Les Miserables'.

Over 15 years our itinerary has included: The Globe Theatre/Tate Modern/National Gallery/The BBC Experience/Houses of Parliament/London

Dungeon/Science Museum/Natural History Museum/Museum of London/Docklands Railway/Tower of London/The Planetarium/Madame Tussauds/Guinness World of Records/Westminster-Greenwich River Trip/The Cutty Sark/Imperial War Museum/Toy Museum/London Transport Museum, Covent Garden/St Paul's Cathedral/National Maritime Museum/Greenwich Observatory/London Aquarium/MOMI/British Museum/The London Eye/The Millennium Dome/Royal Academy/Tower Bridge/National Portrait Gallery/London Zoo/The Design Museum and HMS Belfast.

For Year 8 London Day has included a ticket to see 'Cats', 'Grease', 'Les Miserables', 'Jesus Christ Super Star', 'Lion King', 'Joseph and his Amazing Technicolor Dream Coat', 'Starlight Express', 'Return to the Forbidden Planet' and also Shakespeare's 'Measure for Measure' at the Barbican.

(Since 2000 London theatre visits have taken in 'The Woman in Black', 'The Lion, The Witch and the Wardrobe' and 'Fame').

Nigel Johnson summarises:

The whole school (all 280 pupils and 30 staff and parents) would decamp, en masse, to London for a programme of events and activities over a whole day which would encompass every aspect of the capital city – you name it, we went there! Traditionally, the day for Year 8 finished with a theatrical experience and the shows were greatly enjoyed.

Bob Williams was the mastermind organising (it seemed) every coach in the Soames fleet to arrive promptly at the crack of dawn and embark the children for an exciting day out. Even more importantly were the hours spent booking and providing the detailed itinerary (different for every year group) which ensured the day's success. In the fifteen years that London Day featured on the Autumn Term calendar, I believe that we only 'lost' one child (and, only very briefly!) despite moving children around on the Underground throughout the day. It really was a massive undertaking that was timed to the minute and, logistically, incredibly complicated yet Bob accomplished the exercise each year with a smile on his face, albeit with a huge sigh of relief when the last coach finally made it back through the school gates.

Above: Robin Sampson, for many years led pupils on the Skern trips. A few of the exciting activities are shown opposite – Jeremy Ford and Georgina Seed exhausted on the return journey – bottom.

SKERN LODGE – BY ROBIN SAMPSON

It was back in 1987 that **Sally Youngman** pioneered the concept of an Activities/Adventure Week for our Year 8 pupils, taking a party to the Outdoor Centre in Appledore, North Devon. The Master at the time, Nigel Johnson, was very keen to set up an Activities Week for all the pupils at Brandeston. He recognised the benefits of taking the pupils out of school, out of their comfort zone and providing them with physical and mental challenges, particularly for our older pupils. This was the first venture down that pathway.

The centre was then in its infancy but has expanded over the years and now boasts three accommodation blocks, superb dining facilities and a bar and is now able to cater for large numbers of people. In 1988, by way of a contrast, we took Year 8 to the Lake District. A plague of midges and ticks persuaded us that Skern Lodge really was the better bet and that has remained the way of things for the past 19 years. For the greater part of this period the Group Leader's role has been my responsibility - with **Margaret Kennon** as a very able deputy - (even after she started drawing her pension!)

Early days at Skern Lodge saw us staying in the Farm House. The accommodation was cosy and the food always excellent. From the earliest days the activities were always a challenge. Who could forget the orienteering around Northam Burrows inhabited by sheep, horses and angry golfers! We spent hours searching the area for markers, trying not to get lost and hoping to be picked up by the minibus sooner rather than later. Some of the markers were never found and I am sure the golfers had something to do with it! Kayaking was another demanding activity at the time because it required a long strenuous paddle up the river Torridge from Appledore to Bideford in all weathers. Then having trudged through the mud to put the kayaks back on the trailer we returned to the centre covered in mud for the customary hosing down in swimming costumes before dunking wetsuits in tubs of cold water. The hot showers and hot

chocolate that followed were always so welcome.

The activities offered on-site now include a high ropes course, climbing and abseiling tower, traversing wall, pot-holing tunnels as well as a vast array of minibuses to take groups off-site to use the superb local environment.

The bridge jump remains one of the most popular activities at Skern and the pupils always ask, with much bravado, if it is on the schedule. Suitably wet-suited and equipped with life jacket and helmet, it requires the pupils and Staff to jump off the stone bridge, at Bideford, into the river Torridge... (if they do it, we have to!) The jump is completed at high tide when the water is slack and the height of the jump varies from year to year depending on the height of the tide. Standing on the wall before the jump is the hardest part, because once you have leapt like 'a pencil' there is little else you can do about it. Having made a considerable splash you bob up disorientated and gasping for breath. Having spotted which way to go, a few well chosen swimming strokes take you to the shore. However, despite reminding the pupils to keep their legs together and their mouths shut before they jump off a few always forget and regret not listening to the advice given.

Again, off site, there is a surfing session on Westward Ho!'s sandy beach. Back on the river we build rafts and race them and take our exciting rib ride to the mouth of the estuary. For me the expedition bivi is probably the highlight of the week. Groups are transported out to a farmer's field at Hartland about 40 minutes away. Here we build shelters, abseil off Hartland Quay and traverse (low-level climb) the beautiful rocky coastline. There are a number of tricky obstacles to negotiate on the coastal traverse and I am sure a number of pupils will remember with affection their dip in Jool's Pool. In the evenings the pupils would cook the food provided over methylated spirit burners back at the bivi site. Concorde no longer booms at us in the evenings but as darkness falls we would go on a night exercise to the shore and toast marsh mallows over a fire built from driftwood before slipping back to our shelters for a few hours sleep.

So, twenty years on, and now in the capable hands of **Jan Norton**, we are still going to North Devon getting smelly, muddy, wet, scared and having a great time. What is particularly pleasing to me is that, whenever I speak to past Brandeston pupils, they all remember Skern Lodge with great affection. Fond memories...

Above: June 2007. Year 6 pupils transported back to the 1580s at Kentwell Hall.

KENTWELL HALL: BACK IN TIME TO THE TUDORS, BY JOHN CLOUGH

Brandeston Hall and its West Suffolk counterpart, in terms of age, Kentwell have been linked together for the past twenty-five years by the annual visit of Brandeston pupils to the manor of Long Melford. The owner and restorer of the property, Mrs Phillips, always greets the boys and girls with the words, "Aaah! Brandeston Hall, we always look forward to your visit." Well Mrs Phillips, the feeling is mutual, and it has been a real pleasure and education to me to see how the estate has grown and developed over the past quarter of a century. It has also been interesting to see all the old faces and characters year after year relishing their role in creating what is a superb tableau and experience of life in Tudor England. The pupils always look forward to their visit and more importantly look back too, for many years, on their day of time travel.

Highlights over the years have been too numerous to mention individually but the contribution of some of the following stalwarts and veterans ought to be acknowledged. Firstly, **Mike Vipond** whose Walter Raleigh-like persona and dash combined with his impeccable command of the language of Shakespeare, made him an integral part of the furniture for many summers. Secondly, the erstwhile Master of Music, **John Le Grove** whose superb musical repertoire and ability to knock up many a tune in the style of Byrd and Tallis never ceased to amaze, to say nothing of his hose. Thirdly, the enthusiastic and passionate **Simon Fuller**, who loved Kentwell and whose love of the subject was so infectious to all and sundry. Fourthly, **Carlos Reynell** whose Spanish looks and comical mullet, have rightly been the target of much well-deserved suspicion and mirth. Last, but by no means least, **Claire Goodin** who has taken on board the costume and dance elements with such aplomb, whilst simultaneously being the living embodiment of Spenser's Gloriana in his epic poem 'The Fairie Queene,' as well as bearing an uncanny resemblance to Queenie in Blackadder, especially when petulantly stamping her feet, an all too common occurrence.

Above all, Kentwell is a day out with real educational purpose, lots of fun, involving dressing up and speaking funny words. It also marks the end of another academic year and carries the promise of a golden summer hoving rapidly into view. Year on year the 'Kentwell Experience' is a a real pleasure for pupils and teachers alike.

OTHER EXCURSIONS

Lest it be thought that trips are limited to the above, there are also Brandeston signatures (symbolic, rather than in grafitti form) to be seen across the county, across the country and abroad in places as diverse as:

In Suffolk: The Wolsey Theatre, Sutton Hoo, The Suffolk Show, Theatre Royal – Bury, Duxford Imperial War Museum, Parham Airfield Control Tower, Minsmere RSPB Reserve, Sizewell Power Stations, Aldeburgh, Helmingham Hall, Easton Farm Park, Orford Castle, Lowestoft Fish Market, The National Stud – Newmarket, Thorpeness Mere, Framlingham Castle, Stonham Barns, Woodbridge Tide Mill, Snape Maltings, Lavenham, Banham Zoo, Christchurch Park, Alton Water, Shawsgate Vineyard, Pleasurewood Hills, Foxborough Farm (Suffolk Wildlife Trust). **In Norfolk**: Castle Museum – Norwich, Norwich Cathedral, Sainsbury Centre UEA, Theatre Royal Norwich, Bressingham Railway Museum, Grimes Graves, Blakeney, Holkham, North Norfolk Railway, Dinosaur Park - Norwich. **In Essex**: Lakeside, Colchester Castle and Zoo, Waterworld, Mercury Theatre, Colne Valley Railway. **In Cumbria**: Lake Buttermere, Lake Windermere, Honister Pass Slate Mines, Aquarium of the Lakes, Beatrix Potter Museum, Keswick Pencil Museum, Ravenglass and Eskdale Railway. **In Yorkshire**: Scarborough, Castleton, N.York Moors Railway, National Railway Museum – York, Jorvik, Castle Museum – York, York Minster, Whitby Abbey, Robin Hood's Bay. **Other points of the English compass**: Ely Cathedral, King's College – Cambridge, The Science Centre – Bristol, Legoland – Windsor, Beale Park, Cotswold Wildlife Park, The Henry Moore Foundation, Chessington World of Adventures; Bluewater, Theatre Royal – Stratford, Sadlers Wells, The Thames Barrier, Lyme Regis, Corfe Castle, South-west Coastal Path – Lulworth Cove and Durdle Door, Brownsea Island, Salisbury Cathedral, Rufus Stone in the New Forest, Winchester Cathedral, Knole House, Runneymede Memorial, Royal Opera House, Covent Garden, The Pennine Way National Path, Castleton (Derbyshire), Mam Tor and Peveril Castle, Dartmoor, The London Eye, Cheddar Gorge and Wookey Hole, The Roman Baths, Bath, NEC Birmingham, Lincoln Cathedral, Sherwood Forest, St.Thomas' Pilgrim's Hospital and Canterbury Cathedral. **In Scotland**: Isle of Cumbrae, Ayr, Prestwick, Burns Country, National Sportscotland Sailing Centre on the Clyde. **In Belgium**: Bruges, Bruxelles, Waterloo, The Ardennes, Ghent Cathedral and Castle, Blankenberg, Grottoes of Han – Han-sur-Lesse, Zeebrugge, Antwerp. **In Holland**: Middelberg, Goes, Noordwijk, The Hague – Madurodam, Amsterdam, Alkmaar Cheese Market, Volendam,

Top to bottom, from left:
1975 – first IAPS cruise at Valetta with Jeremy Kemp, Richard Larter and Simon Ferguson; Mykonos, ashore from SS Uganda, 1970s; Braving the North Sea at Aldeburgh – Fiona Kelsall and friends; A good head for heights, Skern Lodge; Crabbing at Walberswick 2007; Small world – trip to Legoland, Windsor, 2008; Touch and feel – at Colchester Zoo; Matt Warren surfing, Skern Lodge 2008.

Marken, Aalsmeer Flower Market, Delft, Rotterdam. **In France**: In Paris: The Opera House, Eiffel Tower, Notre Dame, a bateau-mouche down the Seine, Place du Tertre. Elsewhere: Euro Disney, Futuroscope – Poitiers, Amboise, Loire Valley, The Normandy Beaches, Pegasus Bridge, Arromanches, Bayeux, Caen, Barfleur, Falaise, Parc Astérix, Rouen, Mont St Michel, Avranches, Dinand, Monet's Garden, Giverny, Dieppe, Château Vaux le Vicomte. **In Cyprus**: Kyrenia, Crusader Castle at Kantara and St. Hilarion.

In an age when we are told that teachers are increasingly reluctant to undertake trips because of the lurking threats of litigation, imagine just how many Risk Assessments and Health and Safety surveys will have taken place, and how many thousands of forms will have had to be filled in to give young Brandestonians horizons as wide as the above list shows.

SKI HOLIDAYS OVER THE YEARS

Generations of Brandeston Hall boys and girls have, over the years, enjoyed the ski-slope experience, as members of school parties led by **Mike Anderson, Brian Rosen, Mike Vipond** and **Sally Thomson**.

Ski resorts visited have included: **In Italy**: San Valentino, Piancavallo, Aprica, La Polsa, Andalo, Foppolo, Paso Tonale. **In France**: Les Contamines, Notre Dame de Bellecombe, Courcheval, Alpe d'Huez, Serre Chevalier (Puy St Vincent / Montgenevre). **in Switzerland**: Crans Montana, Zermatt, St Moritz, Leysin, Saas Fee; and in Austria: Maurach, KitzBühl, Zell am See, and Mayrhofen.

Mike Anderson writes –
'Many of my most fulfilling times as a teacher have been spent outside the classroom where the true characters of children come to light. The ski holidays undertaken at Brandeston Hall were perfect examples of this: great fun and very revealing, as many children who were not really team games players learned the excitement of outdoor pursuits. 'Sir' always looked good for the first day or two but was always trailing behind by day three or four!

The first trip of all was to an isolated hotel in the middle of nowhere just above the snow line but the skiing was good and the evenings, spent

Above: Residential trip to Castleton – Year 4 walking up Mam Tor, 2007.

swimming, or sitting round a huge open fire talking about the day, were magical. Clothing was hired in those days and one of the excitements of the trip was the arrival of huge boxes of kit prior to departure. Collecting it in afterwards was never as easy!

Other memories from the early trips include the military music blaring out at the bottom of the slopes in communist Bulgaria, a trip where the children could find nothing to spend their money on and even came home with a profit after selling brightly coloured bobble hats to local skiers. In Les Contamines Didier Six, a current French International footballer at the time, also happened to be staying. He was desperately anxious that no one found out he was enjoying such a dangerous sport when, officially, on the injured list!

Happy days, and I hope trips that led to a life time interest in a wonderful sport.'

(Mike, subsequently Head of the Junior School at both Kings, Ely and Taunton, and his late wife, Janet, really started the ball rolling in planning the first excursion to San Valentino in 1976... and it's still rolling. Not a single year missed, on the slopes, since!)

Mike Vipond writes –
'With the enormous growth in popularity of skiing holidays in the early 1980s Ann and I undertook to lead 'ski novice' groups in order to prepare them for greater things. Aprica was ideal for such nursery slope groups and thus it was that a number of gentle creatures learnt to ski and experience the wonder of the mountains with patient and caring Italian Instructors.'

Brian Rosen writes –
'I must have been on about a dozen Brandeston Ski Holidays, mainly as party leader and, of course, organizer. I almost always returned proud of the behaviour and enthusiasm, not to mention the skiing progress of not just the pupils but the accompanying Staff, who worked pretty hard. We all learnt that, although we were at the mercy of the weather, we could still make progress and also take a pride in our battles with the elements.

My philosophy was not complicated – we all had a common goal, to ski and enjoy ourselves as much as possible but always with safety in mind. It was never difficult to maintain discipline as just a threat of missing time on the slopes brought everyone back in line. Yes, one boy did spend a morning shovelling snow off the hotel steps as a reward for throwing a snowball at a passing Porsche, whose driver, understandably, had become extremely irate!

The holidays were never just about skiing. To get the maximum benefit from the week, the entire party, including Staff and, wherever possible, any accompanying parents, were strongly encouraged to take part in the collective 'après-ski' activities. Thus we organized night descents with flaming torches (carried by adults!) swimming, skating, tobogganing, 'ice hockey' with brooms and balloons, fondue evenings etc.; thus nobody had the slightest chance of becoming bored when they weren't actually on the piste. Then, of course, there was the occasion in 1978 when, after an excellent week's skiing in Piancavallo, we had to vacate our hotel early on the morning of departure and, with a late evening flight scheduled, we decided to grab a memorable day in Venice with **Bob Williams** as our 'built-in guide'!

When I retired I was very happy to hand over the 'ski portfolio' to **Sally Thomson** who had been with me on the last few trips and had been a huge help with the organisation. It is very pleasing to note the number of years that Sally has continued to fly the flag and that the

Top: Brandeston skiers in the chair lift at the Italian resort of Andalo.
Above: Sun on the ski slopes in Italy.

school has now enjoyed an unbroken run of such holidays in excess of 30 years, since Mike and Jan Anderson's first tentative venture of 1976-77. Dear me, I wonder how much that has cost the parents?! Surely, in terms of the overall experience, money well spent!'

Sally Thomson writes – 'After I took over the mantle from Brian Rosen I was helped for the first couple of years by the admirable **Hugh and Margaret Kennon**. Subsequently various Members of Staff have given up their February half terms to assist in a variety of ways. Likewise, parental help has proved invaluable, with **Jon Ford**, now a Governor but then the father of **Jeremy** and subsequently **Michelle**, being one of the longest serving parents. He even joined us on a couple of occasions long after his children had long left the College! **Nick Stolls** was another. He learnt to ski with his son **Matthew** on our trip to Kitzbühl in 1995 and was a regular participant for several years thereafter. He rejoined us in 2003 with Matt in tow – who, by then, had put his GAP year in Canada to good use, having qualified as a ski instructor! A couple of years ago Nick, a dentist by profession, joined us once again, taking charge of the Tuck Shop! (Something of an anomaly here!)

Memorable moments spring to mind both on the slopes and during 'après-ski'. We have had our

Above: James Finney, James Trembath and Stephen Packer. They met West Indian fast bowling legend Courtney Walsh at Lords in 2007.

fair share of accidents – **Harry Mitchell** being helicoptered off the mountain on the first morning of my first trip! – a baptism of fire. Inevitably, the odd broken leg – the most memorable being **James Loveridge** who had one false leg anyway – the look on the piste paramedic's face when the false leg came off in his hand is one I'll never forget!

In 2003 we were fortunate to find a superb hotel in Andalo which we use on alternate years and tend to look for another Italian resort to use in conjunction with it. Last year we hit upon another fantastic hotel in La Polsa but the snow was almost non-existent so that rather took the edge off the week. This is becoming a problem across the Alpine area. We have also been lucky enough to have the same PGL Rep for the last four years and Kenny from Scotland has become an integral part of the Brandeston Hall Ski Trip!

The major difference from my first trip in 1992 to today is the increase in Health and Safety considerations. The amount of paperwork and time spent on risk assessments, consent forms etc. is enough to put anyone off but, as soon as we are away and everyone is having a great time on the slope, all those hassles are quickly forgotten – the joy of seeing the beginners master a red run at the end of the week is always a highlight and one that I never grow tired of!'

VISITS TO SPORTS EVENTS

By way of demonstrating that emulation of top sportsmen and women is the best way to improve performances, Brandeston pupils have seen for themselves the very best of sporting endeavour at:

All England Club, Wimbledon; Twickenham; National Hockey Sports Centre, Milton Keynes; Lords; Essex County Ground, Chelmsford; Saracens RUFC, Vicarage Rd; Northampton RUFC, Franklins Gardens; Wasps RUFC, Twyford Park, Wembley Stadium (Mk 1); Wembley Arena; Leicester Tigers RUFC, Welford Rd; Bath RUFC (The Rec.); Cambridge University Ground, Grange Rd., Coventry RUFC (Butts Park Arena) and ITFC, Portman Rd.

STUDENTS FROM ABROAD

Few Brandeston pupils of the 40s and 50s could be described as anything other than white Anglo-Saxon. In those days most people were ethnically conservative in their views. Just as improved communications across the world opened up the possibilities of educational travel, so did they correspondingly increase the numbers of pupils coming from overseas, not only from expatriate British families but also from families of non-British origins who were attracted by the traditions and benefits of a British education.

With boarding on the decline in Britain, it was important to maintain numbers. High profile recruiting tours were undertaken. For schools, including Brandeston, the educational benefits were massive. Young minds were opened up by growing up alongside youngsters of different ethnic origins, and mutual understanding inevitably increased.

For young people set to inherit an increasingly cosmopolitan world this is of great consequence. Brandeston has welcomed in recent years pupils from Japan (**Emily Sato** a very fine artist), Hong Kong, Russia, Spain, Germany (**Lars Fischer**), China, and Nigeria. The **3 Oguntayo brothers**, sons of Chief O.O. Oguntayo, exemplified the new multi-ethnic world of education. They were one of the first ethnic African families to attend both Brandeston and the College. **Tosin,** the youngest of the three, records his first impressions below, remembering his ready acceptance into the school, something of which all can be proud:

I started at Brandeston in September 1983. As an 8 year old Nigerian boy who had never lived away from home, the whole experience should have been very daunting. However, from the very outset, I felt like I was embarking on the greatest adventure of my life. I distinctly remember wondering why some of my fellow pupils were feeling home sick, when there were so many new experiences to discover and explore.

Despite being one of only two black children at the school, everyone made me feel so accepted that I settled in very quickly, and never really felt that I was different to any of my fellow pupils. An integral part of my being able to settle in so well was the role of the wonderful Miss Rix, our Head Matron. I can still picture her reading to us each evening at bed time. The very first book she read to us was Roald Dahl's 'James and the Giant Peach'. I had never had anybody read to me at bed time before, and so it was something that I really cherished. It also served to bring all the members of my dorm closer together, as it was an experience that we could all share in and look forward to.

I also remember the way that Miss Rix would ensure that we

dutifully folded our clothes every evening, by turning it into a competition and awarding a polo mint, to the person with the flattest and neatest result!

I also recall being fascinated by 'Fred' the school peacock. I had never seen a peacock before in my life, and to watch him spread his wings was mesmerizing.

I can remember enjoying myself so much in my first few weeks that when we reached half term, I was really quite disappointed. I can distinctly remember thinking: " Half Term? How can it be half term already? I want to stay at school!" It really had become a home from home for me within those few short weeks. To this day, Brandeston retains an extremely special place in my heart.

Tosin Oguntayo, Brandeston Hall 1983–88, Constable House.

(Tosin was an outstanding sportsman throughout his time at Brandeston Hall and the College. He still holds the U14 record for the Long Jump. He went on to become Head of School at Framlingham in 1992-93 and is now carving out a successful career as a London barrister).

CHARITABLE CAUSES

It is important that those who enjoy the privileges of a good education should be aware of problems facing those who are less privileged, and of causes which are dependent on voluntary charitable support. That is part of education. When called upon, the Brandeston community has always responded with genuine enthusiasm, in supporting Appeals, not merely through their generous financial support but through extraordinarily imaginative ideas and, often, enormous physical endeavour. Staff and pupils alike have been emblazoned in red for a day, venerable beards shaved, treasured ITFC scarves burned and outrageously attired senior girls strutting their stuff on the cat-walk! It has all been great fun and well worth the effort.

Sally Thomson (For many years the school's Fund-Raising Co-ordinator) writes:

'Summoning both the imagination and the energy to raise worthwhile sums of money, for a wide range of charities, has always been a very important part of life at Brandeston Hall. Over the years we have supported deserving causes overseas, nationally and locally through a variety of interesting and sometimes quite original activities. A perennial favourite has always been the chance to wear something other than your uniform to school. We have had themes - such as wearing something red for the Comic Relief Red Nose Day Appeals (and, thus attired, engage in fund-raising antics including an 'Egg and Spoon' Race around the Cross-country Course!), or the Harry Potter Day as part of 2007 Book Week to support Book Aid, or your jeans on Jeans for Genes Day, but quite often it's just your favourite casual clothes! Always a solid earner; the 'fines' accumulated for dressing down in this manner earned an admirable £1,000 for the Asian Tsunami Relief Fund and a similar amount was collected for the 2005 Pakistan Earthquake Appeal.

In recent years a popular charity event has been the Disco organised by Year 7 pupils. Money has been raised for Cancer Research and, latterly, Suffolk Lowland Search and Rescue of which one of our staff is a volunteer member. In similar vein, the annual Summer Fete organised by Year 8 pupils has also been a major fund raiser. For a period of a quarter of a century, or more, we have seen a variety of innovative initiatives: a fashion show on a recycling theme, an antiques valuation evening and, on one famous occasion, we challenged the pupils to multiply a £1, thus allowing them to develop their entrepreneurial skills! One of the highlights of the past decade has to be the Sponsored Swim in 1999 which raised a fantastic £6,500 for Children in Need, with every child in the school and numerous members of staff taking part, and the highlight of 2008 was the £3K raised via a sponsored Spellathon in aid of the NSPCC.

Our prime charity focus for the past five years has been the Rogbonko Village School in Sierra Leone. In that time we have raised well over £12,000, which has paid for all the materials to build the new school, has equipped every pupil with a mosquito net and has helped to resource classes. A drop in the ocean in terms of Africa's on-going needs but, for this particular village, a lifeline.'

Above: 'Harry Potters' William Simpson, William Donsworth, Sam Tournay-Godfrey and Arthur Getting.

Above: "So those are the Pyramids..." photo taken at Giza in 1982, the year Brandeston Hall's vessel, SS 'Uganda' was requisitioned, mid-cruise, as a hospital ship for the Falklands campaign.

Good Causes supported over the years: The school has supported almost a hundred different charities – local, national and international – often on more than one occasion. The Charities supported have included: several Cancer charities, a number of Environmental charities, Comic Relief, various African charities, Guide Dogs for the Blind, the Asian Tsunami Appeal and other spontaneous responses to natural disasters, Redwings Sanctuary, Mencap, Dr Barnado's and other children's charities, The Red Cross, St John's Ambulance and the Royal British Legion Poppy Appeal.

The IAPS Easter Mediterranean Cruises, by Bob Williams:

I still encounter former pupils who assure me that it was the best holiday of their lives. Certainly, for those boys and girls who had never previously ventured beyond these shores to explore the Med in an action-packed ten days (14 on our first venture in 1975), on the dear old SS 'Uganda', was an intense and exciting learning curve. To sense that tingle in the spine at setting foot on a new continent (Asia or Africa), with its attendant, somewhat alien sensory impact, in what for most were their pre-teens, is not something easily forgotten. Memorable moments would have included sailing out of Venice with a breathtaking view from above the Bridge, steaming into the sea-filled volcanic crater that is the island of Santorini (Was it the original Atlantis of legend??), listening to the proverbial penny drop in the vast Roman theatre at Ephesus (from where St. Paul had to flee for his life after making contentious remarks about the Goddess Diana), in 1982, being met by Kate Adie on the Naples quayside as the ship was requisitioned (in mid-cruise!) for emergency duties in the South Atlantic... or simply being glad of the pretty robust 'sea-sick' bags that were always to hand when the sea occasionally cut up rough!

My IAPS Cruise Diary, for Easter 1976 gives just a flavour of what it was all about:

'DUBROVNIK: A safe arrival. The first glimpse is always breathtaking. A ten minute drive from the airport along the scenic Dalmatian coast road and, quite suddenly, the city is below us. A day and a half before 'Uganda' sails; time to explore what is the best preserved medieval city in Europe. Pedestrians only – no fumes, no noise: wonderful! A circumnavigation of the city atop the walls provides us all with some fine views and the Party Leader with acute vertigo.

NAUPLIA: The weather is immediately kind; the sea like a mill-pond and dolphins are spotted at dawn on the first morning. Around Cape Matapan we follow the Greek mainland northwards making for the small port of Nauplia. Too shallow to accommodate 'Uganda's' 17,000 tonnes so we go ashore by ship's boat, always an interesting feat of logistics. We aim for the theatre at Epidaurus and the hill-top acropolis at Mycenae with its famous Lion Gate and Beehive tomb. Aboard once again at dusk, tired, a little sun-burnt and anticipating our first look at the continent of Africa.

PORT SAID AND CAIRO: Coming alongside is a fascinating business. Our arrival is marked with a military band (including bagpipes!) - re-assuring to know that the trappings of Empire are not entirely forgotten! The bumboats swarm around the ship providing the opportunity for our young travellers to indulge in some hard bargaining over the ship's side. Warnings that our impressions of Egypt will be confused. This is a country of disturbing contrasts: twilight shanty towns; persistent beggars; the awesome grandeur of the Pyramids – what an incredible achievement – (Napoleon's Court Mathematician estimated that there was sufficient masonry in the three pyramids at Giza to enclose the whole of France with a wall ten feet high and one foot thick!); buses overcrowded well beyond the point of danger to life and limb; graceful Feluccas on the Nile; the war-torn Canal Zone; the incredibly beautiful treasures of the Cairo Museum. The sarcophagi, jewellery and death-mask of Tut-an-khamun has, in itself, been worth seven hours of the most uncomfortable coach journeys we are ever likely to endure.

HAIFA AND JERUSALEM: Last minute clearance from the F.O. enables us to fulfil our programme. The troubles on the West bank had caused much uncertainty. Visiting both Egypt and Israel within three days is a contrived coincidence which serves to underline two very differing views of their mutual situation. To set foot in the Holy Land at this time of the year adds a new dimension to an understanding of Easter. Our excellent guide did his stuff with customary efficiency: the Church of the Nativity in Bethlehem, the old City of Jerusalem, the Via Dolorosa, the Holy Sepulchre, Gethsemane and the Garden Tomb – names so familiar, now seen for the first time.

PIRAEUS AND ATHENS: Between ports of call there is rarely a dull moment. Deck Hockey, the Swimming Pool, Fancy dress and Quiz Competitions and the nightly Disco all provide what seems to be almost non-stop entertainment. Over the final two days the Mediterranean abruptly changes its mood. A force 8/9 gale soon provides firm evidence as to who is, or is not, a good sailor. Rhodes, Santorini and Mylos are all viewed from close inshore but we are unable to set foot on these gems of the Greek Islands. Final landfall Piraeus: Total distance steamed – 2,118 miles. A morning ashore in Athens, legs behaving as if they are still at sea. We climb up to the Acropolis and spend our few remaining drachmas in the Flea Market.

A remarkable bonus on the journey home: all are invited (in turn!) on to the flight deck to view the controls of our vintage Comet. Jet lag and a 22-hour long final day fail to dim a genuine regret that the holiday of a young lifetime is over so quickly... Just the 'Cruise Project' to complete now!'

Footnote: SS Uganda. In July 2007 the nation paused to reflect on the Falklands Campaign of 1982. The Framlingham Yearbook carried Bob William's memories of how young Brandestonians were inadvertently caught up in the conflict as their cruise came to a premature end when their ship, The SS Uganda, was requisitioned. In the April of that year they were on the shores of NE Africa, having just completed a memorable day in Cairo, when the instruction came that the ship was to sail within the hour, destination unknown! Full steam from Alexandria to Naples. Here all passengers disembarked, having been greeted by the paparazzi, including Kate Adie. The SS Uganda was to head for the South Atlantic and to become a Task Force Hospital Ship. The early return to Suffolk was similarly greeted by reporters from the EADT and Radio Orwell. Bob still has a recording of **John Fuller's** chirpy interview that went out over the airwaves of Suffolk!

Sadly this proved to be just about 'Uganda's final assignment. The 'floating classroom' turned Hospital Ship returned to Southampton on 9th August 1982. Following a re-fit, she did a further two and a half year spell of duty, ferrying troops between Ascension and Port Stanley – until Stanley's airport was again fully operational. She then lay forgotten and rusting and an ignominious end in a Taiwan scrap-yard appeared to be her fate. In fact she foundered in 1986, in a typhoon off Kaohsiung, before reaching the breaker's yard. She lives on in the memory of those who sailed in her, exploring new horizons.

Over four memorable cruises, a Brandeston footfall was registered in: **Italy**: Venice, Naples; **Croatia**: Split, Dubrovnik;

Greece: Itea – Delphi, Mycenae, Piraeus – Athens, Nauplia – Epidauros, Volos – Meteora, Santorini, Rhodes – Lindos, Mykonos, Crete – Heraklion and Knossos; **Cyprus**: Limassol and Paphos; **Turkey**: Kusadesi, Izmir – Ephesus; **Syria**: Tartus, Crac-des-Chevaliers; **Israel**: Haifa, Nazareth, Sea of Galilee – Capernaum and Tiberius, Jericho, The Dead Sea – En Gedi, Masada, Bethlehem, Jerusalem and Ashdod; **Egypt**: Alexandria, Cairo, Giza, Pt Said; **Malta**: Valletta.

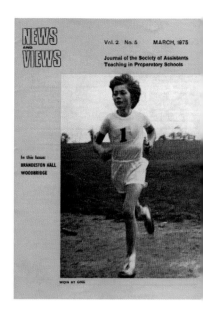

Above: Iain Birrell – Cross-country winner at King's Ely, featured on 1975 IAPS Journal cover. His brother Tim was killed in a tragic skiing accident (see p142).

IAPS (INDEPENDENT ASSOCIATION OF PREPARATORY SCHOOLS)

Brandeston Hall does not exist in an educational vacuum. Staff and pupils are part of the wider educational world, subject to academic demands, responding to outside pressures, sharing experience and evolving as teachers and pupils come and go. The Headmaster has traditionally been a member of IAPS – an organisation bringing together Prep Schools to their mutual benefit.

IAPS organise sports meetings for pupils, run orchestras drawn from member schools, and organise academic meetings for staff. This means that both staff and pupils are involved more widely, and that staff, in particular, can learn from sharing experience with teachers in other schools – professionally important if one's school is snuggled away in the heart of the Suffolk countryside.

The schools take it in turns to host meetings for staff, and Brandeston has done its share of hosting over the years. The pupils have also participated fully in IAPS sports meetings, with many notable successes.

The organisation produces a thrice yearly journal, 'Prep School'. This evolved from the merger, in 1988, of the former 'Preparatory Schools Review' with the 'SATIPS' magazine (Society of Assistants Teaching In Preparatory Schools) to which Brandeston teachers contributed, making Brandeston known to a wider audience.

In 1975 Brandeston Senior Master Bob Williams contributed a blockbusting 6 pages on the school for the occasional series 'In which we serve'.

SPECIAL EVENTS

Sometimes it is important to involve children in events on site, events aimed at reminding them of their heritage or of historic or national events. Notable, amongst many others, in this respect are:

1995, 50th anniversary of VE Day: VE Day Street Party. Major General Jack Dye MC (his MC was actually signed by Field Marshal Montgomery), himself a veteran of the Normandy beaches, came along, together with Robin Wilson MC, a friend and fellow Company Commander, who became Deputy Head of Taverham Hall, and also very much involved in the Snape/Brandeston musical link. Jack had also personally presented a DCM (a near-VC) to a Sergeant who had saved his life, so few people could have been better qualified to personify the experience of heroism.

1998, Jubilee Celebration of the Opening of Brandeston Hall: *Nigel Johnson reminisces:* There was the great '50th' Celebration of Brandeston's Foundation, masterminded by Bob Williams. A weekend that saw so much, with a wonderful Service of Commemoration underneath the War Memorial Plaque above the front entrance to the Hall. It was a wonderful weekend with an excellent exhibition of memorabilia curated by Sally Thomson, a marvellous tea provided by Daphne Elliott – with a special cake ceremonially cut by the well represented 'Class of '48' OFs. We were delighted to welcome many former people who had played a significant role in the school's development over the half century – including Sir Patrick Howard-Dobson, Rachel Kittermaster, John and Wendy Pemberton and that awesome triplicate of venerable former Matrons: Dulcie Wilton, Cherrie Allsop, Joan Rix all expressing their delight at seeing the school achieving so much. Then there was the memorable Golden Jubilee Ball to carry us through to the wee small hours.

The words of Rev Roger Dixon at the Golden Jubilee Commemorative Service on May 30th will have reverberated and continue to reverberate with generations of Brandestonians: "Let us now praise famous men – I wonder how all these young men whose names have been read today would have felt about being called famous... They had no opportunity to prove what would have been their place in life, what would have been their achievements. But when we reflect on that, then it makes this school all the more fitting a memorial to them.

For what they had no chance or opening in their lives to do, is made possible for many boys and girls through their living memorial... What these young men were prevented from doing by their deaths in sacrifice for the liberty and safety of their country, we must achieve for them, and we must provide every opportunity for the young people who pass through this school... to do so too.

...We are celebrating fifty years of the life of the Junior School and look forward to the next fifty years and all the years to follow.... For what was worth fighting for in 1914 and 1939, what was worth handing on to the young for fifty years past, is worth working for in the future".

2008, 60th Birthday of Brandeston Hall School: On September 20th the SOF organised another special birthday celebration at the school, with displays of old photographs, an official tree planting, featuring two of the original pupils, and a fly-over of a Gypsy Moth. Brandeston singers entertained 150 guests at a special birthday supper held at the College, and Brandeston pupils were given a tangible and edible memento of the occasion in the shape of a large iced birthday cake depicting the main school building. Later in the academic year, in February 2009 and by way of further celebration of the opening, the Myers-Allens organised a very successful Hangar Dance, inviting parents, grandparents and staff to re-create the atmosphere of the 1940s, in period dress, to the strains of period music.

CONCLUSION

The education of the young takes place inside and outside the classroom. It takes place in the home, in the school and in the wider world. It takes place as young people are drawn into experiences which help them to empathise with other people, other places and other cultures, as well as understanding themselves and developing their own talents. It takes place as they are brought to relate to the historical context in which they have been placed. They need also to understand the past, and to be led to anticipate the future which awaits them. The process by which they come to take their place in the wider, adult world is a complex one. It can only be regretted that these vital, external dimensions of education are so frequently thwarted by the constraints of our increasingly cautious and litigious culture.

Left to right, top: 50th Birthday numerals. 2000 meeting of the Class of '74: Paul Elliott, Bob Williams, Sarah Elliott (née Blake) June Schneidau, Jeremy Kemp, Sarah McLagan, Ian Tooley, Edward Moore, Louise Kemp, Michael Schneidau, Daren McLagan, Catherine Tooley and Beverley Moore.

Centre: Major General Jack Dye at the 50th anniversary of VE Day, 1995. Rev Roger Dixon conducts the Golden Jubilee Commemorative Service May 30th 1998. General Sir Pat Howard-Dobson and William Hayes, 'Last Post' trumpeter, at the Jubilee Celebrations.

Bottom: The Class of '48, on 30th May 1998: Christopher Martin, John Thurlow, John Edwards, Charles Benson, Keith Handley, Robin Podd, Jim Blythe, Tony Martin, David Risk.
The 60th Birthday cake – an edible memento.

PART 3
PERSONAL PERSPECTIVES

A teacher is one who makes himself progressively unnecessary.
– THOMAS CARLYLE

Right: Bob Williams and John Pemberton,
two of Brandeston's longest serving teachers –
54 years between them.

From the moment I first came to Suffolk in the winter of 1993, Brandeston Hall has held a special place in my heart. With each passing year, its haunting beauty mellows and deepens in my affection. Each season brings fresh inspiration and different, seductive charms – in March, the daffodils break and green shoots and hawthorn dominate the spring palette. In summer, the air is heavy with the sweet smell of lilac and may, and nenuphars daub their yellow splashes on the calm surface of the Deben; the chilly autumn nights are redolent with sausages and bonfires, and on clear winter nights, the tingle of hoarfrosts challenges the efforts of the crackling fires in the massive tudor grates – but pervading all, there is the vitality, exuberance and fun of Brandeston's latter-day chatelains, our youngest Framlinghamians, the children of Brandeston Hall.

Gwen Randall began her Headship of Framlingham College in 1994 and retired in 2009. She was of a pioneering spirit – first female Head of the College, one of the first female members of HMC, and she showed a passionate commitment to the schools in her charge.

On Remembrance Sunday, I look at our two War Memorials and commune silently with the long forgotten shadows of Headmasters of the bleak war years. How terrible it must have been for Stocks, Whitworth and Kirkman to receive the relentless flow of news of fallen Framlinghamians. How young they were, how dreadful their sacrifice, son upon son, husband upon husband, father upon father. I think of each one as the pile of commemorative poppies, one for each life lost, is placed on the altar, a monstrous pile of red on which I lay my spray of white lilies. The memorials in Framlingham's Chapel remind us of the coldness of those deaths, the icy blast of war in the trenches, the chill of the mud, the choking gas, the acrid stench of blazing desert battles, the pain and the fear, the courage, and quiet acceptance of appalling duty. Their deaths must have challenged the spirit of those who were left at home, and each name engraved was etched with love and pride, and a deep sense of gratitude and sorrow. The tragedy of those memorial stones was transformed by the gift of Brandeston Hall – all too youthful deaths translated by a commitment to youthful lives.

The boys who stepped over the threshold in 1948 gave sense to it all. Many generations of boys and girls have spent their young years here and been touched by the magic of Brandeston. It was for their tomorrow that those men gave their yesterday, and those Old Framlinghamians who were spared the ultimate sacrifice of death in war had true vision when they made that perfect gift of Brandeston Hall.

Short trousers, pony tails, conkers, hopscotch, rugby scrums, dance and drama, eggy smells in science labs, croquet on the lawns, times tables, Janet and John, Beatrix Potter, Shakespeare, woodwork and jewellery making, choirs and athletics trials, flutes and fiddles, midnight feasts and fashion shows, pranks played on matron, school reports, merit stars and miscreants, cows in the distance, ducks on the pond, stick insects in jam jars, beetles in match boxes, bloodied knees, prizes and silver cups, granny and the school play – this is the tapestry of Brandeston Hall.

HEADMASTERS OF BRANDESTON HALL

The designation has changed over the years: Headmaster, Master and then Headmaster again. To some degree this can be attributed to politics, and to evolving perceptions of the role of the Head of the Junior School. Whatever the title, the job was the same, a demanding one, but fulfilling too.

Typical of most schools, Brandeston has known periods of the kind of stability that eventually comes to be taken for granted, interspersed with times of relative uncertainty. Headmasters leave their imprint in different ways. They have to respond to the educational currents of their time, and bend to the evolving demands of central government and educational fashion. There also has to be ease of transfer between the maintained and independent systems. Brandeston Headmasters are also part of the wider Framlingham/ Brandeston Foundation. All of this reduces scope for a Head to drive forward a fully individual view of education. Brandeston Heads have served the school well in their different ways. Few successful Heads are clones of one another. The best Heads are quite simply themselves: they embody and communicate values and standards with which parents and pupils can identify. They also inherit the ethos and traditions of a school and build on them.

In selecting Heads, Governors sometimes adopt a pendulum approach: no Head can possibly embody the full range of headmasterly qualities. Thus a Head whose perceived qualities are mainly academic, may be followed by someone more sports-orientated. A kindly, mellow figure may be followed by someone of more draconian qualities. Some circumstances favour an avuncular approach, others a more rigorous view of discipline. In the competitive world of independent education, the ability to market the school is increasingly important. Few human beings embody all the qualities that, at different times and in different circumstances, go to make for a good Headmaster. The best of them play to their own strengths and, by way of complementing them, appoint staff members who, between them, cover all the main requirements of a successful school.

Heads of Prep Schools are expected to imbue their schools with a happy, family atmosphere, and, at the same time, aspire to rigorous standards of academic achievement and good discipline. Few Headmasters come across uniformly to all parents and all pupils. Perceptions are subjective. That said, in a unit as small as a Prep School, the influence and leadership of the Head is paramount, not only in setting down values and standards, but also in leading a happy and effective staff, and in having a vision for the future.

In 60 years Brandeston has had 9 Heads, with an average term of service of close on 7 years. Two have served well into double figures. In recent years, Headships have been shorter, perhaps uncomfortably so. But history tells us that stability will return, and that, perhaps when it is least expected, a period of renewed continuity will ensue. The down-side of stability can be stagnation. The up-side of change can be innovation. The balance always has to be struck. Even as Heads may change, the loyalty and stability of long-serving staff will always bridge the transitions.

Some Brandeston Heads are still with us, and we have their living testimony. Others are now departed, so we have had to have recourse to what they have written, or what others have written about them. What follows is a collage of reflections, tracing the transition of the school from an embryonic independent 10-13 Junior House to a school almost two thirds the size of its parent. With an age range of 3-13, some pupils may spend twice as much time at Brandeston as they do at the Senior School. It is now a school which, while vital to the health of the College, also enjoys such independence as is necessary for it to be considered a fully fledged Prep School. While preparing most of its pupils for entry to Framlingham, it also offers Common Entrance and the possibility to move on to other independent schools.

DAVID KITTERMASTER 1948-1968

David Kittermaster, avuncular, a twinkle in his eye behind those thick-rimmed spectacles, accessible to parents, patient mathematician, enthusiastic cricket coach, an all-rounder who combined a sense of quiet discipline with approachability, was for 20 years the very embodiment of Brandeston. He set it on its way, and inspired the affection that so many Brandestonians maintain to this day towards their school. When he retired in 1968 it was a very special and poignant occasion.

John Edwards recalls how, under his benign gaze, pupils, particularly those with experience of life as a sub-species in the Junior House, were made to feel responsible individuals. Boarding at a young age produced home-sickness; the writing of weekly letters, the infrequent three week exeats needed the palliative of the genial style of Headmastership which David Kittermaster epitomized.

Affectionately known as 'Kippers', he was, in **Richard Overend's** words "a hands-on Head". **John Rankin** tells of DDK's "human kindness", of how he made Maths problem-solving an art

Top: DDK, 'Kippers', eking out the pennies to pupils in the early 50s – just £2 per term – mainly spent in the Tuck Shop. Centre: The commemorative plaque in All Saints Church, Brandeston. Below: David and Rachel Kittermaster in relaxed mode.

form, and how he would occasionally take on the boys at table tennis. John Capon recalls how he first learnt from DDK the rugby skills which were to take him to County standard, and keep him playing at club level until his mid-40s. This was a Headmaster who lived the job and who involved himself in every aspect of the lives of his young charges.

The wives of Prep School Heads play a vital role too, not only in supporting their husbands, but in filling in with those jobs which no-one else officially does. In her own gentle discrete way, **Rachel Kittermaster** filled this role. She was not only housekeeper, but if the cook was off, Rachel would step in and ensure the cook's work was done too. For **Robert le Rougetel**, himself later to become a schoolmaster, Rachel was the flute teacher who introduced him to the profound pleasures of classical music, while at the same time tolerating the playing of 78rpm records of Lonnie Donegan et al. in a hut situated well away from the main school.

Michael Wright, DDK's first Head of School, who had been with him the previous year in the College Junior House, looking after the cricket and hockey teams, remembers how the Kittermasters had corgi dogs, and how the boys kept their distance. One or two, including Michael, had their legs nipped.

There is a commemorative plaque in the church – David Kittermaster is the only Head to be so commemorated. It fell to him to establish the relationship between a new school and the village. He did it well. The links between the school and the church were part of that relationship. Given the position of the church in relation to the school, it could not be otherwise. **Jim Blythe** was instrumental in persuading the authorities to agree to having the plaque, which for generations of early Brandestonians brings back into nostalgic focus the years of their childhood.

RICHARD BROAD 1968-1974

Richard Broad was appointed Headmaster of Brandeston Hall in 1968, following DD Kittermaster. He had previously been Head of Gloucester House, Portora Junior School. During his Headship (1968-74) key initiatives included the introduction of a College Entrance Examination, the demise of the cane as an acceptable form of discipline, the robing of the Chapel Choir (generously funded by the mother of 1969-70 Head of School, **Charles Blackmore**) and the establishment of designated subject rooms/resource centres – and also a school orchestra. His Local History Activity Group produced an exhaustive 'Survey of the Parish of Brandeston' which was enthusiastically received and is still, to this day, a valued source of reference. A Parents' Association was set up and funds raised for the building of a new outdoor, but heated swimming pool. This meant that Brandestonians no longer had to be bussed across to the College or venture into the Deben. Richard was, in 1972, a founding member of the IAPS Orchestra Committee when Brandeston Hall established a long tradition of playing host to this national orchestra while they prepared for their annual concert at Snape Maltings. Other memories from this period may include "Ton" the Broads' independently-minded Jack Russell, power cuts caused by that time of national crisis (storm lanterns strung across the Dining Hall to facilitate the provision of Tea and an attempt at communal Prep), Guy Fawkes nights, the Otter Hounds (a successful protest denying the Easton Hunt Otter Hounds the right of access to the banks of the Deben within school grounds), the involvement of parents in team teas, **John Richards** and the Upper Third, Doctor Allen, and the water coming through the Head's study ceiling from above. And there was the unfortunate cow that was hooked on the other side of the river by an inexpert boy angler. During this time Richard's wife, **Cynthia**, maintained the tradition of strong involvement in the affairs of the school.

Leslie Gillett's History of the Second Sixty Years refers to the friction that developed in the final year of this Headship, describing it as a clash between '"justifiable independence' and 'unacceptable autonomy.' Brandeston is not the only Prep School where this kind of 'big brother, little brother' problem has emerged. Maybe the pendulum effect as described above had swung into motion. Opinion at the time was deeply divided, not least because Richard had enrolled the support of many parents in projects, including the construction of the swimming pool and robing of the choir. Dismay was felt within the student body too, not least because they were losing a fine teacher of History. This was a difficult time for the school. Richard's departure came at the end of the Easter Term, leaving **Bob Williams** as Interim Headmaster for the Summer Term. The July Speech Day of that Summer Term, held in the Old Gymnasium, is perhaps best remembered for Bob's active inclusion, for the first time, of senior pupils in the delivery of the Head's Annual Report. Head of School, **Jeremy Kemp** (a sporting review) and **Jeremy Wade** (a report on the year's cultural activities) both received warm applause for their contributions to an uplifting occasion.

After Brandeston Richard moved to King Edward's School, Witley, where, after a period in the Junior School, he became Head of History in the Senior School. He retired to Dunkeswell in Devon in 1988, where he remains a busy man.

Top: Choirmaster Malcolm Russell with choristers – the robing of the Chapel Choir was generously funded by the mother of 1969-70 Head of School, Charles Blackmore.
Centre: Parents Committee – fund-raising ball for the swimming pool, July 1970.
Below: The result of all the fund-raising efforts – excavation and construction of the swimming pool, sheltered from the north winds by the old garden wall

He and his wife Cynthia were welcomed back to Brandeston for Peter Arbon's 80th birthday in the new Village Hall, meeting up again with Bob Williams after some 33 years. He also returned for the 60th birthday celebrations of the school in September 2008. Whatever the circumstances of Richard's departure, it is clear that he is proud of his contributions to the school's development and that he retains great affection for it.

REFLECTIONS ON THE RW JONES YEARS
(1974-1980)
Joyce Jones, Ron's widow, in conversation with Bob Williams.

Ron came to Brandeston with a fine record not only as an outstanding teacher of Maths but also as a

Top: Brandeston Hall staff c.1968, l-r from back row: Miss J Wright, MH Beard, MA Neville, Miss IM Jenkins, Rev SF Heneker, JG Haslam, Miss O Arther. Front row: GA Ireland, JEL Pemberton, Mrs Aspinall, RP Broad, Mrs R Broad, JT Gilbert, Miss O Field. **Below:** The Golf course in Spring 1994 with James Jackson, Paul Lewis and Edward Maule.

remarkably adept cricket coach. However, by the time he took the helm at Brandeston Hall, he felt that this was best left to younger cricketers on the staff so he set about putting Brandeston on the map as a 'golfing preparatory school'. Ron's first remarks, to **Joyce**, on seeing the school estate for the first time, were "This would make a lovely 6-hole golf course..." He was right. He quickly set about making Brandeston Hall a respected name in the junior golfing world. By the summer of his enforced retirement in 1980, he had produced a patiently coached team, that came within an ace of winning the Stowe Putter, the prestigious annual Prep Schools' Championship. The 3-man team of **Neil Stanhope**, **John Coates** and **David Handley** finished second to Holmewoode House, from

Kent. Neil also finished a mere two points adrift of the winning score out of the ninety-one competitors for second place in the individual competition, earning himself both a hand-shake and a pat on the back from Peter Alliss!

Joyce fondly recalls their six years at Brandeston as very happy years. There was a cheerful Common Room, with staff, both academic and domestic and parents, all pulling in the same direction. Ron was always scrupulously fair in his dealings with all in his care, young and not-so-young. He was admired and liked by all. He was a Head who really cared. It was Ron's hand on the tiller when the decision was taken that Framlingham would go co-ed in September 1977. He was never in any doubt that it was the correct decision to take at the time. Not too many more years were to pass before the lasses were sweeping up the majority of the annual awards at Speech Day.

When Ron took up his appointment at Brandeston Hall, in September 1974, Bob invited him to write an article for the occasional series, 'In which we Serve', for the then annual SATIPS magazine. This reflected on the history of the school up to that date. Twenty-five years on, his credo on the fundamental philosophy of a good preparatory school - and the Preparatory School for Framlingham, in particular, still holds good:

'My first impressions of Brandeston were coloured by a small boy who leapt to open my car door as soon as I arrived, by the

Top: Brandeston Hall staff 1980, l-r, back row: Brian Rosen, Tony Lawrence, Malcolm Foster, Michael Baic, Mike Anderson, David Grace, Michael Vipond, Andrew Cronin. L-r, front row: Miss Janet Blatchly, Miss Riet Stuij (Housekeeper), Revd. Kenneth Roberts, Ron Jones, Mrs Joyce Jones, Bob Williams, Mrs Ann Nesling, Mrs Shirley Robinson. Below: Clock presented in 1998 by the SOF in memory of Ron Jones (1974-1980)

magnificent building - in part Early Tudor and set in the pleasant Suffolk countryside, by a friendly staff and well cared for grounds. The impression was that this was a place to savour and enjoy.

Sitting in my Study overlooking the meadows and woods beyond the River Deben, I still have the same conviction that this has the ideal setting, background and atmosphere to ensure the correct development of boys at a very impressionable age.

Suffolk has the calm and quiet of an earlier age. We have many boys who have their roots in the land, others from service families together with doctors', accountants' and shop-keepers' sons. Such diverse backgrounds enrich our community life.

What of the future? Perhaps within the limits of the essential preservation of personal contact there could be room for controlled growth. Numerically, we presently stand at 105 boarders and 61 day boys. However, any development must be to favour the maintenance of standards of academic excellence, behaviour and general morals and, whilst expansion may lead to a more viable unit financially, the feeling of family must be preserved.'

Ron and Joyce were always extremely generous hosts. An invitation to join them for a glass of something, at the Master's House, was always on the understanding that one really couldn't leave without 'having the other half', as Ron always put it!

Joyce has but one complaint. In a domestic and catering department, very ably run in the late '70s by the Dutch Housekeeper, **Miss Riet Stuij**, bread and butter pudding (Joyce's

favourite!) was all too rarely served, possibly because it was not greatly loved by the pupils.

A further recollection that still raises a smile was of one of the annual Governors' Staff Parties. As per custom, the prefects were on hand to serve food and top up wine glasses. As the last of the guests/VIPs departed it became apparent that, behind the scenes, a number of the prefectorial body, their public duty done, had been engaged in draining what was left of 'the grape'. Ron, possibly falling back on his experience of effective RAF disciplinary procedures, personally supervised the offenders' instant immersion in cold baths and offered them an 'opportunity to explain themselves', in the Study, the next morning!

It was a sad day for the school when Ron was smitten so suddenly and cruelly with a severe form of rheumatoid arthritis, thus having to take early retirement in July, 1980.

John Simpson (*the man who initiated the setting up of June staff parties at Brandeston Hall after Governors' meetings) additionally reflects that*: it was Ron Jones who gave Brandeston its spirit – the spirit of involvement. He was one of the major forces behind the decision to take girls – and was enthusiastic about doing so. Ron was also a great believer in using pupils to engage in conducted tours with prospective parents, something always appreciated by visitors.

John Ives recalls that it was his daughter, Lizzie now **Mrs Lizzie Hillier,** who was greeted by Ron Jones and told that she was the first girl to arrive at Brandeston.

PADDY NEWBERY 1980-1985

Paddy remembers: **Judith** and I still regard our time at Brandeston as a very special period in our lives. The initial five years of the eighties were, I believe, good ones for the School. The main changes that occurred were probably the introduction of girl boarders and the creation of a Pre-Prep class. Both of the changes were implemented without difficulty and they obviously widened the school's range in a positive manner. After a slight dip in numbers in 1980-1981 the school remained full and it sailed along on an even keel offering an enormous range of opportunities.

One of the first things I did was to amend the balance of the winter games programme so as to give more emphasis on hockey (which just happened to be my speciality sport) in order that the College gained from a strong pool of players moving up. The philosophy that hockey has a far greater take-away value for pupils in schools such as ours also came into the thinking but, inevitably, the football enthusiasts amongst the pupils and the staff were not quite as keen as the Master. I think I can fairly say that the objective was achieved.

A contributory factor in the hockey improvement was in the pitches produced by Mike Rutterford. He took over the grounds in the early eighties and what he achieved was truly outstanding. Before he had been with us long, he had made our pitches the best on our circuit and the envy of visiting teams. It was also wonderful to have a groundsman who really knew how to maintain and prepare a cricket square.

The other sport which was particularly strong was Cross-Country Running, brilliantly coached by Bob Williams. He was himself a former Welsh international runner and produced teams which swept all before them in various championships.

Drama played its part in Framlingham life, rising from the depths of the staff pantomime, performed after the annual firework party and a huge hit with parents and pupils alike, to some excellent productions directed by Tony Lawrence and Michael Vipond. For me the highlight was the 1981 joint production at the College of 'Joseph and the Amazing

Above: Paddy Newbery – 'Brandeston has the ability to cast a spell over everyone lucky enough to work or study there'.

Technicolor Dreamcoat' in which Brandeston Hall boys and girls provided the chorus. It was exceptional for a school production.

On the Art front the standard was high with, again, Bob Williams at the helm. Some of the pottery that came out of the school's kiln was magnificent indeed. We still have several fine pieces produced by our own children.

It would be unfair to single out any characters in particular. The staff in all areas of the school were a delight to work with, and their dedication and enthusiasm made it almost impossible for the school to be anything other than a happy, successful one. If I have to single out anyone, I should choose, first of all, my wife, Judith, who did an enormous amount to keep me on the straight and narrow and to engender a family feel within the school. This she achieved by ensuring that she and I had a considerable amount of social contact with parents and also by providing as many motherly touches as she possibly could. She was well backed by Miss Stuij the charming, highly efficient, but sometimes formidable, housekeeper and, over the five years, firstly by Jo Donsworth and then by Anne Hadley who were both wonderful school secretaries. I appreciate them the more because I suffered from far-from-good ones in my next appointment! The importance of these two positions cannot be over-emphasised and I know how lucky I was.

An amusing story regarding my period in office concerns the peacock 'Fred'. Fred had been at the school for many years before we arrived. After a few years the bird disappeared, I know not where. The rumour amongst the pupils was that I had shot it. Where that idea came from I have no idea but when we met friends who were parents during our time at Brandeston Hall they asked just recently if it was true that I had disposed of the peacock. It's a long time to take the blame for something I did not do! May I please scotch that particular fallacy!

Judith and I have nothing but happy memories of our time at Brandeston Hall. It is a truly wonderful place in which to run a Prep School and it has the ability to cast a spell over everyone lucky enough to work or study there.

NIGEL JOHNSON 1985-2000

Nigel reflects upon his Brandeston years. (More of Nigel's memories appear in other parts of this book).

Fifteen years was a long time to be Master of Brandeston Hall. It was a period of growth and development during which the school was hugely supported by the respective Heads of Framlingham College and three greatly influential Chairs of Governors.

My three senior partners were different in every way. **Laurie**

Laurie to a tee – he always supported the best interests of the school as a whole and worked tirelessly to support his teaching staff. However, my best memory of Laurie remains his cheerful and positive approach towards meetings and his irreverent approach towards all and sundry as he sat behind a small coffee table in the smallest of studies!

James Miller had very similar responses. I'm sad that James' period at the helm was such a short one. He was a man of vision and a big spender! James also left me very much alone to manage

Above: Brandeston Hall staff 1992/3 during Nigel Johnson's Headship.

Rimmer was a larger-than-life character and one who gave me the most marvellous introduction to headship at Framlingham: his watchword was trust. If I got it right then he made sure that I got due credit. If I got it wrong then I knew that I was in for a roasting! I well remember my very first Governors' Meeting, which at that time was held in the Athlone Hall. As we mounted the steps Laurie turned to me and said, "Don't speak unless you are spoken to and you are not to say anything at all on the matter of staff salaries" (this was a major subject of debate at the time). This was not something that I could ignore, but when Roger Paul, the then Chairman offered me the opportunity to speak, I did so. Although this was against Laurie's view, he ended the meeting in supporting my comments. That was

the Junior School. The fact that his two boys, **Richard** and **Tom**, were pupils meant that he probably had an insight into what was taking place anyway. He clearly recognised the importance of Brandeston Hall to the College as a whole and it was with his support that Brandeston opened its Pre-Prep with **Liz Tydeman** in charge and **Anthea Smith** as her able lieutenant. The opening of Pre-Prep, with such an experienced duo, was a significant development and ensured the continuing growth of the school to a point where BH reached the significant milestone of 300+ pupils in 1995. Whilst there was always concern that this facility for the very young was expensive (indeed regularly made a loss!) James saw its potential and its importance and supported every request that I made in terms of the development of the school. These included changes and improvements to Alice Hall, to accommodate more girl boarders, and a second floor to the two classrooms overlooking the pond, to house new junior classrooms.

However, it was under **Gwen Randall** that Brandeston really prospered in terms of new and magnificent capital developments. Between 1990-95 the growth in numbers had impacted upon the teaching life at Brandeston. We were pushed for space. In 1995 I was asked to put forward a development plan that would achieve a new Sports Hall and also offer a new and exciting Design and Technology Centre. The opening of the Rowley Hall in 1997 was a marvellous and exciting development, the more so since Gwen Randall agreed that it must not be simply a square box but should complement and add to the marvellous façade of the terrace and the Hall itself. The design, created by the Messrs Hollins of Framlingham, achieved everything that we could have hoped for, with a wonderful space that was used to the full to support a whole range of activities including drama, sport and music. However, it was the linked decision to change the use of the old gymnasium to a new DT suite that was a key initiative, with its mezzanine design floor and lower workshop facility. It was a teaching area that no other prep school in Suffolk could match! The re-development of the Library in 1999, funded by the OFs, was the final piece of the jigsaw and saw Brandeston achieve facilities that any school would be proud to possess. These governorial decisions were a demonstration of a huge confidence in the Prep School and the part that it would play in the overall well-being of the College.

Gwen Randall and I experienced an occasionally strained relationship. Gwen was far more hands-on than her predecessors and expected me to keep her more fully informed of my intentions and my management of Brandeston - something that I was not always comfortable with - but she was right to see Brandeston and the College as one school rather than separate entities. The march of time was inevitable and her determination to recognise the nature of the greater whole was to become a reality under my successor **Stephen Player**.

Buildings and facilities are key components of any successful school but it is always the people and the pupils that make a school and the community what it is. It is difficult to pick out those aspects that make Brandeston the special place that it undoubtedly is - so much is there which is 'special'. Staff changes were significant between 1985 and 2000. 1986 was a key year with the arrival of four people who were to have a huge and ongoing impact upon the life of the school. The departure of **Jim Bidwell** (Head of English),

Robin Williams (Head of Maths), **Nick Stafford** (Head of History) and **David Grace** (Director of Sport), opened the door for new blood to arrive in the form of Heads of Departments **Paul Baker** (Maths), **Robin Sampson** (Sport), **Simon Fuller** (History), **Nigel Cox** (English) and, as form teachers in the Junior Department, **Penelope Kirk**, **Richard Daykin** and **Sally Thomson**. Their impact was immediate and very influential in allowing me to change the nature of the school. Where previously Brandeston had concentrated upon 13+ exit to the College, the educational provision and expectation now became focused at a much earlier stage, with real emphasis being placed upon language and numeracy in the early years. This coincided with the decision to embrace the then new 'National Curriculum' and national tests (SATs) at 7+ and 11+. Paul, Richard, Robin, Sally and Penn became the heartbeat of the 'new' Common Room; they were (fortunately for me!) held in check by their more experienced colleagues amongst whom **Bob Williams** as Second Master, **Mike Vipond** (as Director of Studies) and **Shirley Robinson** (Head of Science) were legendary figures. Bob, in particular, was the most enormous help to me when I was learning the ropes; his quiet good humour and patience offered leadership of the highest quality – and this at a time of massive change in his personal life as he married for the first time and took on a ready-made family in Mandy, Paul, **Leila** (1985-86) and **Helen** (1985-1990). Gone were the tank tops and other vintage garments and in their place came an equally colourful but far more 'up-to-date' figure. Bob kept me in line quietly but effectively. His knowledge of Brandeston was encyclopaedic and allowed me scope to develop my own thoughts. What was equally important was his genuine enthusiasm and his willingness to embrace change and accept responsibility and work load without complaint – but more of that later!

The new staff gelled immediately, as well as dramatically reducing the average age of the Common Room! Paul and Richard's humour and sense of fun carried us through the day. Few escaped the focus of their attention and they were well supported by the boundless enthusiasm of Sally and Penn. Some staff suffered more than others, chief amongst them being our Aussie 'gap' students who were expected to know every Rolf Harris song and Simon Fuller who managed on so many occasions to achieve notoriety completely unintentionally for his actions! I well remember a history expedition to Thetford Castle. Simon had planned the trip for weeks – every last detail had been considered... bus booked, packed lunches on board, clip boards at the ready. **Judi** and I saw them on their way, expecting them to be away for about five hours. Imagine my surprise when they were back two hours later! It seems

During Nigel Johnson's Headship: **Clockwise from top left:** Liz Tydeman with first Pre-prep, 1990. Charlie Simpson crabbing. Robin Sampson. Nigel Johnson celebrating Christmas 1994 , with Elena Zharkova and her Russian cracker. Bob Williams with Olympic swimmer Karen Pickering in 2002. Tree planted in the memory of Karen Buttenshaw on the front lawn.

that Simon gave the children their instructions on attacking the motte and bailey and sent them off charging up the hill – unfortunately straight into a very large wasps nest! As the children ran back and away from danger, Simon's one thought was to protect them – so, as they charged one way, he charged the other! On reaching the wasps nest Simon proceeded to jump up and down on it, both to try and bury the wasps and to stop any more coming out. A brave but ultimately foolish act. Simon was of course stung more than anyone else and covered in bright pink calamine lotion for the next few days. Sadly, Simon was to die, still a young man, in 2005. His death was a loss to the teaching profession.

My time at Brandeston Hall saw the development of a professional body of teachers of the highest quality. This was demonstrated time and again in the results achieved for entry to the College through Scholarship and, of course, through external acclamation in two successful inspections of the work of Brandeston Hall by the Independent Schools Inspectorate.

It is difficult to encapsulate the importance of colleagues like Penn Kirk – who has gone on to become a successful Head in her own right at Portsmouth High Junior School and, currently, at Princes Mead School, Winchester. Brandeston's long tradition of vibrant drama was admirably enhanced by both Nigel Cox and Stephen Player; both acclaimed for very different but equally stunning productions of 'Peter Pan'. Robin Sampson, Richard Daykin, **Carlos Reynell, Margaret Kennon, Mary Vellacott** and Mike Vipond all played their part in providing a breadth of sporting opportunities for the children and, of course, the wonderful input of colleagues like **Roger Dixon**, who was an outstanding, caring and committed Chaplain and a wonderful support to me. His unique delivery in reading stories from Winnie the Pooh (always with a pertinent message) was legendary. And then there was **Joan Ironside** – Matron at Brandeston from 1991 to 2000. She brought with her years of experience of dealing with young people away from home, dispensing huge spoonfuls of T.L.C. whenever it was required. I have always thought that if ever a person was misnamed then it was Joan in her surname – that is unless you crossed Joan and then she raised herself to her full height and one was rapidly made aware that Joan was not pleased! And of course I could not omit my marvellous secretary of 11 years, **Wendy Thomas**, who saved me from making a fool of myself on so many occasions by saying "Do you really want to say that... ?" about a number of letters that I had written, or reminding me of actions that I needed to take to make the school run more smoothly. Her capacity to carry information of pupils and parents in her head never ceased to

amaze me and she was at my side in good and not-so-good times – a truly remarkable secretary and good friend.

Finally, I cannot complete the people-section without commenting on the importance of my wife Judi. She was there at all times, supporting, encouraging, picking up the pieces, listening to parents, supporting and serving match teas, teaching mathematics, supporting the kitchens and the matrons. There was no area of school life to which she did not make a significant contribution and the school would not have been the place that it was without her selfless determination and positive encouragement of the school and every area within it. As they say, behind every successful man... And don't I know it!

And what of the children? There are so many instances to consider of children who made a major impact upon the life of the school, youngsters like **Charlie Simpson** who later went on to become a member of the chart-topping group 'Busted' – a lad whom I was constantly telling to give up his music, and that he would never make a success of it! Or **Jeanine Thorpe** who was the single most talented musician that I have ever come across and **Karen Buttenshaw**, a wonderful Head of School but later to, sadly, lose her life in an accident whilst serving in the army – a job she loved so much. Karen's funeral at Brandeston was a moving occasion and supported by friends and family alike as a celebration of her wonderful life. We later planted a tree on the front lawn in her memory – a tree that still flowers each year. Then there was **Jaime Fraile**, one of a number of excellent Spanish pupils who came seeking to broaden their educational experience. Jaime was so powerful on the sports field (and so popular with the girls).

So many children and impossible to pay true credit to them all, but the youngsters were the life and soul of the school in every respect, and never more so than when we met the 'old enemies', Greshams, Felsted or Orwell Park, on the games field. What matches we enjoyed, what competition!... I still have memories of some fantastic rugby matches played against these schools, intense in every respect, and matches to grace any school playing field. Pride of place must go to an unbeaten 1st XV who carried all before them in 1996-97 and, under Richard Daykin, played some astonishingly hard rugby.

But I guess I saw Brandeston, and the community, at its best during the first Gulf War when **Gareth Ankerson's** father, Bob, was shot down over Iraq. For three days the school waited on tenterhooks to hear news, supporting Gareth, who was a boarder at the time, in every way that it could. Bob was later to come to Brandeston and voice his thanks to the school as a whole for their support for

Right: Foundation House 2004/5 – Elizabeth Tydeman and Nursery Nurse Michelle Wright with their young charges.

Gareth during those dark days before he was released from captivity in Baghdad.

Then there were the wonderful Parents' Weekends. What started as a fathers and sons cricket tea became a major happening. By the year 2000 we had over 650 people in attendance. This event was organized, over the years, with military precision by Messrs Stafford, Fuller and **Cullum**. Memories of parents dancing in wellington boots, long into the night, to the music of Nick Stolls and his band. Folk of all ages having fun.

I have memories too of fierce winter storms when the school and village were cut off for days at a time by snowfall. On one occasion we went out into the village to offer hot soup and jacket potatoes to the older residents since the electricity supply had failed! On another occasion Penn Kirk skied in across-country from Framlingham to support her beleaguered colleagues and the boarding community who were trapped at Brandeston. But we had such fun... stories around a roaring fire in the Old Library by candlelight, mass snowball fights and snowman-building competitions, raiding the kitchens for tin trays to be able to sledge down 'Cowpat Hill', the only suitable incline within miles.

And of course there was the Hurricane of 1987. I had no idea just how bad things were shaping up to be except that I couldn't sleep that night (the only one in my family who couldn't!) and that I kept looking out of the window, but in the darkness it was impossible to determine just what was going on. Only with the dawn could I see the damage and the horrendous conditions that we faced with three giant oaks down across the front drive, and the roads blocked everywhere by other fallen trees. Once again the boarding community and resident staff were left to cope with the situation of a lack of power. Worse still, the failure of the electricity supply meant that the water supply from our own well that fed the school also 'dried up'. Buckets were the order of the day, using water drawn from the school swimming pool to flush toilets. All very unhygienic, but what could we do? We were cut off and there was no hope of anyone getting away for five days – children or teachers. We even resorted to an agricultural water bowser, provided by **Katie Coe's** father, although I have to say that there was a certain chemical taste! The one positive spin-off from the privation we had to endure? It was deemed that, thereafter, we should regularly take a two week half-term break in the Autumn Term. Framlingham was the first school in the East of England to offer two weeks in October, something that is now common nationwide for boarding schools.

A final thought: At Brandeston we encouraged every member of the student body to operate on the simple philosophy that those who put most into life always get the most out. I had a pupil who suffered from brittle bone disease. Her life was a constant round of operations, and the associated pain, to set broken bones; yet she was always positive, always anxious to be fully involved – and always looking to the future. She continues to brush aside what you and I might consider insurmountable obstacles in the logistics of everyday living. She is, currently, making her presence felt, in familiar style, studying politics at York University, a vibrant symbol of that philosophy. (*Nigel retires in July 2009, after 8 years as Head of Terra Nova School in Cheshire*).

STEPHEN PLAYER (2000-04). *Stephen writes:*

Before moving into the hot seat in the autumn of 2000, I had already spent some ten years at BH, at the sharp end, encouraging, persuading and, even, 'gently arm-twisting' sometimes reluctant pupils and ultimately sharing in the pleasure of their success. Success on the stage, in their creative work, on the sports field or in undertaking responsibility within the boarding community in which **Hilary** and I were so closely involved.

Over the preceding fifteen years **Nigel Johnson** had put his own stamp on the school and I was fortunate to inherit a loyal, hard-working Common Room who were all committed to keeping Brandeston Hall in the 'Premier League'. The Governing Body funded a number of exciting initiatives to improve both the appearance of the site and the facilities on offer within the school. The conversion of the old Master's House to accommodate an entirely new Nursery Wing, appropriately named Foundation House, was opened in 2002, with the greatly experienced **Liz Tydeman** as 'Mother Hen'. We were also able to undertake considerable refurbishment of both boys' and girls' boarding accommodation and social facilities. On the back of the relentlessly rolling wave of IT we were able to provide surfers, thirsty for knowledge, with extended computer networks. The groundstaff who

had, since 1948, uncomplainingly put up with an ageing Nissen hut, were provided with a spanking new, state-of-the-art Maintenance HQ - all part of a grand plan which enabled us finally to sweep away the unsightly assortment of semi-derelict buildings on the northern boundary of the estate and provide a fine new tarmac parking area.

Fond memories of these early years of a fledgling new century would most certainly include celebrating, with **Robin Sampson**, his Senior Boys' triumph at the IAPS National Mini-hockey Championships, held at far-away Millfield. I reflect also on some wonderful Leavers' Dinners (invariably a little tearful for the Y.8 girls!); an initiative which has continued to thrive.

May the next sixty years prove equally fruitful for a very fine school.

Bob Williams further comments:

Stephen Player's input at Brandeston, over fourteen years, was considerable. As a Loughborough graduate it was a 'given' that he was a talented games player. A good eye for a ball was most certainly in Stephen's genes (his Dad played professional soccer for Grimsby and Portsmouth). It was, therefore, no real surprise to discover that he was an accomplished coach across a remarkable range of sports – rugby, hockey, cricket, tennis and athletics, although the field in which he himself still excelled was golf (with an honourable mention for his guile on the squash court!). However, a man can only fit in so many hours in the day and as, year on year, the academic demands on his time continued to increase – Head of English and Drama, then Director of Studies, his availability for coaching duties was inevitably restricted. However, seeing his talented young squad lift the Stowe Putter title in 1995, was just reward for his commitment to the development of golf at Brandeston Hall.

Appointed Master in 2000, in succession to Nigel Johnson, Stephen continued to apply his energies, on the wider front, to keeping the school on the boil and in the public eye. By the summer of 2003 the school roll exceeded 300. Throughout his four-year tenure Stephen was also, somehow, still able to find the time to coach and to coax the best out of large numbers of pupils in a series of notable senior drama productions. In September 2004 Stephen was appointed to the headship of Spratton Hall Preparatory School, Northampton. – *Bob Williams.*

His departure marked the beginning of a period of relative instability, at least in terms of leadership from the top. **John Kelsall** (2004-5), having recently retired as Head of Brentwood School and about to join the Board of College Governors, was persuaded that his would be a steadying hand on the tiller. And so it was. John took over at short notice and Brandeston was fortunate to benefit from his wide and lengthy experience, while a permanent successor was sought and recruited. That successor was **Nigel Woolnough** (2005-7) but his tenure lasted just two years before he was succeeded by **Martin Myers-Allen**, (2007–) previously Senior Master at the College, and someone well rooted in the ethos of Framlingham and Brandeston.

In 2009, at the time of writing, everything points to a new period of stability. Governors, staff, parents and students all look for and thrive on stability and continuity, and that has to be an on-going aspiration. With the new Headmaster now in post for nearly two years, the self-confidence projected by the school and its pupils, together with its results from inside and outside the classroom suggest that the school which has sometimes ruefully proclaimed that it is Suffolk's best kept secret is now promoting itself to a wider audience, despite the challenges of the 2009 economic downturn.

The 60 years of history which have gone into building up the ethos and traditions of Brandeston represent secure foundations which transcend such transitory circumstances as are brought about by economic stringency and changes in personnel. The loyalty of so many students from those sixty years, and indeed of long-serving staff, is persuasive testament to that assertion.

Above: Current Headmaster Martin Myers-Allen with Helen Myers-Allen and Lucy Pring, Holly Cartmell and Jack Scott.

A SELECTION OF BRANDESTON PERSONALITIES

It is invidious to pick out individuals who have made their mark on a school. The Heads have their own chapter in this book; a selection of past pupils too, have contributed to it, offering not only their own reminiscences but also adolescent glimpses of the teachers they remember. In this section Members of Staff remember or are remembered, and perspectives offered on the years they spent at the school. This is just a small selection.

BOB WILLIAMS (Brandeston Hall 1970–2001)

Bob must be accorded pride of place in this book. Not only was he Interim Headmaster for a term, but his 31 years at the school make him the personification of Brandeston for half its history. His contacts with past and current Members of Staff, his links with former students, his photographic archive, his prodigious memory, boundless energy, enthusiasm and devotion to the school have made him an indispensable source of information. His persuasive powers have stretched far and wide. Without him, this book would have been very different. Much of its human dimension, together with many of the painstakingly drawn up lists, are Bob's work. There are many references to him in the course of this book, so what follows is really an objective précis of Bob's input not only into the school over his 31 years, but also into this book. Such is Bob's modesty, that the author has felt bound to write this section.

Bob was born in 1941. It will surprise few people to know that he is Welsh, educated at Rydal School, Colwyn Bay. After a brief dalliance with the world of Advertising and Commercial Art in London he was offered a place at Westminster College of Education in Oxford. His first two teaching appointments were at The Old Ride Preparatory School, Bradford on Avon, and then Sherrardswood School, Welwyn. His connection with the College considerably pre-dates his appointment in 1970. His uncle, **Wilfred Gilchrist** OF (1920-21), had produced a design for the cover of 'The Framlinghamian' which was used from 1922-52.

In April 1970 Bob moved to Brandeston and remained there until his retirement in 2001.

During that time he was Head of the Geography and Art Departments, Head of Boarding (1970-87), Housemaster of Constable House (Blue) for 17 years, Acting Head in 1974, Second Master / Deputy Head (1971-99) and Senior Master (1999-2001). He served as Second Master, under 5 Heads/Masters. With such

professional commitments, it is difficult to imagine how he could fit in all his outside interests, listed as: Photography (Past Chairman Deben Camera Club), Walking (Committee Member, West Wilts Group Ramblers' Association), Local Radio (Formerly regular contributor to 'Thought for the Day' on Radio Suffolk), Occasional Voice-Over work (Featured in 'Suffolk and Proud' promotional campaign on Anglia ITV in February 2005), Trustee and Secretary to the Friends Group of the Methodist Church Collection of Modern Christian Art, Quiz Master (his services are still sought after for Fund-raising Quiz Evenings.)

He is also, of course, an avid sportsman. His communications with the author would almost invariably end with a comment about the state and performance of Ipswich Town Football Club. In Bob's own words he has "catholic sporting interests", ranging from a qualification as an FA Referee to a lifelong interest in Athletics. Under this particular banner he has been for 50 years a member of Thames Valley Harriers Athletics Club. Personal career highlights have included, on the track: Welsh Schoolboys International – Wales v. Scotland 1959 and in Cross-Country: Three Full Welsh International Vests – European Championships 1962 and 1965 and the Martini International Event 1965.

He also much cherishes the honour of having twice participated in the Commonwealth Games Baton Relay (conveying The Queen's message en route to the Opening Ceremony): In 1958, along the N.Wales coast (to the Cardiff Games) and in 2002 (Sharing consecutive first two legs with Karen Pickering out of Ipswich to the Manchester Games)… and being dragged off to engage in an interview with 'Weathergirl' Carol Kirkwood on BBC Breakfast News to offer comment on the déjà vu experience!

Away from professional life, Bob has been married to Madeleine for 24 years. He is fiercely proud of his three step-children who, between them, have (so far) presented Bob and Mandy with four grand-children. **Paul, Leila and Helen (Robinson)** all made their mark at Framlingham both in the arts and sporting arenas.

After 35 years as residents of Suffolk, Bob and Mandy re-located in 2005 to Winsley, some six miles from Bath. The call of Suffolk remains strong, and they return frequently to visit their many friends and to share fond memories of bygone days.

Brandeston was lucky indeed to have enjoyed the benefits of Bob's expertise, enthusiasm and commitment for so many years. Indeed the teaching profession itself is fortunate that men of such talents channel them towards the enthusing and instruction of the young. They are the backbone of the very best of schools.

Michael Baic – he taught foreign languages from the early 70s to 2001 – pictured here with Mandy Williams.

MICHAEL BAIC

Reflections on the teaching of modern foreign languages

How times have changed! I began teaching French at Brandeston Hall in the early 1970s and by the time I left in 2001, methods of teaching, educational developments, government initiatives and, most of all, the pupils had altered almost out of recognition.

In the early days, most of the Teaching Staff were expected to wear gowns from morning assembly all through the academic day. I was Head of the French Department; in fact the only member of the French Department until I was joined later, and very ably assisted by **Brian Rosen** and **Anne Nesling;** later also by **Ann Vipond, Agnès Clough, Mme Crane** and **Susie Dring.** In the early days we used, in common with most other Preparatory Schools, the well known book by JR Watson called 'La Langue des Français', now somewhat derided but which did, in fact provide a very sound grounding.

As time progressed and particularly when we moved into the 1980s the old stories and the rigid methodology seemed to date. People looked for something different. Enter the new, widely praised course 'Tricolore'. The format was entirely different. Although grammar was included, it was in a more modern format. One aspect of the course was the emphasis on oral and aural work. This meant that pupils were learning to speak the language as well as write it. The emphasis had shifted emphatically. I think we successfully incorporated the best of both methods, as was evinced by the excellent academic results.

Still later, as all schools, including Brandeston Hall, adopted the National Curriculum, S.A.T.S. and Key Stage Tests, much more pressure was put on the pupils and staff. Detailed study plans were constantly scrutinized and updated. In some cases, it was less beneficial but it did make us all work harder and think how to improve our methods. It also gave a much clearer indication to parents as to the course of study their children would follow. I introduced German to the curriculum in the top two years and this also proved a great success. Not many Preparatory Schools taught German, and Brandeston Hall was at the forefront. Throughout the years I taught at Brandeston Hall, there were always close links with the Modern Languages Department at Framlingham College where the concerns were always to tailor our courses to cater for all abilities.

When I left the school in 2001, we had seen many changes, mostly positive and always with the best interests of the children in mind. Today Modern Foreign Languages are more important than ever and the excellent teaching ethos throughout Framlingham College allows pupils of all levels to achieve their potential and most important of all, to enjoy studying languages as well as learning to understand other cultures.

Michael's father was Richard Milan Baic, descended from princes of pre-Yugoslavia Serbia and Croatia, which both explains perhaps both Michael's name and his linguistic background. He was educated at Framlingham College and in Lausanne, Switzerland. He then studied German in Cologne and Berlin before taking French at the Sorbonne University in Paris.

Michael began teaching at Brandeston in the 1970s as a Modern Linguist and was appointed as Head of French Department and of Administration, a post which he retained until 1998. He remained for a further two years on a part-time basis as Head of German. Michael played a very active role in the critical development of Information Technology when it was first introduced to the curriculum and was also a long-serving Housemaster of Gainsborough (Red) House. In 2000 he moved to the maintained Sector and taught Modern Languages to 'A' Level. Outside the working environment, Michael's hobbies include: Classical Music, Opera, Ballet, Tennis, Gardening, Art, Skiing, Reading and Travel.

JOHN CLOUGH – *A teacher's view*

During my first few years at Brandeston I was often heartened by the tangible family atmosphere engendered by **Nigel** and **Judy Johnson** and their family, including the Labrador. They were ably supported by the likes of **Hilary Player** and her children, **Abigail** and **Katie**. More recently the boarding baton was passed on to **Bruce** and **Ros Wilson** who have provided such consistently excellent pastoral care for the boarding community. There was an inclusive and caring ambience, far removed from my own experiences of boarding school in the 1970s. What also impressed me was the care and attention given to the needs of every single individual child and one had the feeling that the phrase 'every child matters' was much more than a facile New Labour sound bite and more of a daily reality. I was frequently astonished by the versatility and commitment of many of the teaching staff, who included such behemothic polymaths as **MG Vipond, Richard 'Dusty' Daykin, Bob Williams, Monsieur Michael Baic, Shirley Robinson, Margaret Kennon, Mary** 'Marrow' **Vellacott,** and the Venerable **Roger Dixon**. They were teachers who were not only passionate about their subjects but they also liked children, as well as relishing the frequent eccentricities and absurdities of a Prep School.

So has anything changed? In my humble opinion things changed when memos, meetings, working parties, documents, forms (in triplicate, naturally) started eating into contact time with the children and with other members of the Common Room, to the detriment of all concerned. When Brandeston ceased to dare to be different, to be truly independent.... to be a preparatory school in spirit and ethos, if not in name. When it began trying to follow the national obsession of measuring the immeasurable. We all know the story about weighing the pig continually not helping it to put on weight, but what about the seed which is continually dug up to check if it is growing, to the complete detriment of its growth? The national obsession with Inspections and the enrolment of Independent Schools within that process has created uniformity, stress and a dehumanizing of the educational environment.

Brandeston has traditionally been very good at providing a safe haven for children whose parents are working or serving abroad as well as those who have suffered distress from broken homes and for whom a boarding experience can provide a stable and consistent environment. I was also touched to see how the pupils, by and

Brandeston's Headmaster Martin Myers-Allen as Moses on a Harry Potter Day.

large, accepted into the community all kinds of children, irrespective of their race, creed or difference. 'Back to basics' was a campaign launched by the hapless John Major - surely the living embodiment of Peter Cook's character EL Whisty. This at a time when his premiership was rapidly descending into chaos and being derided. Perhaps 'Back to basics' wouldn't be a bad mantra for Brandeston in the years ahead. When I came for my initial interview Nigel Johnson very firmly but fairly pointed out that this was a rural, seven day a week, twenty four hours a day Prep School and not a 9am-4pm urban primary school. What made Brandeston special and can make it special again, was the absolute lack of a cafeteria culture where members of staff could pick and choose their input. Ironically, this led to much more togetherness and more time for contact, quality contact, with the pupils, and for pupils, to discuss their welfare. Similarly, the mania for filling every spare second with febrile activity, no matter how meaningless, needs to be curtailed. To quote WH Davies: How awful if we have… "No time to stand and stare."

Bring back fun and spirituality and eccentricity (or tolerance of it), half-days for staff and nicknames and tree climbing and conkers and snowballing and a sense of proportion and true educational and cultural values, not the debased coinage of the worst of the state educational system. As DH Lawrence wrote in his 1918 essay about educating children, "first leave them alone,... then leave them alone and,… finally, leave them alone." **Martin Myers-Allen** is steeped in these values and he deserves the support of all in his quest to lead the Brandeston diaspora to the land of milk and honey, all and sundry being impressed by his dressing as Moses on the recent Harry Potter Day. A restoration has begun and I'll wager that there is a massive market for such a school in the 21st century. Amen to that!

John was Head of History at Brandeston, from 1994-2008 and an inspirational teacher. I have never seen an Inspector so animated as the occasion that the gentleman in question observed John deliver a lesson perfectly, yet subtly, 'differentiated' to the range of learning abilities within the class concerned. John's penchant for detailed planning also ensured the success of the Kentwell Hall visit year on year. Likewise, following Roger Dixon's retirement from both school and parish, when we had to soldier on without a Chaplain of our own, John shouldered much of the responsibility for the continuity of Morning Assemblies, the annual Carol and Leavers' Services and the spiritual well-being of the school community. – Bob Williams

Rev Roger Dixon with Brandeston Hall's Director
of Music, Martyn Lane.

Simon Fuller with Gerard and Eileen Hollebone at a
Historical Exhibition in All Saints Church, 1991.

REV ROGER DIXON

Roger Dixon was a much loved and very effective school chaplain. He also ministered to the village. For the majority of his time he also had an RE slot on the timetable. The following is an extract from the 1995 Brandeston Hall Magazine and includes the nub of **Nigel Johnson's** Speech Day reference to Roger Dixon's retirement.

Nigel Johnson: 'Over the past thirteen years there have been many occasions when I have recognized just how lucky I have been to have had Roger working alongside, but it is the children who have benefited most from his love and care, whether it be the "high five" offered to youngsters as he walked down the long corridor or the wonderful repertoire of stories we heard in Assembly – and, incidentally, you haven't lived until you have heard him telling stories from Thomas the Tank Engine! He was held in the greatest affection by all who came into contact with him. Indeed, Roger was singled out by the Social Services Dept. during their inspection of the Junior School, in 1993, as "the single most important member of Staff and the one to whom almost all children said they would turn to if they have a problem". However, Roger was more than that. He was a School Chaplain in the true sense of the word: he looked after his Common Room and his parents as well. All of us used his shoulder to cry on at one time or another. He simply shouldered the burden and gave the comfort, support and encouragement we all needed... His determination to support the child in difficulty, at Staff Meetings and, always see the very best side, will be an abiding memory.'

SIMON FULLER (1987-1994)

The tragically early death of Simon Fuller meant the loss of a schoolmaster and historian of great commitment and enthusiasm. His historical survey covering the time of the Lords of the Manor down to the founding of the school has been heavily drawn upon in this present work, and it is appropriate that full tribute should be paid to Simon's memory.

He was appointed in 1987 as Head of History and Housemaster of Britten House. He is remembered as a dedicated 1st XI Cricket and Colts Rugby Coach. Squads of mud-encrusted youngsters were regularly reminded that there is "No gain without pain". He was one of those boarding school teachers for whom the definition of working hours simply did not exist. His life was the job.

In 1994 he organised an Activities Week educational visit to Normandy, marking the 50th Anniversary of the D-Day Landings. This week-long visit made a great impression on all involved. Simon moved from Brandeston to Edgarly Hall, Millfield Junior, and then on to a post in the USA where he fell victim to the cancer which led to his premature death.

At his funeral service in Cardiff, Nigel Johnson, The Master throughout Simon's time at Brandeston delivered the eulogy which included the following:

...."Always one of the first to volunteer for any responsibility, Simon was the driving force behind the development of the June Parents' Weekend into the social highpoint of the year. He was an outstanding teacher of history, who believed in bringing the subject to life. I well recall emerging from my study one morning prepared to remonstrate with a teacher who had seemingly lost control of a particularly noisy class. I found Simon with a group of 9-year-olds vigorously re-enacting the battle of Hastings – and guess who was playing the part of William the Conqueror!

I have no doubt that, up there in the great classroom in the sky, Simon will, even now, be organising extra coaching, sorting out Activities and plaguing his historical heroes with all the 'classified' questions that he had long sought an answer to.

PENN KIRK – *reflects on life outside the classroom*

Pony Trekking: When I arrived at the school in 1987, a tradition had been established, by **Mary Vellacott**, to take pupils on trekking holidays in Wales. I was delighted to join such a trip in 1989. The minibus was loaded up and twelve keen riders climbed aboard and we set off for South Wales. We spent five days riding in an idyllic landscape, often in very wet weather. Brandeston seemed a world away as we explored high peaks, crossed rivers and fords and enjoying watching the sheep on the moors.

Tending the Allotments: A further enthusiasm that I shared with Mary Vellacott was the encouragement of interest amongst the young in gardens and gardening. Our Gardening Club not only provided the opportunity to grow organic vegetables and flowers in individual 'allotments' but, in addition, ensured that the school looked bright and colourful, thanks to the hanging baskets created by members of the club. What fun it was to take the club members to the local nursery and return with the school minibus fully loaded with plants of all shapes and sizes – a greenhouse on wheels!

Activities Week for the Juniors: Each year, a week was set aside for all the pupils in the school to experience something different, whether it be Year Groups travelling to various points of the UK with the Year 8 leavers doing their own 'special thing' – adventure training, in Devon. Due to the young age of the pupils in the Junior Department it was decided to introduce them to the delights of camping within the school grounds. The camp was established near to the back gate of the Master's house. This ensured that at night, when the children were supposedly asleep, **Nigel Johnson** could bring fortifying refreshments to the Staff who were also camping with the children! The children enjoyed camp-fire singing, charcoal-flavoured sausages cooked on a large barbecue and open air assemblies, courtesy of **Roger Dixon**. One of the highlights was the 'yomp' from Brandeston to the College with the opportunity, en route, to listen to the song of the skylarks with **Richard Daykin**.

Kentwell Hall: These trips were organized, in my time, by

Top: Penn Kirk with Mike Vipond, Kentwell, 1993.
Above: John and Wendy Pemberton at Peter Arbon's 80th Birthday celebrations at Brandeston Village Hall.

Simon Fuller as Head of History. No expense was spared in kitting out pupils and teachers alike in period costume. I still have a 1993 photo of myself in the company of a very elegant Tudor Gentleman, alias **Mike Vipond**!

History Trip to Northern Cyprus and Turkey: One of the highlights of my time was travelling to Northern Cyprus and Turkey with Simon Fuller, escorting a mixed party of boys and girls from both Brandeston Hall and Felsted School. Simon was the most enthusiastic historian I have ever met. His passion for his subject brought the trip alive as we visited the Crusader Castles at Kyrenia, Kantara and St Hilarion, in Northern Cyprus, and the awesome Ephesus, near Kusadasi, in Turkey. One of the scariest moments was the boat trip! Due to the change in weather conditions, most of the staff and pupils opted to return to the hotel by coach. An intrepid group of pupils and myself decided to return from the 'nature reserve picnic' by boat which, after forty minutes, broke down. No one can possibly forget the impromptu disco held on the boat as the party waited, helpless and drifting broadside onto the waves, to be rescued. Rumour has it that, upon our eventual return to the hotel, I had (on medical advice!) to be fed copious amounts of local brandy, such was the trauma of the adventure. Happy days.

Penn Kirk was a member of the Brandeston Hall Common Room from 1987-1993, latterly as Junior Department Coordinator. She was appointed Head of the Junior School at Portsmouth High School GDST in 1993, and subsequently, in 2002, to her second headship and current post, at Prince's Mead Preparatory School for Girls, Winchester.
– Bob Williams

JOHN PEMBERTON

To the best of our knowledge, John is, in 2009, the only surviving original member of staff from 1948. He and his wife **Wendy** have been a rich source of memories of those early days: the old classrooms, the other teachers, their strengths and their foibles, the playing fields, the challenges faced.

They lived the life of the school – Wendy had been a matron when John married her – and there was little opportunity to get away from the school in term-time, such were the transport difficulties. They lived in the ex-NAAFI Girls' bungalow (now used for storage), and had two sons who both went to Brandeston and the College. John was Housemaster of Green and ran the House Competition. He taught RE, Latin, Geography, PE and Games. This involved organising Sports Day and taking swimming parties once a week to the College in Summer. He escorted trips abroad with **Mr Hewitt**, ran a Stamp Club and was responsible for the annual firework display with the help of **Peter Arbon**.

John and Wendy left Brandeston in 1971 after 23 years and now live in Woodbridge. He and Wendy were special guests at Brandeston's 60th birthday celebration supper in September 2008 and John celebrates his 90th birthday in August 2009.

JOAN RIX

Joan Rix was a larger-than-life character who is sadly missed by all who came into contact with her across the county. She is best remembered as a wit, broadcaster and raconteur, talents that were invariably exercised in the interests of so many good causes, both local and national (Red Cross etc). The polished performance was invariably a double act with one or other of her good friends, Mary Moore, as piano accompanist, or **Margaret Doe** in a renowned comic routine. Her Memorial Service, held at Brandeston All Saints on Jan 15th 2000 was a fitting celebration of the life of "a grand lady who loved a good mardle", as the EADT reported on the day.

At Brandeston Joan was Head Matron, twice. She had, as all effective Head Matrons do, a fierce reputation, but one delightful story, told by the beneficiary, shows another side to her. When **Terry Hunt** (Now Editor of the EADT, then an LEA 11 plus Direct Grant pupil), was offered a place at the school, the clothing list, implying some degree of expenditure, automatically accompanied the offer. For a household of very limited income this presented an insurmountable problem. Joan Rix came to hear of it and, from

Above: Joan Rix – 'a grand lady who loved a good mardle' – East Anglian Daily Times.

the dark recesses of her Linen Room, she quickly gathered together serviceable second-hand items of the required uniform for the young Hunt. He was thus able to embark upon his schooling at Framlingham.

Joan lived in Park Cottage, just over the River Deben where, in retirement, nothing delighted her more than a surprise visit from her former charges – with the 'naughtiest' invariably receiving the warmest welcome!

SHIRLEY ROBINSON

Shirley, although not full-time until 1972, is believed to be one of only three Members of Common Room to have served in excess of 30 years. (The other two are **Tom Fleming** and **Bob Williams**). *Here is an extract of what Bob had to say at Shirley's Farewell Presentation:*

'An unequivocal believer in academic excellence in her particular discipline, Shirley always maintained that rewards had to be earned.'1' or '2' grades in Physics and Chemistry may have been thin on the ground but always greatly valued by the recipients. A not entirely apocryphal story records that, on one occasion in the mid-70s, she credited a young man by the name of **Ian Fulcher** with an 'A5'... "Undoubtedly the brightest pupil I ever taught but, oh, so lazy!" It was rumoured (rumour confirmed by the 'victim') that he subsequently got a First at University but only after being sent down for failure to work!

Quite how Shirley managed to avoid the nickname 'Stats' Robinson I'm not sure. For more than 20 years, for the most part in a pre-computer era, she processed most of Brandeston's vital statistics: Termly Grades, House Points Totals (averaged out to three decimal places in order to be scrupulously fair to each House), General Knowledge Quiz percentages, Cross-Country and Swimming events and the forest of figures thrown up by the various strands of the Inter-House Athletics Championships. She was always at her best wrestling with numbers in a race against the clock.

I don't think any of us can quite believe that Shirley's withdrawal from the fray means that the Inner Sanctum (Science 'Prep Room') is about to reveal its treasures to the wider world. The new Head of Science will no doubt feel not unlike Howard Carter when first casting his eye upon the contents of Tutankhamun's tomb!'

BRIAN ROSEN – *From Woodwork to advanced Technology*

I arrived at Brandeston in the late seventies, as an ex-engineer, to teach science – and any other subject as required! At that time the boys did woodwork with **Tom Fleming**, whilst the girls, still relatively new at Brandeston Hall, retired to the kitchens to learn cooking. However this arrangement produced problems with 'Health and Safety' requirements and thus the girls were required to study woodwork – quite a bold step in those days!

The established pattern, over very many years, was for 'T Flem' to share his teaching between Brandeston Hall and the College, as indeed it had been for his predecessor and Brandeston's first appointed woodwork teacher, **'Doody' Day**. With the numbers in the school growing, it became apparent that Tom could no longer fit it all into his timetable and I was asked if I would take on some of his lessons (I had spent some years doing metalwork as part of my engineering apprenticeship.)

I readily agreed and I carried on in the same manner as Tom, using the same traditional drawings that produced the tanks, the bird boxes, the spice racks and coffee tables that had flowed from the workshop since days of the Ark – and I suspect that we probably even had a set of plans for that! Prospective parents were invariably brought to see the woodwork hut, always an impressive sight with boys and girls busily sawing, chiselling and hammering away furiously, dreading the bell that would ring ten minutes before the end of the double lesson signalling that work must stop, tools put away and benches cleaned up and left tidy. The girls quickly proved that, where workshop skills and technique were concerned, they were the equal of the boys.

Then a new subject appeared on the national curriculum – CDT, craft, design and technology and one of the first IAPS subject conferences, covering this new discipline, was held at Brandeston. "Ideally you require a retired

Above: Brian Rosen – at Brandeston from 1978 to 1993 – also a former President of the SOF.

engineer on your staff" we were told... I relinquished some of my other subjects and became Head of the CDT Department!

The changeover was not too dramatic. I insisted that all groups became familiar with the various tools for working with wood, metal and plastic. Thus all learnt how to handle different materials and only then were they ready to design and build their own projects. The pencil and drawing board soon became the most important tools. I have to admit that I was amazed at the ideas and the enthusiasm that this new subject attracted, and much work was now possible outside the timetabled lessons. Computers were just starting to appear and even at this early stage some very professional-looking design studies were being produced.

Thus the nature of the work that flowed from "that old cowshed", as it was later unkindly described by a new Head, had changed out of all recognition. When I first set foot in the workshop, it had cracks between the floorboards big enough to lose pencils and rulers through and was a perishingly cold place to start the teaching day. It was some comfort, early on a winter morning, to see smoke billowing from the small chimney, as if from the Sistine Chapel. Proof that **Frank** that won that particular day's battle with the boiler!

Latterly, money was found for a minor face-lift: a skin of hardboard over the floor, fluorescent lighting, central heating and a partitioned-off drawing studio. It at least ensured a briefly extended life for the venerable old hut of which I have very fond memories.

Throughout my time we had a very close relationship with the College CDT Department and our work was organised to ensure a smooth transition when the pupils moved on to Framlingham. Happy days indeed.

It was an appropriate tribute that, at the 1993 Brandeston Speech Day, **Nigel Johnson** *should couple his farewell remarks, to Brian, with the College's*

*understandable pride in the announcement that **Andrew Gemmill** and **Alex Henney** – also with a more recent claim to fame in the 2007 Race to the North Pole – had, in the face of nation-wide competition, been awarded prestigious Arkwright Scholarships. Both had commenced their steep learning curve under Brian's tuition.*

Brian Rosen was a member of the Common Room from 1978-1993. He is himself an OF (with three sons, a daughter and a grandson, all former Brandeston Pupils) and a former President of the Society of Old Framlinghamians. – Bob Williams

'DOODY' DAY

Perhaps it is the name, but 'Doody' Day is remembered vividly by many of the early students. **John Ives** remembers being in a class when Doody came into the workshop and muttered the immortal words: "Who writ Doody on my door?" This was transmuted into a jingle with the words "Who writ Doody on my door, doo-dah, Doody, Day" sung to a tune which will be quickly recognised. John also recalls the words of a Doody Day Woodwork report which bluntly asserted that he, John, had no idea, and didn't intend to have. John ruefully recognises that this was a fair assessment – and that the truth did no harm.

PETER ARBON (Hon OF) – An 80th Birthday Celebration

The name of Peter Arbon occurs many times in this book. By way of recognition of his having stamped his personality on the lives of so many

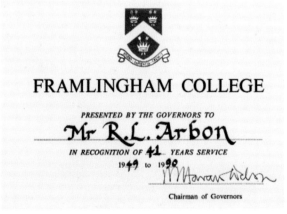

FRAMLINGHAM COLLEGE

PRESENTED BY THE GOVERNORS TO

Mr R.L. Arbon

IN RECOGNITION OF **41** YEARS SERVICE
19**49** to 19**90**

Chairman of Governors

Brandestonians and village residents, we include this edited report of his 80th birthday party.

On Sunday, 14th January, 2007, some ninety villagers, OFs, friends and family members gathered in the Village Hall for a surprise birthday lunch for this much loved member of the local community. The day was organised by Peter's nephew, very much as an expression of gratitude to the folk of the village who have done so much to support Peter in recent years.

Peter spent virtually his entire working life, some forty-eight years, the greater part of it as Head Gardener, maintaining the estate at Brandeston Hall, particularly from 1949, when it became the Junior School of Framlingham College, until his ultimate retirement.

Among the guests present was a generous turn-out of former colleagues and former pupils, a number with links back as far as 1949. A birthday toast was proposed by **Bob Williams** with entertainment provided, in the traditional manner, by Ray Hubbard of the Suffolk Horse Society. An expression of thanks to the Arbon family, for the provision of a magnificent lunch, was made by **Richard Broad**, former Headmaster of Brandeston Hall who, together with his wife **Cynthia**, had made the long journey from Honiton in Devon to be part of this very special day.

Peter recovered from all the excitement, in time to celebrate his official 80th birthday on the 17th January.

OFs present included: **David Risk, Jim Blythe, Tony Martin, Derek Hill, Andrew Ward, John Pemberton** (Hon OF), Bob Williams (Hon OF) and Richard Broad (Hon OF).

Above: Brandeston's Head Gardener Peter Arbon, a much loved member of the local community.

JO DONSWORTH
(Secretary to The Master 1973-1983)
– *Memories of Brandeston Hall*

I have been associated with Brandeston Hall for thirty-four years, as Secretary to the Master, as a parent and now as a grandparent. I joined Brandeston in 1973 as Secretary, at first to **Ron Jones** and then **Paddy Newbery.** I stayed for ten years before going to work at Framlingham College. I can honestly say that they were the happiest years of my working life. I loved the building, the work, the friendship of all the Staff and everything that Brandeston stood for.

One of the high spots was Common Room Tea – on the terrace in the summer – a short break in a busy working day. One of the low spots was the awful duplicating machine – producing papers for examinations always left me covered in black ink. How grateful I was for our first photocopier!

When I joined the staff **Peter Arbon's** vegetable garden was producing vegetables and fruit for the kitchen. I was very sad to see it go. Peter's shed was always a haven for lonely or homesick boys who were assured of a welcome and a glass of orange juice. I am sure my son's delight in growing things stemmed from the hours he spent with Peter in the garden. In fact when my son was at the College in 1976 he made an appointment with the Head to ask for a reprieve for the condemned vegetable garden, but to no avail!

I have so very many happy memories (and a few sad ones). Brandeston to me will always be a very special place. I regularly pick up my grandchildren and see the many changes that have been made. How I would love to go back thirty years and be part of it all again.

NIGEL COX – *Staff Reminiscences*

Looking back on my career to date, I have no doubt that the four years I spent at Brandeston Hall have been the happiest, and that the school at that time was particularly successful and well managed.

I was appointed just as **Nigel Johnson** was reorganizing the boarding accommodation into three separate "Halls". My wife, **Sue**, and I were to run

Above: Nigel and Sue Cox at christening of daughter Catrin in All Saints Brandeston.

Kittermaster Hall, assisted by **Paul Baker; Mike** and **Ann Vipond** were in charge of Austin Hall, assisted by **Simon Fuller. Sally Youngman** (later replaced by **Sally Thomson**) was head of Alice Hall. Nigel had a deep belief in the value of boarding and we all, together with the boarders, were made to feel that we were at the very heart of Brandeston.

So many memories crowd in when I think of those years in the late eighties that it is difficult to know where to begin. Here is an entirely random selection:

It was a time of quite spectacular weather. There was the hurricane which effectively sealed off the village. The boarders had to sleep downstairs at first because there was concern that the barley-sugar chimneys would topple though the roof and top floors. There was no power in the village for a time and no water pumping around the house so we had to organize a gang of boarders carrying buckets from the swimming pool. In the evenings we sang songs and read stories by candlelight in the Boarders Common Room. Villagers without power came and ate at the school as we still had gas to the kitchens. The school slowly emptied of pupils as we were able to contact parents, and the roads into deepest Suffolk were cleared.

A similar Dunkirk spirit prevailed the winter when we were snowed in. The boarders had the school to themselves and after makeshift lessons we all crossed the river to slide down one of the farmer's fields on fertilizer sacks. There were also floods at this time – I recall water lapping against the terrace wall one winter.

How could I forget the beauty of the school's location? Winter mornings with mist hanging over the river, poppies in the cornfields at summer, the silence of the grounds in the frosty moonlight. Not that there wasn't plenty of fun, especially once the golf course was established. On warm evenings there was almost always the chance of a couple of holes with another member of staff and of seeing yet another expensive golf ball slip quietly beneath the surface of the Deben or, even worse, being sliced straight over the roof of the school. **Simon Fuller's** driving was always more powerful than accurate. Christmas was particularly special, with the tree being placed in the Black and

White Hall so that it could be seen the minute one swung into the drive.

Nigel and **Judi** loved a party and were the consummate host and hostess. Never have I felt as welcome at a Head's house as when we were invited by them and were ushered in by a smiling Nigel. There were the big events too – the summer Parents' Weekend with the huge barbecue, live bands and parents' caravans parked up all around the fields. For the boarders, Nigel instituted the Boarders' Hall Dinners with seating plans, superb food such as ribs of beef, guests, speeches and entertainment – at least a film, but quite often something riotous dreamed up by the evening's host Hall. This was invariably followed by cheese and port in the Staff Common Room while a few luckless bodies took it in turn to put the children to bed. Then there was the whole school Christmas Lunch where the tables extended all the way into the White Hall and beyond, singing carols and on one never-to-be-forgotten occasion seeing Nigel in a dressing gown and with a carrot nose performing "Walking in the Air" to accompaniment by **Andrew Bushell**. There were some great staff parties too – one on a particularly sublime summer's evening at **Mary Vellacott's** house, **Michael Baic**, immaculate as ever, and thrilled that another year of success for "Maison Rouge" (Red House, to the uninitiated) could be toasted.

Was it really more fun teaching then? I fear so. There were Paul Baker's jokes, his feuds with Sally Thomson, Mike Vipond's talks to the boarders about table manners and dire warnings of a "spoonioptomy" (surgical removal of a spoon from the nasal passage) if one neglected to remove the teaspoon from one's mug before drinking. When **John le Grove** joined the music staff, I recall with great pleasure his playing of hymn tunes which became increasingly florid with each succeeding verse or the time it took him to wind down whichever piece he happened to be playing on the piano, once Nigel and **Roger Dixon** entered the Assembly Hall or Church. The superb team of matrons, led by **Juliet Adams**, added enormously to the boarders' quality of life and the jollity of the staff. Was there ever a medical helper with a quicker wit than **Clare Collieson**?

Another one of Nigel's innovations was 'London Day', just before Half Term in the Autumn Term. The boarders had to be up in the dark, Day pupils arrived in the half light and then it was on to buses and away to sample the delights of the capital. We never lost a child – or not for long at any rate(!). The whole event was exhausting but a fantastic team effort and a major boost to staff morale – once we were all safely home and had half term to look forward to.

Then there were walks across the fields to the Post Office, visits to Framlingham, the sight of the castle reflected in the Mere, the excitement of a **Tony Lawrence** production in the Athlone Hall, strawberries after Speech Day…

Golden Days indeed. I count myself blessed to have been a member of the Brandeston team at such a happy time.

Nigel Cox came to Brandeston in 1987 from Beaudesert, Minchinhampton, where he had been Head of History. Initially i/c Kittermaster Hall, he succeeded Mike Vipond as Senior Boarding Master; he was also an inspired Head of Drama. In 1991 Nigel moved on to Maidwell Hall, as Assistant Head, also responsible for Drama, English and History.

A further move took him to Arnold Lodge, Leamington Spa, for a number of years (Head of Studies and, again, Head of English and Drama) before taking up a post at King's, Canterbury, as Head of Boarding and Head of English in the Junior School. – Bob Williams

ROBIN SAMPSON
(Second Master since 2000)

What follows serves as a summary of developments and changes over the past quarter of a century. Who better to summarise this period, putting into a broader context (and occasionally reiterating) the framework of the above, than Robin Sampson, who has witnessed so many of the changes.

The strength of a school is often reflected in the quality of its Common Room and Brandeston has been fortunate in having an outstanding team throughout the greater part of its history. The wonderful environment is an obvious attraction. Who could fail to be charmed by the view as you access the school through the front gates? However, for staff teaching at Brandeston, the demanding hours and the expectation of a maximum involvement in the life of a busy day and boarding school, the commitment has to be total. Some quickly discover that it is not for them, but the vast majority do stay, sometimes for a considerable period of time, and contribute significantly to making Brandeston the special place it is – and always with a philosophy of putting the needs of the pupils first. It is very rewarding to see so many Old Framlinghamians returning to Brandeston to admire the many improvements to the campus and to revive old memories. They all talk affectionately about the school even if some of their own experiences evoke an image of the earliest days as both spartan and a touch draconian!

In the autumn of 1985 **Nigel Johnson** took over the reins from **Paddy Newbery**. As with any new Head, some staff moved on and a number of new faces appeared. **Richard Daykin** arrived as a Year 1 class teacher, assisting in later years in the boys' Boarding House and is still with us, now as Head of Geography and the longest serving member of Common Room. In 1986 **Penelope Kirk** arrived to teach in Year 5 and was, shortly afterwards, appointed to the post of Junior Department Coordinator and Senior Mistress. **Sally Thomson** and **Melissa Wardle** both arrived to teach at the junior end of the school. **Paul Baker** replaced **Robin Williams** as Head of Mathematics and **Simon Fuller** replaced **Nick Stafford** as Head of History/Housemaster of Britten and to coach 1st XI cricket. **Nigel Cox** took over Kittermaster Hall and taught English and Drama and I took over from **David Grace**, who had served ten years as Head of PE and Games – in the days before it carried the rather grander title of Director of Sport! New faces were all well and good but the core of the Common Room remained, with **Bob Williams** as Second Master (and Head of Art and Geography), **Michael Vipond**, running the boys' boarding and leading the English Department, **Mary Vellacott** teaching mathematics and heading up girls' games, the inimitable 'Mrs R' (**Shirley Robinson**) running the Science Department, **Sally Youngman** teaching Mathematics and running Alice Hall and **Michael Baic** i/c Modern Languages. Then, of course, there was the much loved **Roger Dixon**, as School Chaplain, looking after our spiritual needs – and responsible for the teaching of RE. All very experienced Members of Staff and always with the best interests of the school at heart. They made all new arrivals rapidly feel welcome and part of 'the team'.

Exciting events evolved during this time, with considerable effort and involvement from all the staff. Bob Williams coordinated the 'London Day' trips where the whole school went to the capital and experienced the various attractions on offer. 'Book Weeks' and visits from such luminaries as David Kossoff (surely the definitive story teller?), and charity fund-raising events such as 'Red Nose Day' were all featured on the termly calendar. Cricket tours to Yorkshire became a feature of the

Above: Robin and Christine Sampson, with children Emma, Tom and Katy.

Summer Term as did Activities' Weeks (an action-packed 'Adventure Week', at Skern Lodge, for our Year 8 leavers).

Year on year, our legendary Parents' Weekend grew like Topsy: (Sports Day in the morning, cricket, rounders and tennis and, the obligatory Tea on the Terrace in the afternoon before the day ended with a giant barbecue and knees-up). School plays ('Beowulf' and 'Peter Pan' being two of many memorable productions) and Speech Days are two highlights of any school year. I particularly recall the Speech Day/Prize Giving of nine years ago when we had Gyles Brandreth as Chief Guest. This brought the curtain down on the 1998-99 Academic Year in some style.

Staff numbers continued to increase with the introduction of Pre-Prep in 1990. **Elizabeth Tydeman** was appointed as Head of this important area with **Anthea Smith** teaching alongside her. Initially, Brandeston opened classes for 5 and 6 year olds but as numbers grew, **Barbara Hamilton, Sarah Stephenson** and **Claire Anderson** also became key members of this department. It was during this period that it was felt that the Jones Room, which was being used as the Common Room, was not large enough to accommodate all the staff and that a new location had to be found. The Common Room moved to the old Library and this remains its location today. The old Library is of course the oldest part of the school with lovely window-seats, ornate panelling, painted ceiling and a large inglenook fireplace. Traditionally, a log fire burns during the last week of the Autumn Term but, with so many deadlines to meet, there can be no surrender to the soporific atmosphere; a lunch-hour nap in front of the glowing embers must, with difficulty, be resisted!

Brandeston has always had a strong boarding community and after Michael and **Ann Vipond** finally stood down, the subsequent Heads of Boarding retained the essential home-from-home family atmosphere. Simon Fuller took over in Austin Hall followed by **Simon Cullum, David Brook, Nick Prowse** then, ultimately, **Bruce Wilson** and his wife

Ros. Kittermaster Hall was run by Nigel Cox before his departure to Maidwell Hall as Deputy Head in 1991. Responsibility for the Hall passed to **Margaret Kennon** and, subsequently, Paul Baker before the very capable present Head of Boarding took over the running of both boys' Halls. Sally Youngman was in charge of the girls' boarding house, Alice Hall, before the baton was, in turn, passed on to Sally Thomson, **Hilary Player** and, currently, Barbara Hamilton. House tutors and matrons provide essential support in the boarding houses and are really key members of the pastoral care team.

During the nineties and early years of the new millennium more staff arrived and a number of staff either retired or moved on to seek opportunities elsewhere. In 1992 **Brian Rosen** retired after fourteen years' service to the school. Brian was Head of DT, a teacher of science and languages and was also a master of numerous sports both 'wet and dry' and an organizer of numerous ski trips to various parts of Europe. At the same time Penelope Kirk moved on to become Head of the Junior Department of Portsmouth High School for Girls.

1993 saw Simon Fuller depart for Edgarley Hall, Millfield Junior School, in the West Country. Simon's boundless energy and enthusiasm was an unforgettable feature during his time at Brandeston. He succeeded Nick Stafford in running the very popular Parents' Weekends and his passion for teaching, coaching and just life in general, was infectious; he was loved by all who knew him and he was greatly missed after his departure. Sadly, Simon's health deteriorated a few years later and he died in April 2005.

After thirteen years service, to both the school and the combined parishes of Brandeston and Kettleburgh, the Reverend Roger Dixon retired.

In 1996 three ladies, with a combined sixty-five years of service between them, also retired.

Above: 'The Three Graces' – from left: Mary Vellacott, Shirley Robinson and Margaret Kennon, with a combined 65 years service between them, retired in July 1996.

Shirley Robinson was a mathematical genius who, where Inter-House Athletics and Swimming Sports stats were concerned, remained unconvinced, almost until her retirement, that the computer could improve upon the speed and accuracy of her own 'grey matter'! She had begun teaching science at Brandeston in one of the ex-army Nissen huts and, in all, put in thirty-two years, for the most part, full-time teaching. Mary Vellacott (eighteen years), teacher of mathematics and geography, Head of girls' games and champion marrow grower (affectionately known as 'Mary Marrow') also retired. Another member of the mathematics department who also called it a day in the same year was Margaret Kennon (fifteen years). Margaret was also an enthusiastic (nay, fanatical!) athletics and cross-country coach. The turn of the century also saw the retirement of Michael Baic and the departure of Melissa Wardle (to become Mrs Bouverie). Michael had been teaching French at Brandeston for twenty-nine years, been Head of Gainsborough House as well as taking his turn in boarding. Melissa had been a junior teacher as well as art specialist, was a tutor in Alice Hall, been actively involved in the College CCF and made a significant contribution on the sports field.

2001 saw the retirement of Michael Vipond after twenty-two years at Brandeston. Michael had been Head of English/Drama, 1st XV Rugby supremo, Head of Wolsey House and Head of Boarding. His contribution to Brandeston was enormous.

These long service personnel were, in turn replaced by a number of new faces. **Catherine Gassmann** took over the French Department (and re-introduced a spot of Latin which proved very popular), **John Clough** – history (John has just left us after some fourteen years), Simon Cullum – DT and, subsequent to my sideways move to front the Science Department, **Carlos Reynell** was appointed Director of Sport. **Mary Proctor,**

Alison Millington, Jan Hipsey and Jan Norton also joined the Brandeston Common room and, in so doing, helped to drop the average age of those within!

In 2000, after fifteen years as The Master at Brandeston, Nigel Johnson departed to take charge of Terra Nova Preparatory School in Cheshire, with Stephen Player taking over the reins here at Brandeston Hall. Nigel had taken Brandeston Hall forward in so many ways during his period of tenure and all those who worked under him had the utmost respect and admiration for everything he achieved. He worked us hard but was always appreciative of staff input. He was a firm believer that the learning process could, and should be fun for pupils and staff alike.

Nigel's Second Master, Robert Williams, retired in the summer of 2001 after thirty-one dedicated years of service. He had seen the school through a number of changes during that time and been an outstanding servant of the school. Vastly experienced and always the diplomat, Bob was always the cool head in a storm and someone to whom staff could always turn for sound advice. After retirement, Bob remained very much in touch with the school in his capacity as Team Photographer.

Stephen Player introduced the Foundation Stage to Brandeston Hall in 2003 with Elizabeth Tydeman given overall responsibility for the new unit. The then Master's House was transformed into a wonderful, safe and exciting environment for our 2+ aged children. When Liz retired in 2004 Ruth Steggles became the new leader of this educational stage and Margaret Graystone the overall Head of Pre-Prep. Such is the success of the Foundation House nursery that a new purpose-built block is about to be completed.

In September 2007, we were delighted to welcome Rob Rogers back to Brandeston as Director of Music. Music remains on a very strong footing, thanks to the input, in recent years, of the likes of John le Grove (also noted for his eccentric dress sense on the games field!) and Caroline Atherton, but Rob is a veritable dynamo and already pushing music, on all

Above: Brandeston's Director of Sport Carlos Reynell with Richard Daykin, in his MGB Roadster.

fronts, up to a new level. A retrospective view of the 'Academic Engine Room' would not be complete without paying tribute to those who have served on the Management Team since its inception some twenty years ago. Now standard practice in most educational establishments, a committee of senior personnel, representative of key areas within the school, should, if working effectively, provide both a conduit and safety net for the full Common Room constituency. Being on 'Management', by implication, involves a considerable time commitment but brings with it a certain satisfaction in helping to ensure that the school is operating to its maximum efficiency on all fronts. Those charged with this responsibility, as Brandeston enters its seventh decade, are Robin Sampson (Second Master), Paul Baker and Bruce Wilson (Joint Senior Masters), Sally Thomson (Senior Mistress) with Nick Chaplin and Andrew Payn providing the Financial/ Bursarial expertise. Barbara Hamilton (Junior Prep Coordinator) and Margaret Graystone (Head of Pre-Prep) are co-opted members of the Senior Management Team with, of course, The Headmaster himself generally in the Chair.

Somewhat in contrast to a longish period of continuity within Common Room, the good ship 'Brandeston' has seen a number of new captains on the bridge since the turn of the century. Following Nigel Johnson's fifteen year period of tenure, Stephen Player spent the last four of his total twelve years at Brandeston Hall, as Master, before moving on, in 2004, to become Head of Spratton Hall near Northampton. John Kelsall, who thought he was retiring from Brentwood School, was asked to front a 12-month inter-regnum before Nigel Woolnough completed a two year spell in charge. Most recently, Martin Myers-Allen was appointed Master in September 2007, having served some eighteen years at the College. Martin has injected much needed humour back into the Common Room and with his hand firmly placed on the tiller, I am sure Brandeston is in very good hands for the foreseeable future.

THEY ALSO SERVED

This section was put together by Bob Williams. His 30 years service at Brandeston put him in a unique position to understand and appreciate what goes on below the surface of a school, and how much is owed to those often unsung but essential contributors to its smooth workings. It should not be forgotten that the school has been a significant employer in and around the village and that many of the names mentioned above are well rooted in local folk lore. These links also strengthen the bonds between school and village.

A successful and well-run school is nothing less than a team of loyal and often multi-talented personnel. Taking a 'good, well-qualified Common Room' as an accepted pre-requisite, Brandeston Hall has been exceedingly fortunate in the calibre of the ancillary staff that we have had on board, for long periods, over the past 60 years.

It is always something of a mine-field to name names but, if long service medals were on offer, then the following have given us, at the very least, something approaching a generous decade of their working lives, most over twenty years, some topping thirty with, of course, **Peter Arbon** the joker in the pack. He first took up spade and fork in May 1949, a mere eight months after the school opened its doors to the first pupils in September 1948, and subsequently put in 42 years, 8 months and 14 days in the employ of Framlingham College, the majority of those years as Head Gardener of the Brandeston Hall Estate... and the enormous depth of his knowledge on all things arboreal and horticultural is still sought today.

Little learning is possible on empty stomachs. These needs were met, within the Catering Department, by the likes of **Agnes Ransome**, **Marion Horn**, **Isabel Ross**, the two 'Queenies' – **Hoy** and **Farrow**, **Joy Parker**, **Audrey Freeman** and **Janet Abbott** (née Doe). **Frank Carsbolt** (with his extraordinary capacity to memorize everyone's car registration plate, both current and previous models!), **Bob Smith** and **Joan Cable** (née Adams) have been among the longest serving support staff within the kitchen. Joan, still a loyal employee at the College, has put in nigh on 40 years covering both sites. This important little empire was overseen, over the years, by Housekeepers/Heads of Catering **Rachel Kittermaster** (the while also fulfilling her duties as Headmaster's wife!), **Olive Field**, **Riet Stuij** and, most recently, the evergreen **Daphne Elliott**.

Rude health, one hundred percent of the time, is a big ask in any close-knit and largely residential community of this size. (Scanning through the 'Brandeston Hall School Notes', penned

termly by David Kittermaster, for the Framlinghamian, there was not one term in the sixty over which he presided as Headmaster, when he did not commence with a paragraph devoted to the particular virus or contagion – invariably more than one – which had just swept through the school). In this respect the Matronal Department had, therefore, an enormous responsibility. In the early years this rested upon **Dulcie Wilton** (alias 'the Green Dragon') supported by her team of three assistants, **Wendy Pemberton**, **Pam Smith** and **Joy Winch**. (Dulcie, Wendy and another stalwart of the Linen Room/ Sanatorium, **Jean Wright**, also put in some years at the College). Thereafter, **Joan Rix**, **Pam Sullivan**, **Marjorie Peters**, **Juliet Adams** and **Joan Ironside**, amongst others, gave selflessly of their time. Support in the Linen Room was provided, over many years, by seamstress **Elsie 'Bubby' Williams** who patiently repaired holes and tears in hundreds of socks, pullovers and grey trousers – long and short!

Staff who have given of their best in a dual role that has taken them from the Kitchen or Domestic side to the Linen Room, or vice versa, include **Cherrie Allsop** (née Middleton), **Gill Muttick** (née Rush), **Julie Tye** and **Sally Wilson**.

Keeping loos and flues flowing smoothly, boilers stoked (in the days of solid fuel) chairs and desks repaired, internal and external paintwork in good order – a similar requirement to The Forth Bridge... start at one end, work through and then repeat the whole process again... and again! – also required a dedicated team of Caretakers and Maintenance Staff. In this respect, the names of **Frank Bedwell**, **Walter Parker**, **Ron Hamon**, **Les Inger**, **Laurence Calver** and **Peter Hogg** effectively covered the entire six decades. Frank Bedwell was, in fact, a trained plumber who kept the old pump house operating in the 'pre-mains water' days when we were entirely dependent upon the deep bore. His native skills were legendary: '... always ready to tackle any job, from erecting goal posts to sweeping chimneys'. (Framlingham College: The Second Sixty Years. LG)

Small boys – and even some girls! – are, by nature, untidy little beasts. That the school (public areas, classrooms and dormitories) invariably looks pristine, and not just for high days and holidays, has been down to the remarkably long years of service by the Domestic Cleaners, including **Nancy Rawlings**, **Marjorie Durrant**, **Joan Arbon**, **Margaret Doe**, **Barbara Read**, **Freda Calver**, **Eric Martin** and the recently retired **Patsy Saunders**.

To complete the circle there has always been a sturdy and skilled team of Ground Staff and Gardeners: **John Turner**, the first Head Gardener had been 'inherited' with the estate and, therefore, already put in a good number of years dating back to pre-war days. He continued to ensure an annual bumper harvest from the garden

until his retirement in 1954. **Roy Kingham** and **Leslie Linnell** (who could also turn his hand to pretty well any task required – and actually lived in one of the old, now long-demolished huts, on site, until his eventual retirement) were also long servers. The current team of **Mike Rutterford**, **Ray** and **Tony 'Tiger' Pike** can account for over 50 years' service between them, maintaining, as they do, a 1st XI Cricket Square and 9-hole golf course, both of which are the envy of every school in East Anglia... and, of course, the aforementioned Peter Arbon. Peter took great pride both in his legendary vegetable garden and the

Above: Brandeston Matrons – (from left) Joan Rix, Juliet Adams, Dulcie Wilton and Cherrie Allsop at Brandeston Jubilee Celebrations.

flower beds on the Terrace. His carrots and dahlias won prizes across the length and breadth of Suffolk!

The concept of continuity of service, not uncommon within a rural community such as ours, is perhaps best exemplified by the 55 years (and counting!) delivered, over two generations, by Margaret Doe and daughter Janet.

Between them all I am sure they could tell a tale or two, sufficient to fill a book of their own. Their collective role, in seeing the school through to its 60th birthday, should not go unacknowledged.

OLD BRANDESTONIANS LOOK BACK

The following have kindly delved into their memories to paint a picture of Brandeston, most of them from its early days as a school: **Chris Bellamy, Jim Blythe** (his extended memories are part of the conclusion) **John Capon** (first name Curtis, aka "Joe"), one of the original Brandestonians. He returned to Brandeston after over 50 years, when his grandson **Sam Bigden** joined the school); **Geoff Bland** (later to become a Headmaster – see also Musical moments), **David Carr** (accomplished sportsman and OF Treasurer), **Bob Clayton** (Clayton's chain of Sports Shops), **John Edwards** (Governor, ex-SOF President and Chairman in 2009 of F and GP), **Terry Hunt** (from an EADT article – he is the Editor), **Nigel Hyde, Chris Keeble** (designer of this book), **Jeremy Kemp** (Head Boy in the time of Richard Broad), **Peter Liell** (for many years an SOF Trustee), **Tony Martin** (one of Brandeston's original pupils and some time SOF archivist. His grandfather, **James Mason Martin** was a great benefactor of the College. He and **Col. EP Clarke**, were the two men deputed by the Governors to seek out and find a building appropriate for housing Framlingham College's Junior House), **David Newson**, (Veterinary Surgeon in New Zealand, and one of three brothers (with **John** and **Andrew**) who attended Brandeston Hall, the sons of the late **Major General Alan Newson**, Former President of the SOF), **Roland Nice** (one of the originals), **Richard Overend** (SOF President 2001-03), **Bruce Pearson** (Leading wild-life illustrator), **John Rankin**, (Captain, medical officer with 4th Regiment RA in Malaya and Sarawak and then General Practice in Dovercourt). **Robert le Rougetel**, (55-59 – teacher, mostly as Head of Economics and Politics at Merchant Taylors, Northwood). **Charlie Simpson** (moved on to Uppingham and achieved musical fame with 'Busted'), **Peter Stewart** (the first boy to cross the threshold in 1948), **John Worland** (one of the first dayboys), **Andrew Wright** (the youngest boy in 1948), **Michael Wright** ('44-'53 – his brother and the first Head Boy), and **Charles Machin-Goodall** (now a barrister).

These recollections, some over nearly 60 years old, show how early experiences become a vivid part of the fabric of memory: how they remain indelible; how the memories of childhood adventures, the sounds and friendships of those years, and the kindly treatment at the hands of adults have an enduring effect. This is the world of Huckleberry Finn, a world of adventures untrammelled by concerns about health and safety issues, and regulations imposed by authorities ever-fearful of the litigious consequences of failing to

anticipate potential dangers and legislate for them. This is the spirit of childhood which explains the success of the recently published 'Dangerous book for boys'.

The Brandeston of the late 40s and early 50s was a school finding its feet, a school which offered freedom to young boys, and a school where much of the education came from the surroundings and from outside the classroom. And of course the final memory recalls the pride experienced as young men move further up the school ladder, and, probably a nostalgia for memories of childhood which linger on throughout life. The poignancy of those memories is increased probably by the fact that boarding Prep Schools offer the first experience of life away from home, and an alternative 'family'. That sense of being a school with a happy, family-based ambiance and tradition is something cherished by parents and Old Brandestonians.

FIRST IMPRESSIONS

Peter Stewart: Yes! I was the first boy to cross the threshold at Brandeston, purely through the happenstance of bus timetables. I seem to remember catching the bus with my mother to Ipswich, then the bus to Framlingham, then a taxi to Brandeston – and we arrived around 2.00pm instead of the planned 4.00pm for the opening Autumn Term.

Michael Wright: I went to the Junior School at the College in 1944 and after 4 years transferred to Brandeston Hall when it opened in September 1948. I was appointed Head Boy. In the Summer Term

Left: John Edwards with Heads of School, Brandeston Speech Day 2008.
Right: The last 'Fram Flyer' of 1954. Framlinghamians and Brandestonians with HL Baly and HM Irving.

before Brandeston opened, the boys from the College who were transferring visited BH for the day to be shown around, and my first impressions were of a lovely old country house with very large chimney stacks and the village church nearby. This was in great contrast to the towering red brick building at Fram. On entering the main doorway, the entrance hall was very impressive with panelling and a painted ceiling and a large staircase. In contrast there were a number of old army hut buildings in the grounds which were used as classrooms and they were very spartan.

There were two sports fields and we were introduced to rugger. During the first term boys became lost and not sure where to go at times, but there was a very happy atmosphere and having been at the College previously and being under ten, it took some getting used to the fact that there were no senior boys to look up to or to chase us to keep us in order.

John Edwards, *long-serving Governor, Chairman of the Finance and General Purposes Committee, and one of the first Brandestonians writes:*

1948 – was it really 60 years ago? Having been in the Junior School at the College since 1945, the adventure of moving to a new venue and a new school was extraordinarily exciting to me as a 10 year old. The Junior School was, on reflection, a very daunting place for us youngsters. Although we were under the control of our own Head, Timber Hull, we were very much in the daily presence of Senior boys in the Main School.

Autumn Term 1948 provided us with a new dimension and a whole new outlook on life. I will always remember building camps of new-mown hay on what is now the 9 hole golf course, with the likes of **George Gooderham**, **Charles Benson**, **Roy Farmer**,

Neville Bromage, **Jimmy Blythe**, **Keith Handley**, **John Thurlow** and many others. It was, in fact, like escaping from prison.

Tony Martin: I had already had a year at Framlingham College when I entered Brandeston with the very first intake. I took no entrance exam and I think my father's friendship with **RW Kirkman**, and possibly their common interest in Freemasonry, got me enrolled earlier than intended. The College, so soon after the war, was a fairly tough place for a small boy, but I have no memory of unhappiness, sheltered as we were, in a Junior School separate from the rest under the benign tutelage of **Quentin Cuckoo**, **Miss Brownsword** and **Mrs Podd**. I do not recall **John Pemberton** from this time, but I do remember **Wendy Milne** in the linen room with **Ma Barnes** and **Ma Meakins**. When we arrived at Brandeston there was a sort of continuity, because John and Wendy married in the holidays and arrived as a couple.

Andrew Wright: September 1948 – my first day at boarding school and the first day of the first term of the new Brandeston Hall. At 9, I was the youngest (and smallest) boy in the school and I found my elder brother, Michael, was Head Boy. The excitement started a week before, with the Southern Railway lorry coming to collect our trunks and tuck-boxes to go PLA (Passengers Luggage in Advance) to Suffolk. They arrived in a huge pile with all the other 'London boys'. It was 'essential' that my tuck-box arrived, because it contained my favourite cake, Mother's Eggless and Sugarless Cake (still rationing in 1948).

The journey to school that day was fascinating and of course, it became familiar each term. Our parents took us from Kent to

Left: Andrew Wright, on left, was the youngest pupil (at 9) in 1948. He relates the story of the 'Fram Flyer' from Liverpool Street.
Right: John Rankin in 1965, leaving Singapore, having spent time in Malaya and Sarawak with 4Rgt RA.

Liverpool Street Station to catch the LNER express to Gt Yarmouth, via Wickham Market and the branch line to Framlingham. At Liverpool Steet it was just like Harry Potter, except for platform 13 and a half, with a great steam train and 'hundreds' of children in uniform, lots of new caps, and parents all saying good-bye. Smoke and tears. The highlight of the train journey (LNER we were sure stood for Late and Never Early Railway) was when we passed Manningtree, and saw all the huge white Sunderland flying boats parked on the water.

John Capon: There were prefects. The first prefects had spent time at the College before the move to Brandeston and had learnt their trade and sometimes 'brutal' methods at the College. At the College 'tanning' was permitted, informally called BRAs (Boot Room Afterwards). These prefectorial methods filtered down for a while to the Junior School. Life was not easy, and for some deep scars remained, with enduring images of particularly harsh treatment. No-one would ever forget, for instance, one particularly nasty punishment, that of having to eat 'rook shit' from the rookery in the grounds. Life is sweeter now.

David Carr: I went to Brandeston Hall in September 1967 (aged 10) and the first two boys I met were **Tim Mitchell** (whom I still meet at SOF Suppers) and **John Le Grove**, also on their first day.

  DD Kittermaster was Headmaster (his last year). The fees were £108 per term. By the time I left The College in 1974 the fees were £625 per annum, but rose to £975 per annum in September 1974 on going Independent. The classrooms seemed brand new, not the Old Stable Block, but we still had the old **T Flem** hut for woodwork.

Richard Overend: The first boy I met within ten minutes of my arrival was **Peter Liell** and we became lifelong friends.

THE GROUNDS AND THE RIVER

Michael Wright: In the grounds there were two firsts for me: I saw my first kingfisher on the pond over the road opposite the main gates and my first pike in the Deben – the biggest fish I had ever seen.

Andrew Wright: Life became fun at Brandeston, without parents and home, at weekends we built wonderful camps in the grounds, swimming in the river, (catching pike if we could), frogspawn in the pond outside the classrooms, leaf cigarettes behind the bonfire in the autumn – and the sun seemed to shine all summer long. **Peter Arbon** was the gardener, always sweeping leaves with a witches broom and allowing us to get the peaches from the greenhouse if we could. I also remember Church on Sundays in the beautiful village church adjoining the school and huge noise from the giant rookery in the trees by the church.

John Rankin: I remember the River Deben – Its beauty of course but more particularly, swimming in a dammed-up portion of it was heaven. I loved watching the brightly coloured dragonflies as we swam. One Sunday several of us went on a Riverside walk: (nothing unusual in that.) We were in our Sunday suits and the Deben had been dredged. Being small boys we walked near the edge where the mud had been heaped up. Of course we got into difficulties and were quite scared since two or three of us were sinking and we had to form a chain to pull the more deeply embedded ones out. Arriving back at school covered in caked mud we were very worried, but when those in authority heard what had happened they were kind to us, and made us warm and really spoilt us.

Tony Martin: Being a town-bred boy, I had very little experience of the 'countryside'. Because the grounds were intact and very much as

Left and below:
The River Deben at
Brandeston – here
we once swam –
here they once
boated.

On the "Thames". Brandeston
Muriel Annesley. 1900

the army had left them, with the walled gardens still containing the fruit espaliers on their wires, the place seemed to me like Heaven. There was a mumps epidemic in the first year, I think, but I only had 'Half mumps', and, although I was kept out of classes, I was told to 'lose myself' between meals. Therefore several of us ran around like little savages through the woods and along the river for what seemed like days on end. My special friends at the time were **BA Scrivener** and **CJ Martin** (no relation). We made dens in the ditch to the west of the playing fields where the footpath goes down to Five Bridges. I have never understood why these were so called, as there are still only three.

Robert le Rougetel: The hut was one of many scattered about the grounds, remnants of the army's use of the Hall during the war. One was given over to model-making, and those of us keen on this had the run of it, with no adult supervision. It was all very relaxed and free, I suppose, from the kinds of legal restraints and obligations which current heads have to contend with. In Summer

we swam in the Deben, not minding the odd leach, and made 'huts' in the wooden strip which bounds the grounds to the West.

Richard Overend: I have four vivid memories: 1/The river was a great source of fun. A friend and I went fishing and caught a few pike. One Sunday in February I fell in, wearing my best suit. It was cold, and I had to run back for a bath and change of clothes. 2/ The dens that we built from wood with turf roofs. None ever seemed to collapse on top of us. 3/ The stream which was dammed to make large lakes and then torrents. 4/ The rooks in the trees by the church. I cannot hear rooks in a rookery (We have one next door to us now), without remembering Brandeston. The church bells have a similar effect.

Tony Martin: I think we all remember Peter Arbon, who looked after the garden and grounds with great affection. He became something of an institution at the school and in the village. His 80th birthday which I was privileged to attend in 2007 was a moving testimonial of gratitude for the kindness he bestowed on

Opposite: Chris Bellamy's autograph book of 1958/9 showing signatures of most of the staff of that period.

small boys recently removed from the warmth of their homes. There could not have been a more suitable 'alma pater'. He would give us peaches and apricots picked straight from the walls and still warm and there were strawberries and apples too, in season. He made great bonfires beneath the rookery and we got potatoes to bake in them. We made 'gasper' cigarettes from Bronco toilet paper and oak leaves and I sometimes think that acted as a lifetime deterrent to smoking later on, rather than the beginnings of a habit. A four-tined garden fork was left to keep the fire 'rounded up' and I remember painfully **David Summers** driving a tine through my big toe. I had a couple of days in bed, I think, perhaps an anti-tetanus jab and some dressings administered by Dr Craig from Framlingham.

To conclude this passage, we publish the memories of **Bruce Pearson**. *Since his first visit to Antarctica, with the British Antarctic Survey in 1975, Bruce has continued to travel to many of the world's remotest and most spectacular locations as ecologist, film-maker, writer and artist. He earned the accolade of Wildlife Illustrator of the Year (1983); Bird Illustrator of the Year (1984), and was elected President of the Society of Wildlife Artists in 1994, serving 10 years.*

I can't remember a time when I've not had a deep interest in wildlife, landscape and the natural world. And mostly through luck and happy circumstance (plus a little bit of hard work and a simple ability to paint and draw). I have been able to turn the bird watching, bug collecting, insect chasing, mammal trapping enthusiasms of boyhood into a life-long career as a professional artist, sometimes writer and occasional wildlife film-maker. I'm not sure that my times as a pupil at Brandeston Hall and Framlingham College made that happen entirely, but they were both perfect in their locations, routines, and educational underpinning for a boy more than a little interested in natural history.

The Brandeston experiences are all now jumbled memories. A notebook with hand-drawn sketch maps of the school grounds showing locations of some of the more common breeding birds' nests I had found; watching Peter Arbon shooting out rooks' nests from the high trees around the church and reading, for the first time, an edition of Tarka the Otter, by Henry Williamson, that included wonderful illustrations by Charles Tunnicliffe... (then keeping a close watch on the river Deben behind the school in the forlorn hope that an otter might pass).

Once at Framlingham there was a similarly positive experience, becoming involved in the Natural History Society that then allowed access to the meres. This was the wonderful wetland below the school which was covered in coots and moorhens and various duck species in winter and where I once found a whitethroat's nest in the Summer Term.

A few years ago when I had to write an opening chapter for a book about bird migration, that needed to introduce the idea of people long ago believing that swallows disappeared each winter into the mud and reeds surrounding marshes and ponds(!), I returned to Suffolk for a day and walked along the river behind Brandeston and re-visited the meres at Framlingham, to immerse myself in suitably atmospheric wetland locations. Both the landscape, as well as memories of some great school days, were once again a source of inspiration – as they had been over 25 years earlier.

How many schools can match such stunning locations?

Bob Williams *acknowledges Bruce's on-going interest in, and support for, Brandeston Hall. From their first meeting in the early 1970s, Bruce has regularly made time, within his busy schedule, to come and talk to the pupils about his globe-trotting experiences; introducing the young (through his quite stunning photographs) to a number of the world's remotest places – Antarctica and the Sahara being the most spectacular. Two of Bruce's limited edition prints make up part of the school's art collection.*

A further footnote: Bruce would be delighted to learn that there are, indeed, otters to be seen once again on the river Deben.

WARTIME RELICS

Michael Wright: During the first year there were two or three occasions when old wartime smoke bombs and ammunition were found in the grounds and the army was sent for to remove them.

John Capon recalls when the authorities came to explode phosphorous bombs outside on the tennis court. The pungent smell lingered on.

Another vivid memory is of the changing rooms in the old army Nissen hut – a very hot stove sat in one corner of the hut, and it had to be negotiated by boys wishing to get past it. One day John inadvertently placed his hand on it (unguarded and unprotected) and the tortoise pattern was scorched into his hand.

Tony Martin: At weekends, we were left much to our own devices and there was much delight to be had in exploring the extent of the boundaries and the remains of military occupation within them. We discovered phosphorous bombs in the pond which, stabilised when submerged, were lethal when extracted and the glass bottles broken. Curiously I do not remember what happened when we did this, nor the smell of the gas which would have escaped. With hindsight, I can see that they might have killed us, as that was their wartime purpose.

The pond also contained enormous eels which, somehow, we managed to get to the bank.

THE STAFF

Many of these reminiscences are memories of an era in education now long forgotten and overtaken by what many would consider to be more child-centred theories of education. Teachers of earlier times were perhaps permitted greater eccentricity and disciplinary licence and they were subjected less to the uniformity of establishment expectation. Personalities they certainly were, and maybe that is why they are recalled with greater clarity, and indeed, very often, great affection. Others inspire darker memories. It is also interesting to note how many members of the non-teaching staff are remembered, showing how important they were in the lives of young boys.

These reminiscences are necessarily selective, perhaps, even invidiously so, and we can only record a small cross-section of them – to give a flavour of the times. Nicknames are retained, where they cause no offence, as these are part of the fabric of schoolboy memories.

Some teachers make a positive impact, and they, and what they teach, linger on in the memory. Others are colourless and are soon forgotten. Yet others loom large in the memory, for all the wrong reasons. It would be dishonest to try to expunge such memories.

Chris Bellamy was at Brandeston in the late 50s, and has always been a splendid hoarder of archive material. This copy of two pages of his 1958/9 autograph book, showing the names of most of the Brandeston staff of those years, displays not only his early interest in collecting memories, but also his admirable ability at storing them away.

Peter Liell: Being sent away to Brandeston at the age of 12 was probably no bad thing but the teaching staff were of the Evelyn Waugh kind! Now is not the time or place in which to speak of these idiosyncrasies, but I could expand on this if I knew that all the teachers I'm thinking about are no longer on this litigious earth.

Tony Martin: The staff was quite small in number. David Kittermaster was Head, over 'Daddy' Craig, John Ferris, John Pemberton, Ma Podd and Ma Brownsword.

I believe 'Doody' Day came from the College to teach us woodwork, but I seem to remember that he was soon superceded by Tom Fleming. I am still grateful to these two for instilling in me

Left: A young John Capon, proudly
carrying his woodwork piece - a
chicken feeder, made under the
'occasional' supervision of 'Doody' Day.

an ability to use my hands constructively which has stayed with me all my life. Leslie, whose surname I have forgotten, looked after the boilers etc, and lived in a hut beside the yew hedge on the roadside and we would sit in there with him on cold days. It was very cosy.

 Bertie Manthorpe came from the College, weekly, I suppose, and took art lessons. I remember him with affection as a diligent teacher at Brandeston, and later at the College. He had a propensity to throw a heavy bunch of keys towards dreamers and an ability to hold a Vick inhaler in place with his tongue when clearing a nostril.

Andrew Wright: That first day at Brandeston Hall, we were all assembled in the little hall in front of the Dining Hall, where the stairs go up, and suddenly the chatter was stopped by Mr Ferris, 'barking' at us from half way up the stairs. I was terrified of him from that moment on. He was always red-faced and could be ferocious if roused!

Roland Nice: My academic fortunes took something of a tumble after Brandeston. Miss Brownsword's efforts brought me to the top of the form but, on transfer to Framlingham, I slumped to the bottom.

Michael Wright: Mr Kittermaster had been teaching at the Junior School for the year prior to the Brandeston opening and so I got to

know him as he looked after the hockey and cricket teams. The Kittermasters had corgi dogs, and I remember that the boys kept their distance – a couple, including me, received a small bite on the leg!

Andrew Wright: The Headmaster, Mr Kittermaster, was warm and affable (from the way he hit golf balls down the playing fields in the evenings, he was obviously a great sportsman too) and his wife taught recorders. We knew she was a good musician, but we didn't understand her music in those days. Best of all, they had a lovely golden retriever dog, much loved by all, in contrast to a corgi who regularly ran down the main corridor biting boys ankles.

Robert le Rougetel: David Kittermaster - a genial, gentle soul.

Bruce Pearson: We did Art in an old army hut with **Mansell Beard**, but I distinctly remember Mr Manthorpe's occasional presence as well, (perhaps when he adjudicated the Framlingham Entrance exam?).

David Newson: I was at Brandeston Hall, between 1954-58, during the Kittermaster years. I recall that DDK was very good at shopping for the boarders, going into Ipswich once a week with a very full order book. His wife, **Rachel**, taught me the recorder, one of the instruments played right through to my last year at Framlingham. We always used to do very well at the Suffolk Music Festival.

Andrew Wright: I was lucky enough to have John Pemberton as my housemaster, (an Oxford Blue for athletics, we thought) and the kindest of men, who lived with his lovely wife Wendy in an old Nissen hut, down by the playing fields.

John Edwards: The only downside was our introduction to one, Mr Ferris. I am sure, from the safe distance of 60 years, that he was a perfectly decent man, but our first impression left a lot to be

Right: John Capon with Sam Bigden, grandson, currently at Brandeston, his banjulele – which he has never learnt to play!

desired. I will say no more... but those who were there and who might read this will know what I mean!

I remember French lessons with 'Daddy' Craig, PT with Mr Pemberton, Mrs Podd and Miss Brownsword – they all feature strongly in my memory, together with Wendy Milne (now Mrs Pemberton), **Prudence Chapel**, **Buffy Lee**, (now Mrs John Austin) – all as matrons, together with the sick bay under the supervision of a lady whose name I have forgotten, when I had mumps in 1948, and recall hearing that Prince Charles had been born.

Tony Martin: We seemed to spend much time with Miss Brownsword on the reproductive system of the worm, in Nature Study – and sometimes we went for nature walks – but term always ended just before we were told how the worm actually did it. Mr Craig took us for French with limited success, and the only word I can remember is the French for 'armchair' – fautauille. Probably I still cannot spell it but I remember it because he made us laugh when he said it.

Peter Liell was only at Brandeston for four terms, but clearly remembers the remarkable David Kittermaster – such an unassuming man. He remembers, as if it were yesterday, David's shambling walk to the piano in the Assembly Hall (or whatever it was called). He invariably wore boots with crepe soles – today they would probably be hush puppies – and a light grey suit with a tie. Peter remembers the slip-catching practices, with a testing machine in the shape of a rowing boat (generally known as a slip-catch cradle!). At assembly, he played through the hymn tune on the piano to get the assembly (hymn and prayers) going. David and his wife Rachel were gentle, civilised people.

Andrew Wright: There was a gorgeous blonde assistant matron, **Marie (Fanny) Few**. All the boys were in love with her. She always wore a white doctor's coat and we wondered what else!

Roland Nice is another of many who remembers the 'gorgeous'

Marie Few. All would love to know what became of her. John Capon recalls her banjulele playing and how she used to play the instrument to the boys in the dorm. John still has his banjulele but has never to this day learnt to play it!

Tony Martin: Marie Few must have been only about 10 years older than we were but several of us fell deeply in love before we were twelve years old. She was, I believe, from a farming family in Cambridgeshire and it is still she, of all the domestic staff, whom most of us remember. She was quite a well built girl, but very attractive to us in her features. Jim Blythe still goes quite hot at the mere mention of her name. She laid him in her bed one night when he was feeling particularly unhappy! He was about 11 years old at the time.

Our ills and accidents were dealt with by Dulcie Wilton. She wore a bright green uniform, and, although she was not unkind to us, she suffered no nonsense and perhaps inevitably, came to be called 'The Green Dragon'. There was a sick bay where daily medicines were administered and our cuts and bruises dressed. One or two small rooms with a single bed were reserved for those with more serious illnesses. The queue at sick parades was always longer for Marie Few than it was for The Green Dragon and boys would work quite hard in advance at being unwell if they knew her duty was imminent.

On some evening we would see a small car come down the

drive and we somehow knew that a man was seeing Marie Few. It wasn't until we moved up to the College that we saw 'Dibber' Hague driving this car and we knew who the man had been. I don't suppose that anybody knows the outcome of this affair but Hague remained a bachelor to his death. How nice it would have been if something had developed between 'Dibber' and Marie so that their lives could have continued as did John and Wendy Pemberton's.

Ian Fulcher: Challenged by the story about his A5 grading awarded by **Shirley Robinson** (see p122) Ian responded with the following: I find myself looking back on Mrs Robinson's science lessons with an extremely rosy glow. Her enthusiasm was infectious. And yes, the subsequent part is indeed correct.

I am now running a small computer company in Kentford, Newmarket, and still regret not finding a job in which I could use Mrs Robinson's science teachings on a daily basis. She was somewhat strict and one knew not to muck about, so it made it much worse that I chose her lesson to throw **Malcolm Willett's** pencil case out of the window into the (out-of-bounds) garden. I can't remember the punishment but I do remember thinking that I wouldn't do it again!

For **John Rankin** Mr Ferris was a terrific teacher but unfortunately unable to keep his temper and therefore much misunderstood. Nor was he as effective as he would otherwise have been. He tried to teach us in Form 5 about romantic poets. Liking history, I found it interesting but even then realised that it should have been much later on in our education. He was desperately disappointed with our response and behaved as if he had never been a boy himself.

John Worland: My own 'Ferris' story: I remember meeting 'Stinker' Ferris, as he had been known, some time after I had left the College. He told me the story about his red and green pens. The red pen, which was used for corrections, had to be re-nibbed every year for the start of the new term because he had worn off the 'blob' and the pen was worn down to the gold base. The green pen, which was used for commendable work rarely had to be re-nibbed.

Mr Ferris was a stickler for accuracy. There was one occasion when I should have received a 'Good Copy' (These contributed to House points). I had done a perfect essay. However, Ferris had dotted every single 'i' and crossed every single 't'. Demanding as ever, Ferris proclaimed to the class:"Worland would have received a 'Good Copy', but I will not let him have it because of his lack of crossed 't's and dotted 'i's." The rest of the class enjoyed it! I have never forgotten it.

Tony Martin: Not all was sweetness and light and fun. John Ferris should never have been a schoolmaster. He was short-tempered and vindictive and had a vicious streak. He would lose his temper in class, turning a bright red in his rage. He really did frighten us. He wore thick, horn-rimmed glasses and his nose was pointed in his narrow face. His mouth turned down in a disdainful expression as if he had no time for small boys.

LESSONS AND ROUTINE

Learning from Failure: *In 2007 a Suffolk teacher ignited controversy by suggesting that failure should be rebranded as "deferred success".* **Terry Hunt**, *Old Brandestonian and Editor of the East Anglian Daily Times, responded by recalling his own experiences at Brandeston and the College...*

I remember the moment as if it were yesterday. In fact it was more than 35 years ago, but it has stuck with me through the ensuing decades.

I was 13 years old and in my second year at Brandeston Hall. In those days, exam results were posted on noticeboards for all and sundry to see, and laugh at in some cases.
I knew I hadn't done well in the Chemistry exam. To be honest I had a pretty good idea that I'd had a nightmare. It was a subject I found almost impossible to understand. The practicals, with all those mini-volcanoes and games with Bunsen burners, were quite fun. But any kind of theoretical work or, horror of horrors, exams, were quite beyond me.

So, as I slouched along the corridor to join the growing gaggle of small boys straining to see how they had done, I wasn't overly optimistic. I waited until they'd gone, and then scanned the list of names and marks.

In true pessimistic fashion, I started my search for the name at the bottom of the list. I didn't have to look for long. There it was Hunt, 10%. Bottom of the class. The worst student chemist in the form. The most clueless boy out of the 20-plus in the class. I'd probably got the 10% for turning up at the right exam and spelling my name correctly.

In truth, it was a crushing moment. To have to deal with that level of failure and public humiliation was difficult at the tender age of 13. Small boys being small boys, my classmates weren't exactly sympathetic. I don't suppose many of them have taken up counselling as a profession.

For **John Capon** 'not much of the academic input remains'. He learnt to write with **Miss Brownsword**, (a lady whose nickname reflected the ampleness of her upper body). French was a closed book. Later on, in 5D one third of the class achieved 0% on French Mock 'O' levels. Reading the lesson at morning assembly was a trial, particularly when more demanding members of staff were on duty –having to get one's tongue around all those difficult Old Testament names.

The photograph on p56 shows John learning how to operate the 'grinston' (Grindstone) with **'Doody' Day** in the old Woodwork hut. That was as advanced a machine as was available. No metal, no power driven machines, no goggles, no code of Health and Safety. But practical skills were central to the lives of many of the students. The tradition of crafts and design has continued to flourish, with students at the College still achieving the highest of standards. John's design for a chicken feeder (echoes of the origins of his surname perhaps!) shows early practical creativity. It should be remembered that in the 50s the largest Club at the College was the Young Farmers' Club, and that the school had a day off for the Suffolk Show, such was its importance at the time.

David Carr recalls that Exeats were restricted to 4 per term, just on a Sunday from the end of chapel (10.30am) and you had to be back by 7pm. Usually, on a Sunday evening, there was a film arranged by Mr MH Beard – 'War Wagon' (John Wayne) and 'The Dambusters' were two. He was also lucky enough to be allowed to go with the Ellerby family to see West Ham (his team) play at Portman Road.

John Rankin remembers PNY Craig's French Grammar text book – How marvellous to write a book! He also remembers Mr Craig's boxing occasions, which John did his best to avoid, and Form 5 with **Michael Sparrow** (whom he would love to contact), Brian Scrivener and **Michael Clarke**. He thinks Jim Blythe must have been there as well and recalls his wonderful sense of humour and fun – and what a memory! No matter how hard I tried I could never beat Brian Scrivener in the Fortnightly order!

Robert le Rougetel: Three of us who were academically able were fast-streamed from the entry form (bizarrely named Remove) to the top form within two years, spending our last two years in that form (then known as the Third Form). DDK taught us Mathematics very well, and a brilliant and brittle teacher, John Ferris, taught us English, History and Geography, to whatever level he felt he could stretch us. We encountered plenty of Shakespeare, the poems of

Marvel and Pope, and the horrors of the English Civil War. I think even then we recognised that JPF was out of place in a Prep School. I discovered that he had been a member of the Bletchley Park code-breaking team during the war. Eventually he left for his métier, History Research at UCL, spending his last years writing part of a massive History of Parliament.

SPORT

John Rankin remembers learning rugby on the 5th section hilly ground amongst all the numerous molehills. He also remembers **Rodney Crabtree's** father in the Fathers' Match hitting a ball John bowled an awful long way, straight, then gazing in admiration and asking him very unwisely if he could repeat the feat – which he duly did. He also recalls listening to the Middleweight Title fight between Randolph Turpin and Sugar Ray Robinson in New York and the return in London on Crystal sets. Reception was a bit unreliable. Also: Teas on the terrace were always a highlight for me during Home Cricket fixtures. The tea itself was magnificent as was the view. When one had been batting for a long time or in the field on a hot day this was really living. There was an old Beeston bus that took us to the College for swimming each week.

Peter Liell: I remember the day when the coach took us cricketers to Eversley in Southwold. I found when we got there that I had forgotten to bring my cricket boots. So **Michael Spencer** lent me his spare plimsolls – which were at best one size too small. Thanks to the Spencer plimsolls I performed well enough to be awarded my colours.

Andrew Wright: For me, learning cricket, hockey and rugby (how many hours did I spend trying to perfect my flying scrum-half pass?) were indelible parts of Brandeston life, much more than the French and Latin.

Richard Overend: I remember the Horse-riding lessons with Miss Galli/eon (I never did know how to spell her name!) The horses were hacked over by her from the stables at Framlingham station. They were lazy horses on the ride over, but went very fast on the way home.

The major sports contribution is from **David Carr**: Football was the Christmas term sport and the coach was **Allan Watkins**, Glamorgan (and England) cricketer. He could score a goal by shooting from the other half of the pitch – amazing to me as a little boy. I made my 1st XI debut in my first term and scored seven goals in my first game! I was captain in 1968 but **Simon Bloomfield** was captain in 1969 when we had a really successful side – we won something like 8 out of 10 matches including beating Nowton Court 16-0 and 8-0, but lost twice to Orwell Park 3-2 and 2-1. RHS Holbrook was always a daunting place to go to – the opposition were always about six inches taller than us and twice as fast. Usually, we played on a pitch that was in the middle of about 50 other pitches – their facilities were amazing, but we somehow managed to win each time. Other opponents included Eversley (Southwold), Moreton Hall, Culford, St Josephs, St Edmunds (Kesgrave) – some probably no longer in existence.

Rugby was played up to half term in the Spring term and hockey for the second part. We either always had snow or a flu epidemic so I do not remember any school matches in 1968 or 1969. **Richard Broad** would take the 'first section' for a walk through the surrounding picturesque countryside if there was snow on the ground and a match was cancelled. I also recall, about the only time I went in there, watching the 1969 F A Cup final in the Headmaster's house – it might have been the only TV at Brandeston Hall then. In 1970 we certainly had one school rugby match and several hockey matches.

Cricket was the important sport in the summer term. I was captain in 1969 and 1970 and think we were undefeated in 1970. The highlight was the Fathers' match – I think it was **Peter Giles'** father (an OF) who used bring fresh strawberries to eat after the game. In one school match in 1969, Peter took seven wickets for two runs with his left arm bowling. In a house match in 1969, Yellow batted first and scored 13 – Blue were all out for 10. Athletics – for the high jump, the landing area was just sand and **Charlie Blackmore** and **Andrew Payne** suffered broken collar bones as a consequence.

Swimming was at The College, and we were transported there by Thompsons (the Tommy bus). More 'upmarket' coaches were provided by Soames of Otley.

EVENTS

Andrew Wright: On Opening Day, I do remember the speeches and ceremony outside the front door – and brother Michael's speech. We thought Princess Alice was a charming lady, but a bit old to be 'a princess'.

David Carr: DD Kittermaster retired in Summer 1968 and the parents, staff and friends raised almost £250 for a leaving present – an amazing amount at that time.

Jeremy Kemp's recollections remind us of the way in which tragedy can sometimes strike a school and its community. In Jeremy's time the school was stunned by the tragic death of **Tim Birrell**, in a skiing accident in Switzerland. National, foreign, as well as local newspapers reported the story. A snow cat overturned, killing Tim outright and seriously injuring his two young brothers. One brother, **Iain**, was a close friend of Jeremy's. Newspaper cuttings were kept, together with a letter from Timothy's father, saying how Iain would need his friend's support in the term to come. Such tragedies cut deep into the soul of a school. It is friendship that helps people eventually to come to terms with the consequences. It is also part of education to learn the life is fragile and that part of education is to understand that fragility.

According to newspaper reports, a record 500 people attended the 1974 Speech Day. All stood in silence in memory not only of Tim Birrell, but also of two other Old Boys of the school, **Brian Arthur** and **Bryan Ellis**, both of whom had lost their lives in the Paris air disaster of that year. Both had been fine rugby players and had flown to Paris for the Rugby International.

David Carr: The Village fete was held on the front lawns – it was always exciting trying to win on the bottle stall.

FOOD

Some of the experiences remembered below were common in schools immediately after the war but, reassuringly, rarely occur nowadays at Brandeston or anywhere else.

Indeed choice – hot, cold, vegetarian, and healthy eating is now the order of the day. Post-war food was very limited in its scope, and rationing meant that plates had to be cleared. Wastage was frowned upon. Rationing continued until about 1953. A shortage of Sweet Coupons limited between-meals snacks.

Bob Clayton: A 'Ferris incident' occurred in the dining room when leeks were on the menu. Having been brought up in the country appreciating the taste of fresh vegetables, I decided to have a second helping. Since the Assistant Matron wanted to go, she emptied the remaining large quantity of leeks from the container on to my plate telling me to leave any which I didn't want.

Consequently I consumed a small amount leaving the rest until Mr Ferris came along, calling me a very greedy little boy and insisting that I stayed until all the leeks had been eaten After a flood of tears (mine not his!) he eventually allowed me to go, along with 'three bad marks', leaving the remaining leeks, feeling sure that I had been taught a good lesson! I have never eaten leeks since.

John Rankin recalls "having to eat herring roes which I hated. Mr Ferris said I had no option but to take them on my plate". To compensate for that, there was a Tuck Shop. Being rarely able to buy chocolate (it was rationed) meant that some of us, when we did eat it, made ourselves ill from the sheer quantity eaten.

Richard Overend, too, remembers the tuck shop "where you could buy the sort of sweets and foods considered bad for you nowadays. Also the shed where the tuckboxes were stored. (Everyone had a Tuck Box in those days). You could get in by slipping a penknife into the yale lock on the door."

John Capon remembers getting hold of illicit peaches by jumping out of the stable block classroom window. There were also black grapes to be had from the greenhouse – woe betide you if you were caught by '**Crankypants' Turner**. These little treats were wonderful. Food in those days was basic – food rationing was still in operation. All the more surprising that so much unpalatable food found its way down through the holes in the heating grilles, either to fester or to be gleefully consumed by whatever vermin lurked there.

Nigel Hyde: Hunger! Many of us were often hungry and the time between 'lights out' and breakfast seemed interminable. In a sad attempt to earn some 'cred' in the dormitory I would get onto the roof at night, go down the fire escapes, and raid what was then the walled kitchen garden. I never came back with much, and to this day I have never eaten celery again.

Tony Martin: Because of Mr Ferris I cannot to this day eat parsnips. He forced me to eat them and stay behind at table until I had done so, sick though I was during the consumption. The man did the same with tapioca pudding which certainly looks like frogspawn and probably tastes the same. Bob Clayton (so I heard) and I put many parsnips, leeks and tapioca pudding down the heating grid that ran round the dining room at Brandeston and the trauma left me with an enduring hatred.

MISDEMEANOURS

Bob Clayton: I remember an incident involving a ticking off from DDK which occurred after a playful water-fight in a bathroom situated above his study. There were two baths situated side by side in this bath-room. Whilst the assistant Matron was attending to another matters elsewhere, leaving two eleven-year-old boys to their own devices, one of us playfully flicked some water at the other with devastating consequences. On her eventual return the Assistant Matron found to her horror that the bathroom floor was covered in several inches of water. It further transpired that a large quantity of water had seeped through the floor to the room underneath which, sadly, was the Headmaster's study!

Mr Kittermaster was not amused but did no more than reprimand us for unruly behaviour unbefitting of two young gentlemen!

Nigel Hyde: When I arrived at Brandeston Hall as a 10 year old in 1955 domestic help was provided by local ladies known to us as Skivvies or Skivs. One morning Headmaster Kittermaster addressed us sternly. The Skivvies, he said, were no longer to be addressed as Skivvies and anyone found referring to them as such would be severely punished. I think we took this advice without objection, recognising that Skivvy was not a very nice name to call someone. It was just that we had not thought about it before. I did not know where the ladies who provided domestic help came from, but imagined that they came from Brandeston village. I remember them arriving at the Hall in a group; all talking at once, like a flock of starlings as they came down the drive. They seemed very nice and I regarded them enviously because they came from the outside world. (The domestic ladies used the word 'La' amongst themselves; a word that the dictionary explains as 'an expression of surprise or emphasis'. I have never heard it used since. Even at the time I thought it archaic and at least Shakespearian in origin).

Roland Nice was one of the first generation of Brandestonians. He was at the school in the days before corporal punishment was banished, and remembers being 'tanned' by David Kittermaster on his birthday. He and **Brian Woolley** were the only two to put up their hands as being responsible for an incident when DDK would not allow them any special cakes. DDK dealt him four slaps with his hairbrush – the marks came out later! Corporal punishment was indeed administered, but few claim to have been permanently scarred by it – for most it was the expected consequence of poor behaviour.

Chris Keeble, *the designer of this book, has two passions which survive and thrive to this very day: motor cars and, naturally, design. These interests were in embryonic evidence during his days at Brandeston. His precocious interest in fine cars resulted in a ticking off, but also in a story to last a lifetime. In his own words:*

Even while I was at Brandeston, I was already hooked on cars, particularly competition cars. In those pre-television days, boys used to collect all sorts of leaflets and badges – creative hobbies which passed the time. Because my particular interest was cars, I wrote to Rootes Group (Howes), in Ipswich, requesting leaflets and badges on the new Sunbeam Alpine. This was, I believe, the vehicle which had won the Monte Carlo Rally that year (1954).

Some days later, two men in smart white coats showed up, unannounced, at Brandeston Hall, looking for a Mr Christopher Keeble, presumably having deduced from my letterhead that I was some grand, possibly titled, landed gent looking for, and well capable of affording a new sports car. I can't really believe that my youthful letter was as impressive as the letterhead!

The upshot of this was inevitably that I was given a ticking off and, in order to avoid similar confusion in the future, pupils were asked to head their letters from then on as 'Brandeston Hall SCHOOL'.

John Capon's tale of creative naughtiness is of sunbathing on the ivy-clad roof of a lean-to shed. Sunbathing was not allowed, so the boys removed a few tiles in the roof of the shed and made their way up to their own private sundeck through a hole in the roof. A disused pipe was used for intercom to warn of any passing teacher – the Latin word 'Cave' was widely used as a term for 'Watch out – beware' – and this would be urgently whispered along the pipe.

Partners in naughtiness were **David Summers** and **Patrick Wheatley**. He also used to go riding on the ponies belonging to Miss Galliane at the Brandeston Queen, and deliver beer with Mr Ablett from the Queens Head, who also sold the boys cigarettes. These could be sold on for a fat profit. Cut-rate smoking could be enjoyed by wrapping up wadges of oak leaves in toilet paper.

Above: The Rootes Motor Group sent down a spanking new Sunbeam Alpine to be viewed by Chris Keeble, thinking he was a landed gent looking for, and well capable of affording, a new sports car.

Inventive too was the method of cooking baked beans and soup on a fire of boot polish pinched from the shoe room – it burnt well.

THE ARTS

Peter Liell: DDK played the hymn tune to start the day: I think the short service (hymn and prayers) preceded breakfast. David and Rachel Kittermaster were gentle civilised people. I remember that Rachel used to make recorder music with **Marjorie Gillett**, Geoffrey Bland, **Stephen Baylis** and others.

Tony Martin: There were rudimentary music lessons on an infrequent basis from a Mr Hall and Mrs Kittermaster, with her friend Marjorie Gillett, who taught some to play the recorder. To this day I cannot hear a recorder without thinking what a dreadful noise it makes.

Geoff Bland: Strangely enough, it was the dreaded Mr Ferris who made me realise that I could act. Our form presented a play in which (prophetically) he cast me in the leading role as a schoolmaster in charge of a class of unruly pupils. I absolutely loved it and, though I say it myself, I think I did it well. At any rate, it was the start of a lifetime of amateur dramatics for me, culminating in parts like Polonius and Touchstone on the local stage here in Cheltenham.

Re: **David Newson**: The Framlinghamian of 1962-63 makes an interesting reference to a very successful concert, at Brandeston Hall, by returning Old Boys (joined by Messrs **Deryck Cox** and **Roger Radice** on two pianos)... 'a skilful rendering of melody and rhythms'. David, on trumpet, was one of their number.

Charlie Simpson: One of my fondest memories of Brandeston Hall was Parents Day 98'. It was my first ever real public performance with my band 'Natural Disasters' with **Casper Williamson**, **Hugo Horvath** and **Ian McLaren**. Those weekends were always very special because it would follow on from Sports Day which was always great fun. When I look back at my time at Brandeston H all, I am filled with the happiest of memories. There were always so many things to do and there was never a dull moment. One of my favourite times at the school would have been the production of Bugsy Malone in which I played the role Fat Sam.

Early evidence of artistic talent is shown in this

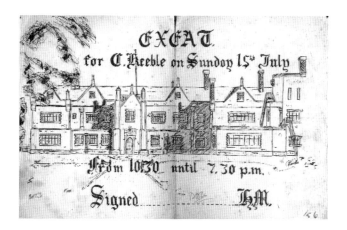

Chris Keeble-designed 'arty' Exeat, *(above)*, duly signed by DD Kitttermaster. On Sundays, when boys were not out on exeat – and there was a strict limit of four exeats a term – everyone, however reluctantly, had to sit and write a supervised letter home. It was the receiving of some sort of communication rather than the quality of the writing which assured parents that all was well.

David Carr: School productions in my time were 'Emile and The Detectives' and 'Alice through the Looking Glass', both produced by **Mr JG Haslam**. Mr Beard did produce some films, one being 'The Witchfinder General' – *see page 16* – based on John Lowes and the Brandeston witchcraft saga. The sixth form (nine of us in 1970) had an outing to The Theatre Royal, Bury St Edmunds to see 'Hamlet'.

Robert le Rougetel: We were taught science (in one of the Nissen huts) by a marvellously eccentric and entirely unqualified man, Dennis Early, whose real talent lay in writing and producing plays for us to perform. Hs career would have been curtailed abruptly in today's climate by an incident backstage, when he required an explosive sound effect, and arranged for a Thunderflash (a military practice grenade) to be detonated in a dustbin. The noise terrified the audience, and the explosion filled the auditorium with a thick smoke. And this was during an inter-schools Drama Festival, held, oddly enough, at RAF (USAF) Bentwaters. He got away with it, somehow.

Charles Machin-Goodall: Recently I was listening to Radio 4 when they began to discuss a little remembered film called 'The Hireling' based upon a book of the same name by LP Hartley. I remember 'The Hireling' as a school film. It was an unusual choice for a boys' prep school, based as it was on the story of an aristocratic woman released from a psychiatric hospital in the 1920s being driven back to her old home in Yorkshire by her chauffeur with whom she develops a relationship. As I say, it was an unusual choice – it was also an unpopular one. Boys more used to 'The Italian Job' (original version) or 'Charge of the Light Brigade' (1960s version, there being an earlier one, surprisingly made in 1912) did

not take kindly to a film based upon thoughts rather than action. I also remembered how popular films were applauded at the end, not by a round of clapping but by vigorous stamping of the feet on the old wooden floorboards of the Hobbies Room, next to the White Hall, where school films were shown.

DAY BOYS

John Worland - *one of the original dayboys:*
For those who had passed their 11+ East Suffolk County Council paid the fees and means-tested their parents before they were issued with a County Council bicycle. If you were 'given' a bike, it was inspected by County Council bike inspectors every term to ensure that it was in good order. If not, it was taken away, repaired, and your parents would be sent the bill. My 'bike' was a 'bog standard' model with no 3 speed gears. I think the handlebars were 'black' and not chrome-plated.

There were rules for travelling to and from the College or Brandeston. If you lived up to three miles away (I was living at 23 Castle Street, Framlingham), you walked – that made 6 miles walking a day. If you lived up to 9 miles away, you had to cycle – up to 18 miles a day. If you lived over 9 miles away you lived in the 'Hostel' in College Road. Therefore on Mondays you cycled to Fram or Brandeston from home, then cycled/walked to the Hostel from Monday to Friday night and then home on Saturday after school. No wonder day boys were as fit as fleas.

I started at the College in September 1947, then Brandeston September 1948, and on to the College in September 1950. I left in Summer 1952. When we started at Brandeston, the boys I cycled with were Messrs **O'Farrell** and **Stephenson**, **Martin Plant**, **Gordon Reed**, **Chris Brain**, **Mike Allen**, 2 or 3 **Taylors** and others whose names I have forgotten.

STORIES

Peter Liell: One particular memory is of **David Belcher**, a fine artist and thespian, performing the dance of a whirling dervish on the cricket field, combining it with a track-and-field hammer throw – the only problem was that David's hammer was a golf club and he toyed with Brandeston's swallows and house martins as he performed this ritual. I remonstrated with him, but I don't think there was any malice involved and I don't remember that any bird was injured.

John Capon remembers the tale of Iki the ghost of Brandeston Hall, supposedly the ghost of a young man who hanged himself in the toilet at the start of the tunnel (blocked off) leading across to the church. Iki reputedly hanged himself by suspending his braces from the overhead toilet chain. On the same subject (different spelling) David Newson remembers how 'Ikey Night' was always an excuse for mayhem. Once a year the senior dorms would attack the junior dorms, armed with pillows. "I well remember the occasion when we were all caught, en masse. The punishment was a detention, for everyone concerned, in the Library – thus missing a film!"

The Lost Tooth: (contributed by one of the girls). It happened on the pitch behind the old tennis courts whilst playing hockey one afternoon. I was playing in defence and **Roberta Scott** came charging towards me heading towards the goal. As the ball flicked up I miraculously stopped it, unfortunately with my mouth! I remember looking down on the grass to see my whole tooth, roots and all, laying there. My teacher, whose name escapes me, picked it up, wiped it on my PE skirt and insisted that I put it back in my mouth! Off I went up to **Miss Rix**, Matron, leaving a trail of blood behind me along the long corridor. The tooth was then taken out and thrown away. As I was waiting for Matron to contact my parents my games teacher then came up and took me immediately to her dentist in Debenham. Half way down the stairs to the White Hall I believe **Emma Gravelius** was told to retrieve my tooth from the bin and once again it was put in my mouth. It was a long and bumpy ride as the road was being re-surfaced but thanks to a fantastic dentist my tooth was restored. However, I didn't enjoy wearing a permanently attached gum shield for six weeks, especially as it was just before team photos!

Tony Martin: JLP Ferris fancied himself as something of a sportsman and umpire. He seemed to be all over the field at once and I recall being pushed about by this small wiry figure with the thin legs and baggy shorts. He delighted in getting us to push the heavy cricket roller on the hottest days. I think we were the ones who were not good at sport, and this was a sort of retribution for our failings. I remember being ill and confined to the sick bay with a high temperature. The school was told to be very quiet below my window. Not long before she died, I asked my mother what had been wrong with me and she said that I had been told to push the roller by 'that dreadful man', and I had suffered sunstroke as a consequence. I clearly remember waking one morning knowing that I was better and feeling well again. I looked out of the window, just at daybreak, when it was slightly misty. The air was cool and the

rooks were calling. The purity of the moment has stayed with me to this day.

REPORTS

Peter Liell: AR Manthorpe's last report on my Art was 'I would not call him gifted.'

Bob Clayton: On one of my History Reports Ferris wrote that 'during the term Robert has cheerfully plumbed the depths of imbecility', much to the amusement of my father who quoted it on many subsequent occasions, pointing out that at least I was cheerful about it.

John Capon's final report suggested that it was time to move on: he had acquired 'grown up habits' – in brackets (smoking).

Chris Keeble's Maths report – 'Sleeps with his eyes open'. Soccer – 'Runs about the pitch a great deal, but seldom kicks the ball'.

Neville Marsh's English report in 1956 (by JP Ferris) – 'His physical attitude in class and his writing both suggest a slipshod and indolent approach'. *Professor Neville Marsh finished up as acting Vice Chancellor at Adelaide University.*

CONCLUSIONS

Charles Machin-Goodall offers a broad conclusion in his contribution: Sounds from a Prep School Past. I thought of the beginning of term with boys running excitedly up and down the main staircase. Trunks and tuck boxes being carried at either end. Of boys greeting friends from the previous term and speaking hurriedly of adventures during the holidays.

I thought of the roar that went up from the long line of boys on the front lawn playing British Bulldog as they run towards the single capturer at the beginning of the game. That was like the Charge of the Light Brigade! How, on other occasions, the front lawn was the picture of serenity as two peacocks on either side of the main drive would sit to preen themselves and squawk their eerie cry. Then there was the sound on a quiet night of the water running constantly over the weir; or on a stormy night of the leaded panes rattling in the window frames. The glass panes lying loose in their places after years of gentle vandalism – boys peeling the lead frames back to try to release them.

There was the sound of the master's footsteps on the stone corridor giving warning of his approach as you were meant to be standing with your face to the wall in the Black and White Hall, or the screech of chalk against blackboard or the clanging of the old brass hand-bell to mark the end of a lesson.

There was the happy reminder of the end of the first Christmas term and the Carol Service and the singing of 'The Lord of the Dance' sung with evangelical fervour – not because of any particular evangelicalism but because of the excitement of returning home for Christmas. And there was the last assembly of the last term when the hymn with the words, '... who from our mother's arms' was sung with more mixed feelings.

Charlie Simpson: One of the people I had a great amount of respect for during my time there, was the Headmaster, Nigel Johnson. I think the school was always striving to get the best out of us. Looking back I couldn't imagine a better prep school for my parents to have sent me to.

Andrew Wright: A few collected memories of four very happy years. How lucky we are still to be in touch with so many old Brandeston and Framlingham friends, some 50 years later.

Tony Martin: The experience of Brandeston prepared me for the College; the experience of the College enabled me to make the best of National Service; and National Service really did make a man of me.

For **John (Joe) Capon** school was about character-building, sport and practical lessons for life. For cleaning out the Pembertons' chickens, he received a bar of chocolate. He also learnt how to use a handkerchief – Daddy Boo (Craig) insisted that you should start in one corner and work your way round rather than begin in the middle. No disposable tissues in those days – you had to wait for the next laundry call!

Regular attenders of Speech Days will know how the speeches by Head Boys and Head Girls are now one of the highlights of these occasions, and an opportunity to show-case the talents and confidence of the best of the school's young products as they prepare to move on. Jeremy Kemp was Head Boy when Headmaster-Elect, **Ron Jones**, was introduced by **Laurie Rimmer**, Head of the College. After Bob Williams, acting Headmaster, had

given his report on the year, Jeremy in his speech spoke proudly of the success of the table tennis players. **Jeremy Wade** spoke of the drama programme, and of the school's success with ceramics and music. Jeremy then performed the traditional task of presenting a bouquet – to **Mrs Jones**. (*Jeremy is now a Director of Savills.*)

Richard Overend: I remember how proud I was going back from the College as Captain of the Old Brandestonians XV to play Brandeston.

Lest it be thought that this history is an exercise in wearing rose-tinted spectacles **Tony Martin** *reminds us:* Despite the generally happy atmosphere there are still names which I remember with displeasure. There were times when boredom was experienced, and there was little encouragement to foster interest in other activities – certainly not by early 21st century standards – if one was not very bright and disinclined towards sport. I suspect that most schools were the same at this time.

The final reckoning: **Jeremy Kemp** kept a copy of fees. In 1971 a term's fees amounted to £138-6-8., but they were inflated to £147-14-7 because of extras: Insurance for two terms: £5-10-0; entertainments 2s-6d; Tuck Shop 19s-0d; Bootmaker 2s; tailors and cleaners 1s-9d, travelling expenses, pocket money etc £1-19-2 and finally Haircutting 19s-2d. The 1974 bill amounted to £241-00 (Britain went metric during this period).

John Edwards: Once one starts to unlock the memory it all comes back. Happy days. It was a wonderful privilege to have been part of it all, and I really do consider myself very lucky still to be heavily involved, as a Governor, in Brandeston's future.

Robert le Rougetel: Enough rambling – You can see that those formative years were blissful, stimulating and wonderful to recall.

Above: "Lot's of us – good players – and we've all got our own table tennis bats". Evidence for a speech by Jeremy Kemp, Head Boy, 1976. (Julian Pollard captain, centre back)

MY BRANDESTON – THE CLASS OF 2007

In 2007 we asked present pupils to give us contributions to 'My Brandeston' – to have a cross-section of up-to-date views on the school. The Summer term also saw the first issue of 'The Brandeston Buzz' – a magazine with a pupil news team under the direction of **Mrs Vass**. What follows is a cross section of memories expressed:

"The disco for Sulsar was a great success. We managed to raise a whopping £670. So many people having fun, and raising so much money for a worthy cause proved to all of us the true side of Brandeston." **Milly Hopkinson and Holly Cartmell**.

Horrors for scholars with 'The Woman in Black' – London visit 2007:
"The play was set in two halves. The first half was the setting of the scene and preparation for the horrors that awaited the audience in the second half. People say you are only afraid of what you don't know! In the interval we sat in our seats chewing our fingernails. The play was terrifying. It was a play not to be missed by anyone. Even though the most petrifying scenes were enough to make the toughest person scream. It really was a night to be remembered." **Christina Welsh**.

Extracts from an Interview with **Derrick Allum**, *for 6 years a much loved caretaker who retired in 2007 – by* **Camilla Ball, Vicky Paulley and Meg Wells-Furby**:

"What was the most exciting time at Brandeston?"
"The most exciting time is when all the children do plays and when I get to watch the house competitions. I love sport – and watching it in such lovely surroundings – it gives me a real buzz!"
"What part of the grounds do you like the most?"
"The grass and the golf pitches. I love down by the river too. I always loved rivers – I'm a country man born and bred."
"What will you miss most about the school?"
"I shall miss the kids most – all ages, all of them – and the teachers. My favourite teacher was 'Mr Mac' or 'Supermac' as I called him – he was a lovely man." (*John McIlveen* – Editor)

"The happiest moment at Brandeston Hall was when the Physics papers were collected and we were free from Common Entrance. No more work, Prep or effort – life is about to get so much better." **Lewis Myers-Allen**.

"The sporting opportunities were fab – netball, hockey and rounders. The academic variety was amazing. I had never done structured lessons before. The music has been fab as well. Finally – meeting all the great people along the way – friends and teachers. **Mimi O'Neill**.

"My funniest memory was of the French trip. I sneaked up to the boys' dorm with a few of the girls to steal sweets. While I was trying to make a run for it, clutching some strawberry laces and chewing gum, I got sprayed in the face with Lynx. I immediately yelled "I smell like a man!", and ran downstairs to spray myself from head to toe in WOMAN'S perfume!" **Olivia Cowley**.

"The best memory I have of Brandeston Hall is the time we played a Ukraine team. One of their players caught chicken pox and they needed a substitute. I was asked to play and accepted. We lost the tournament but it was a great experience." **Ben Easey**.

"Science week was really fun! We made slime and set off helium balloons. When we made the slime it felt all squidgy and soft as well as bouncy. I turned my slime green." **Christopher Walwanda**.

"We set off helium balloons. We put a tag with our name, school and email address and then went outside to launch them. After we had launched them, most of the class ran after the balloons and got into big trouble... oops!" **Cressida Sowerbutts**.

Elliot Waring *and* **Katie Rutherford** *won book tokens for their contributions, extracts of which appear below:*

"When my uncle was young, he came to the school and said that it was great, especially the sports. My favourite memories are of the sports and of the trips we go on, especially the London trip and Skern Lodge. The boarding is amazing. It is great for making friends, doing new activities and, most of all, enjoying yourself with your friends.
The special occasions we have are really fantastic. We dress up in our own clothes and have fun activities all day long. Occasionally we have extra-special events, like Leavers' Dinner, Skern Lodge and Sports tours. These are some of my favourite memories. Another favourite memory is of being House Captain, and of all the opportunities that came with that." **Elliot Waring**.

"I had been wanting to go to Brandeston for ages. When I was in

Year 5 my parents told me I could go in Year 7. I told them I couldn't wait that long. I had no friends in my year. They reconsidered and I went in Year 6.

On my first day I remember going into assembly, so scared that I was shaking. To be honest no-one was really friendly and my 'guardian' abandoned me within a few hours. I know how hard it is to make room for another person to join in and to be accepted, so it was understandable.

My first tutor was **Mr Reynell** who was understanding, but hilarious with it. Every morning we would watch Scooby Doo before a very boring assembly. One addition to my school life was the fact that Saturday school was compulsory – that was one disadvantage. But Brandeston has brought out my love of sport, even if I wasn't very good at it.

By Year 7 everything had evened out and I knew everyone, including the teachers. **Mr Daykin** was my Tutor. I knew he was nice but he refused to smile, and thought it was unnecessary. When he got married he became a lot happier – and I think we had a part to play in his transformation!

My favourite trip was the French trip. The journey dragged on and on, but the trip was awesome. We did some hilarious stuff together. You must go to France.

In year 7 we did 'The Pirates of Penzance'. There were also many school concerts.

Year 8? Well, what can I say? A year of revising and exams – but not just those dreaded things. It is also full of things to do as a year-group, such as Skern Lodge. This was the best trip ever. The activities were thrilling. We all had to support one another and cooperate in order to complete our tasks.

The Leavers' Dinner was a night to remember. Everyone looked really fabulous, and after the dinner we had a disco.

Over-all Brandeston has been a really wonderful experience and I want to thank everyone, including the staff, who have helped me over the years. I will never forget anyone." **Katie Rutherford**.

At Speech Day it has become traditional for the Head Boy and the Head Girl to address the parents and guests at the end of proceedings. Daunting though this must be for 13 year olds, they take the platform with great aplomb and show the maturity and poise achieved at the end of a Prep School career. In 2007 the Head Girl, **Eleanor Smith** *summed up how it felt to be leaving Brandeston:*

"There is sadness, as some of us who are going our separate ways are leaving the family at Brandeston behind. However we all know that the strong friendships we have made here are genuine and will endure well into the future. Making friends and getting on with people is one of the main qualities that Brandeston has taught us. We have a sense of pride at what we have achieved in so many aspects of Brandeston life... Brandeston's key lesson is that doing your very best and always being prepared to have a go, will stand us in good stead for the future... Finally, perhaps our lasting emotion will be one of happiness, because this is a happy school, and Brandeston Hall is a testimony to the fact that smiling is contagious, as this school is full of smiles.

Top: Christopher Walwanda as Mark Anthony. **Above, l-r, back row**: Tom Carpenter, David Echazarra, Vicky Paulley; **middle row**: George Starr, Meg Wells-Furby, Lucy Pring, Milly Ball; **front row**: Giverny Bussey, Jack Wright.

Left: An early Fathers Cricket Match, 1951. Fathers: Watson, Palmer, Whitfield, Thomas, Rankin, Crabtree, Shepherd, Fuller, Hayward, Sparrow, Cunliffe. Boys: Boyle, Parker, Cairns, Crabtree, Jay, Capps, Nelson, Stedman, Wright, Hayward, Rankin.

PARENTS

Without parents there would be no pupils. In an independent school parents pay the fees. Without fees there would be no independent schools. In 1948 parents, fee-paying or not, handed over their children to a school, into the professional charge of their teachers and let them get on with educating the child – few would confront a teacher – teachers were daunting, to parents as to pupils. In 2008 that has changed. Fees are high. Fee-payers expect value for money. If a school fails to deliver value, complaints will be made. Teachers can no longer feel secure behind a cloak of professional inscrutability and unaccountability. The public have been educated to question, to expect high standards, and to complain if those standards are not met.

60 years ago parental contact was limited. There were Fathers' cricket matches. Reports (handwritten, and sometimes illegible) were received just once a term – with little chance of their being challenged. Parents' Meetings with the Head and class teachers were rare. Nowadays parents expect to be fully involved with the education of their children. Regular parental meetings with staff, ongoing assessment of a child's progress, invitations to school functions, parents' gatherings – all are now accepted as standard. Much is for the better. Perhaps for Brandeston the watershed was twenty five years ago with the introduction of Parents' Day. **Nick Stafford** *explains how it all began:*

The seeds of an idea – turning the clock back a quarter of a century: It began one early summer term, 1984 – or was it 1985? The volcanic **Robin Williams**, Head of Maths and 1st XI Cricket coach, asked me, (nay, told me) to organise some sort of drinks/food 'do' for parents and boys after the 1st XI v Fathers cricket match. He had some vision of me producing my home-brewed beer and wine to help a barbecue go down after the serious business of playing with willow on ball. Actually this is more or less what we did, but the problem was that we enjoyed ourselves too much and promised

to take it from being a gathering of twenty odd like-minded adults to share with a hundred or so... like minded adults.

The barbecue equipment had to grow with it. So did the catering staff – teachers and their wives/husbands could no longer be relied on to feed everyone safely. Alcohol had to resemble something less than US Prohibition hooch or anti-freeze. Also we had to please mums and dads who liked playing other summer sports, such as tennis. Parents' Weekend was thus born in 1985 – or was it 1986? What really did it were the caravans. Parents were invited to bring their cara/campervans and encouraged to make a party of it...all weekend. The rationale behind it was that, after the eating bit of the evening, Robin Williams and I wished to conduct 'parental consultations' in the splendour of such temporary homes. Naturally hospitality was of the highest quality and there was much to-ing and fro-ing between the vans.

In my final year at Brandeston Hall, I was determined to take the whole event as far as possible. Practically every sport was played – any excuse to prise the most unsporting out of their deck chairs and away from their caravans. No expense was spared – I purchased a second hand ice cream freezer and dispenser from some junk yard for a quid. A quid went a long way in those days. Both Saturday afternoon and the Sunday had activities planned, including a stroll to Church on the morning after and continuous swimming in the pool.

That last one was memorable. The ground staff, ably led by **Mike Rutterford**, produced a huge awning to protect us from the threatened rain. The catering facilities had become entirely professional, satisfying over 600 stomachs that Saturday in June. Parents '87 ended with Robin, me and my wheelbarrow stumbling across the outfield of the 1st XI cricket pitch with our ill-gotten gains. The wheel barrow was full of money. All day we had been selling ice-creams, cold drinks, raffle tickets, barbecue tickets and who knows what else. I had no container big enough except Mike Rutterford's wheel barrow. Whether we made it home or not, I don't remember, but the wheelbarrow did, and, crucially, the books appeared to balance!"

Nick Stafford was Head of History, Head of Britten House and Boarding Tutor, between 1983-1987, before taking up a Headship near Windsor. He is now a successful, independent brewer of fine Yorkshire ale. In 2007 he won the 'Best Regional, or National, Retail Initiative' category at the BBC 4 Food and Farming Awards Ceremony... beating off Premiership opposition (Messrs Tesco AND Sainsbury's) in the process!

... Firmly established by Nick, Parents' Week-end went from strength to strength in the organizational hands of the late **Simon**

Right: Nick Stafford – home brew to award-winning real ale.

Fuller and, latterly, **Simon Cullum**. Ever bigger marquees, some pretty impressive live bands playing on stage and Firework Finales became the order of the day. Through the 90s the event was combined with Sports Day - a very busy day for all concerned! As the Summer Term became ever shorter, and ever more congested, the curtain had to be brought down on the concept of an extended Parents' Week-end, but the memories linger on.

This section would not be complete without the testimony of at least one or two parents. It would be an injudicious editor who sought out uncomplimentary testimonies – and, to be sure, in no school will all parents feel that a school has transformed their son or daughter into the hoped-for prodigy. The following must suffice.

Howard and Paddy Gallagher look back

Although it is some twenty years ago since we first drove through that lovely pillared gateway, we both remember saying 'Oh, what a fine looking place'. It reminded us both of our own schools in Northern Ireland.

We were shown around the school by a young but extrovert girl pupil who betrayed no interest in showing us the class rooms, dormitories or anything else 'scholarly' for that matter, but was far more interested in pointing out the best trees for climbing! Of, course our lips are sealed as to whom that may have been but our families are still very good friends.

There are other memories such as playing cricket and those very enjoyable cricket tours. Any father whose son was in the cricket team must surely remember the joy in being invited to represent the Fathers XI, playing cricket on one of the loveliest grounds in England, let alone Suffolk. We toured with the boys, three years in a row, to Stamford Boys' School, Gilling Castle and St Peter's, York. 'Pimms' at St Peter's with the wonderfully hospitable Headmaster (and fellow Ulsterman), Trevor Mulryne, provided a memorable end to a most enjoyable day! Memories of Paddy having to avert her eyes whilst we were bowled out for about 68, but missing out on seeing a very proud father watching whilst **William** nearly single-handedly bowled out the opposition, taking 7 for 21... what a day! - that particular year merited a mention in Wisden's Almanac. **Robin Sampson** always endeavoured to teach the boys to behave as graciously in victory as in defeat. Such a shame that the tours stopped.

Brandeston teas were an institution! Nothing pleasanter than taking a break from all the nervous energy being expended, watching your son or daughter playing their chosen sport, only to be revived by all those sandwiches, cakes and buns. Going away to other schools was always such a disappointment by comparison.

Our biggest headache was what to write on the 'Parents' Comments' section of the report cards. **Sarah's** was straight forward but William's was always a challenge; Hope springs eternal... the carrot better than the stick... wishful thinking... Churchill failed Latin... are choice quotes that spring to mind! After we were told that our comments were being posted on a noticeboard in the Common Room we made them a little more circumspect!

Our youngest nephew is currently at Brandeston, happily following in the foot steps of his three elder sisters. And that's it, until the next generation!

Mike and Vivien Jones: parents and grandparents

All four of our sons (**Andrew** (Head of School 1970-71), **Tim, Philip** and **Matthew**) went to Brandeston Hall in the period 1969-1974. The education they received at Brandeston gave them a very good start in life. This was instilled by Richard Broad, and was essentially based on 'the whole boy' – respect for others, hard work, self-discipline and tidiness of person – shoes clean, hair brushed and, in the summer, sleeves neatly rolled up! Diligence was encouraged with academic work and active participation in sport and outdoor activities. On the practical side we still have wooden items the boys made under **Tom Fleming's** instruction, which were really useful and well constructed.

An active Parents' Committee encouraged parents to become part of the school's community. Various events were held to raise money for the swimming pool, opened in 1971, and quickly proving an invaluable asset We have fond memories of the annual 1st XI v. Fathers' cricket match and assisting the costume department in support of school drama productions. The presentation of Britten's 'Noyes Fludde', in the Athlone Hall, was a particular highlight for which **Graham Ireland** worked wonders with his young trebles.

The grounds and surrounding Suffolk countryside were always a delight. **Peter Arbon**, the groundsman, is still fondly remembered by our sons. It was a lovely setting for the boys, and even for the grown ups to have pool parties on summer evenings!

We were delighted when one of our sons, as an Old Boy, sent his daughter, **Emily**, to the school in 1996, and we had reason to revisit several times.

PART 4
WIDER HORIZONS

In every man's heart there is anchored a little schooner.
– HENRY MILLER

Right: Brandeston village sign depicting, on the left, the timber
frame thatched cottages of the village, and on the right the
Church and the gruesome execution of John Lowes in 1642

THE VILLAGE: ITS ORIGINS AND EVOLUTION

Brandeston is first mentioned in the Domesday Book as Brandestune. The name may come from the Anglo-Saxon word 'tune' – referring to the construction of ditches and hedges to protect property from attack by Viking invaders. People had probably settled in the area originally because of the fertile soil, the waterway and bridges over it, together with abundant supplies of timber for building.

John Clough gives us another historical view: for him the name Brandeston emphasises its Anglo Saxon foundation. 'Ton' means farm/village and the first part of the name may either refer to the Saxon god/king Bran or come from the Norse word 'brandr' which was a kind of market. As Brandeston was a place where there was, and still is, a ford across the Deben, it may have been a meeting place where goods were exchanged. Further down the Deben is Sutton Hoo, the royal burial place of Raedwald, so the Deben, which passes through the Brandeston grounds, was probably something of a sacred river for the Saxons.

In the 14th century the Black Prince, son of Edward III, hunted in Brandeston with the de la Poles. During the time of the Black Death (1348-9) the populations of the villages to the south of Brandeston were decimated (Monewden, Hoo – both still little more than hamlets) whereas Brandeston was spared the worst of this scourge. After the Black Death Suffolk became a sheep-rearing area and very wealthy as a result. Many fine houses in the county such as Brandeston, Kentwell, Hengrave were built at the time of the wave of prosperity derived from wool. In later history the names of John Lowes and Margaret Catchpole resonate well beyond the village, while Lloyd-George is reputed to have 'visited' a lady of the village in the early 20th century. So Brandeston does have an historical 'footprint'.

The agricultural nature of the village and its surrounds survives, even though few villagers now depend on the land for their livelihood. The population has varied over the years, peaking in 1831 with 569 inhabitants. Agriculture used to be a labour-intensive business. In 1991 the population had shrunk to 221, reflecting a pattern of rural decline and exodus to the larger industrial towns across the country. By 2007, however, the population had increased again to 225 adults and 80 children. Villages are now once again in demand. Rural life is viewed as a pleasant alternative to the hustle and bustle of towns. In Brandeston several new houses have been built. Older houses have been modernised, extended, and cottages doubled up to form one dwelling. The lives of the inhabitants have changed. Few work in the village – many drive to work or indeed take the train to London. Others come to the village to retire amidst its tranquil surrounds.

How things have changed! Continental invaders no longer threaten. The soil remains fertile – people still take a pride in their gardens – but much of the agricultural land is contracted out, and planted with non-traditional crops. The sense of social hierarchy is much diminished. Many shops and crafts have disappeared. Public transport is difficult – a car is a virtual necessity. Nowadays, it is perhaps the sense of village community which is a major attraction in an increasingly urbanised and depersonalised world. That is best exemplified in Brandeston's splendid Village Hall, focus of many village events.

THE EARLY LORDS OF THE MANOR AND THE VILLAGE

When Andrew Revett purchased the Lordship of the Manor from Henry Bedingfield in 1543, he built Brandeston Hall and this became his Manorial seat at the heart of an established social structure. The concept of Lord of the Manor dates back many centuries. Feudal society had been hierarchical, with allegiances duly sworn and obeisance expected. This structured society evolved, but Lords of the Manor, owners of large estates, were powerful figures. They were still owed, indeed expected, the allegiance of the farmers, peasants and craftsmen of the villages on their estates. The Bill of Sale above shows the extent of Brandeston's Manorial domain in 1920, when much of the Estate was sold.

Above: 1920 Poster showing parts of the Brandeston Manor up for sale. **Opposite from top:** Summary of the Valuation of the whole estate in the 1820 Survey. A shooting party – note the bowler hats, moustaches, the uniformed policeman and 'smock' uniforms of the beaters. Full village turn-out gathering at the Hall in 1904, best clothes de rigueur.

THE HALL AND THE VILLAGE SCHOOL

The Hall had been associated with educational enterprise well before 1948. Charles Austin I was closely associated with education, and his role in the development of education in the village was central. In the late 19th century educational opportunities had increased, often under the auspices of village notables, like Charles Austin.

To put his involvement in a wider context: It was the Forster Education Act of 1870 which ushered in the birth of the modern system of education in England. Forster was a Liberal MP. It was felt, not for the last time, that better education would improve industrial output. Opponents of the scheme were hostile to the idea because they felt that mass education would make the labouring classes dissatisfied. But the Act was passed – education became compulsory from 5 to 13, with the key elements being Reading, Writing and Arithmetic. This not only gave rise to a national system of state education but also assured the existence of a dual system – voluntary denominational schools and non-denominational state schools. The Act required the establishment of elementary schools nationwide. These were not to replace or duplicate what already existed but supplement those already run by the churches, private individuals and guilds.

A tribute to Charles Austin's educational interests is made in the following extract from an item in The Fortnightly Review, Volume 17, 1875. The sentiment expressed is complimentary to him, if not to the local inhabitants:

'He took under his special care the

For Home and Country.

The BRANDESTON and KETTLEBURGH

Women's Institute.

1922 PROGRAMME.

MEETINGS FIRST MONDAY IN EACH MONTH AT 7 O'CLOCK AT BRANDESTON HALL.

President—Mrs. WENTWORTH REEVE.
Vice-Presidents—LADY LARCOM, Mrs. AUSTIN.
Hon. Treasurer—LADY LARCOM.
Hon. Secretary—Mrs. F. WIGHTMAN.

COMMITTEE—

Miss Agnr.	Mrs. Davies.	Mrs. Pulham.
Mrs. Bilney.	Mrs. Kemp.	Mrs. Reid.
Mrs. Bradlaugh.	Mrs. J. Meadows.	Mrs. Taylor.
Mrs. Button.		

From top: 1922 WI meetings were held at the Hall. Embroidered kneelers in All Saints Church celebrating two Headmasters. Local Historian Wilda Woodland checks factual accuracy in the first proofs of this book.

middle-class College at Framlingham, where he made one of the best of his later speeches, in defence of educational endowments. Nor was his zeal for education confined to that of the young. He strove – warily, indeed, but on that account all the more effectually – to admit some Liberal twilight into a neighbourhood which stood sadly in need of it, a neighbourhood almost literally made up of agricultural peasants and Evangelical parsons.'

So he was involved not only in the setting up of Framlingham College, but also in the running of Brandeston's Village School.

Wilda Woodland's documents tell us that the first recorded Brandeston School teacher was Samuel Leeds (1793-1864) – and that he kept a small school, probably in his own home: 50, The Street. The old Village School in Mill Lane was built in 1852 by Charles Austin. The 1871 census, taken in the year after the Forster Act, showed that the Schoolmistress was Miss Read, battling on with 73 schoolchildren. Charles Austin's own daughter, Jane, on the other hand, had an Italian Governess, Senorita Gonino, all to herself. Brandeston Hall National School closed in 1943. Today the building survives as a private residence, duly modernised, and is called 'Fenners'.

LORDS OF THE MANOR (SQUIRES) AND THE VILLAGE

The Lords of the Manor lived in the Hall but were not necessarily in permanent residence. Commuting to the capital has now become common

place but it should not be forgotten that in Tudor times through to Victorian times too, the gentry of Suffolk spent time in the capital. Their absence seems not to have diminished their local influence and involvement. Squires were at the centre of village celebrations and took their responsibilities seriously. Conversely, villagers must have felt an obligation to show due deference and to participate dutifully in such occasions, judging by the turn-out in the picture on p155 of a village fete taken in the grounds of the Hall in 1904. Best clothes were the order of the day.

The life style of the Squire was very much that of the traditional gentry, as the picture (on p155) of a shooting party demonstrates. Note particularly how the The involvement of the Hall in village affairs continued even when the occupants were tenants rather than owners. Mrs Wentworth Reeve (1920-25) assumed Presidential responsibilities for the WI, and the Conservative Association. The 1922 leaflet shows how the WI meetings were held at the Hall.

There were other sporting occasions within the grounds. A letter to John Booth in 1947 as he was preparing his Appeal Booklet suggests that there was a field in the Brandeston grounds which had been used for cricket 'in olden times', and that there was even a Cricket Week, somewhat of a 'county' nature.

LEA-supplied bicycles used by day boys in the 40s and 50s are but a memory. Walking may be healthy but is not popular and is time-consuming. When Brandeston Hall was predominantly a boarding school, many pupils arrived on a special train from London. Most pupils, day and boarding, now arrive by car. Cars used to come along at the beginnings and ends of terms and for three-weekly Sunday exeats. Now the main local concern is about the traffic generated by the high proportion of day pupils. Cars come and go on a daily basis, creating demands for car parks and causing a degree of congestion on local roads. They drive fast, and it all happens during the rush hour. Many villages suffer in the same way, and the problem cannot be exclusively attributable to the school run.

Involvement with the church: The Hall and the Church sit side by side. Over the centuries The Lord of the Manor and the Church played parallel, often interlocking roles in the lives of villagers. The Squire and the Vicar personified this relationship. Relationships between them over the years fluctuated in terms of cooperation with one another. This interdependence continued after the Hall became a school. School Services are held in the church and villagers made welcome. **Richard Broad** recalls that after the Morning Service villagers were invited to coffee and home-made cakes in the Hobbies Room. Likewise, the school has long participated in the November Remembrance Day observations. **David Kittermaster** was Churchwarden for a while and a keen supporter of the church. He is the only Head to have a commemorative plaque in the church. He and **Ron Jones** are remembered in embroidered kneelers. The churchyard almost blends with the school grounds and school groundsmen have for many

1948 ONWARDS – BRANDESTON HALL AND THE VILLAGE

Pupils: In the 1940s and 50s the Local Authority sponsored significant numbers of 11+ pupils from across the county. Several came from the surrounding villages, often as day boys. There were only twenty of them and they mostly cycled to the school. Some, like **David Risk** (see item at the end of this chapter) walked to school. The

Top: All Saints Church Brandeston c1900.
Above: Members of the Scrimgeour family, former tenants of the Hall, return to a fete in 1952.

years maintained the churchyard as a reciprocal arrangement for regular use of the premises.

Roger Dixon, (in his dual role as School Chaplain and priest for Brandeston and Kettleburgh), also did some teaching at Brandeston Hall and part of his stipend was paid by the school. He did his best to bring the parishes and the school closer together. His successor, recently-retired Graham Vellacott had no teaching role but was responsible for the parishes of Brandeston, Kettleburgh and Easton, and took a keen interest in the affairs of the school.

Fetes: The school's involvement with the annual July Village Fete goes back to David Kittermaster's time. Historically, this event was always well supported by staff and pupils – and free-spending parents! In the Kittermaster and Broad era (and, briefly in Ron Jones' time) the school provided an ideal venue with its ample acres – and roomy interior, should the weather prove inclement. Traditionally, the proceeds have been shared between the needs of the Church and Village Hall.

With the Summer Term now ending so much earlier the direct involvement of the school is all but impossible and, for the last twenty-five years or more the Fete has been held on the Coronation Field or, most recently – and very successfully, in the grounds of the Queen's Head.

The school has also supported the village Christmas Fair. Richard Broad remembers that at least 20 children were involved in setting up a huge stall, offering toys and books.

Local History: The Historical survey conducted in the 70s not only gave field-work experience to pupils at the time, but ensured that a useful historical snapshot of the village could be passed on down. Copies of the survey reside in various libraries and homes as testament to these endeavours. Tim Rosen remembers undertaking investigative visits around the village, and particularly to the house of Hector Moore, the village blacksmith. Nicholas Broad and Alasdair Hamer-Philip, covered the east end of Brandeston, probably the Kettleburgh Road. It is recorded that publication of the Survey of the Parish of Brandeston –1st edition – was in 1971 (51pp incl. photographs). It was reprinted in 1972 – revised with additional material such as churchyard inscriptions and duplicated in 1974. The publication was reviewed at length in the EADT on 18th April 1974 by Edmund Orwell who wrote: 'This longer and more comprehensive survey is an even greater contribution to Suffolk Local History; local residents, record offices, students and others interested throughout East Anglia will be anxious to secure themselves a copy'.

It should be noted that the claim on p15 of the survey that Winston Churchill stayed at 16 Low Street is a joke – he didn't! This was probably a prank perpetrated on the investigators by the inhabitant of the property.

The Queen's Head: Inhabitants of the Hall enjoy the close proximity of the Queen's Head. Off-duty soldiers from the Hall ensured brisk trade during the war years, and friendships with local girls naturally ensued. Brandeston Hall staff similarly have almost immediate recourse to the relaxing facilities of this pub. One of the first members of staff, nicknamed 'Daddy Boo' Craig, could be expected at the Queen's Head at 6.00pm every night... But of course, in those days of limited transport, there was not much else to do off-site in the evenings. Subsequent stalwarts who brought considerable colour to such regular occasions of social intercourse, at 'The Queen', have included John Richards, Robin Williams and the ever youthful Carlos Reynell. In more recent times the inn has provided an excellent meeting place, inside and outside, for both parents and staff, before and after special occasions.

Interdependence: A busy school has limited scope for active involvement and inter-action with the locality, but Brandeston Hall realises how integral a part it plays in the life of the village, and does its best to be part of it. Both before the Hall became a school, and afterwards, it was a major employer of local people. Peter Arbon reflects both on the continuity of the link between Hall and village, and the involvement of village residents in the affairs of the Hall. His 80th birthday party in January 2007, held in the Village Hall, was attended by villagers, former Headmasters, teachers and former pupils. It was a fine occasion, and demonstrated the closeness of those links.

Reciprocally, teaching staff at the school have been involved in village affairs. Heads have, invariably, been offered a position on the Village Hall Committee. Nigel Johnson was, for a period, Chair. Even after retirement from that post he returned to argue in favour of the new Village Hall, so persuasively that he is said to have swung the meeting. Other members of staff have lived in the village. Ground staff used to cut the grass on the village playing field from 1952/53, again a reciprocal arrangement in exchange for playing football on it. This had to stop when the road became too dangerous.

David Risk remembers how the village was totally cut off for two days after the 1987 hurricane. Villagers went down to the school for sustenance: tea, soup, rolls etc. In the aftermath, David remembers how his chainsaw was kept busy clearing up fallen trees

for days on end, as was Peter Arbon's and **Mike Rutterford's** both on the estate and around the village. Furthermore 200 gallons of milk were trapped in the village, as there was no way of getting it to suppliers. Local people were invited to help themselves rather than letting it go to waste.

The school has in the past offered the use of rooms for local WEA classes. In a similar spirit, help has been provided with preparations for the Best Kept Village Competition.

On June 10th 2007, continuing the tradition of involving village people in the affairs of the Hall, a village tea was provided on the terrace. Best hats were put on and the boarders were fully involved in hosting the guests.

The Hall has long been central to life in the village and its residents have inter-related with the village and its affairs in many constructive ways.

CONCLUSION – DAVID RISK

One of the first providers of information for this book was David Risk. David is well qualified to provide a conclusion for this section. He was a day boy, living locally, when Brandeston Hall was opened in 1948. In fact he was the first boy living in Brandeston to attend the school. His father was a tenant farmer of Charles Austin III and was in the Home Guard. He was also responsible for ploughing up the fields to grow potatoes during the war and involved in clearing the pond of phosphorous bombs thereafter.

David himself, farmed locally. Both he and his father had considerable involvement in the practical affairs of the school. David still lives in the village. He has been on the Parish Council since 1960, became Clerk, and has been Chairman since 1990. He is especially well placed to offer an over-view.

Reverting to his schooldays, David remembers how he had been initially taught by a governess – Miss Raynham – and had never mixed with 'rough kids'. Then he found himself taking the Brandeston Entrance Exam – the fees at the time were about £30 a term.

There were only twenty day-boys and they mostly cycled to the school. David himself walked to school. The staff seemed to regard dayboys as a bit of an imposition.

When he left school he carried on farming, taking over from his father.

As for the farming side of the family's involvement, he remembers how the war-time potato fields were ploughed to turn them back to grass surfaces. Curiously, furrows were left, as the governors insisted on traditional ploughing. This left the surface uneven. The problem was only solved when drains were laid in the old furrows and this raised them up to the level of the rest of the field. The Risk family used to cut the hay at the back of the school before it was turned into a golf course. David remembers getting stuck in the mud (down by the river) and being mocked by pupils from the upstairs windows.

There used to be a little wooden footbridge across the river, which was replaced by a large concrete bridge to enable cattle and tractors to cross as the river had been dug out and cattle and vehicles could no longer go along the front of the school and cross the river, as the 'hard' way was no longer there. The cattle used to be taken along the front of the school, through the water to graze on the other side of the river. David also has memories of the swimming area, well away from the cattle crossing, at the western end of the school stretch of the Deben, with steps down from the bank, which was boarded. You were only allowed to swim in the river once you had obtained your 'swimming leave' at the College on one of the weekly visits. David used to plough the kitchen garden dividing it up into four patches. The Risks stopped farming in 1993.

In his view village attitudes towards the school have evolved. Initially the school was viewed as a source of employment. Now it is a more of a generator of traffic, and provider of custom for the pub. Generally the school is regarded as a local asset, something with which the village can relate, and, as over the centuries, still feel occasionally involved in its activities.

Top: David Risk – one of the first day boys in 1948 – wine-waiting at the Village Hall in 2007, at Peter Arbon's 80th Birthday – pictured smiling below.

BRANDESTON HALL AND FRAMLINGHAM COLLEGE

On the occasion of the official opening of The Hall in 1949 **Dr Rendall** stated that "Brandeston Hall is indeed a very part of our Foundation and it would be impossible to think now of Framlingham without it."

The sub-title of this History implicitly acknowledges the link between the two schools. Historically, they are inextricably bound together. Brandeston Hall owes its inception as a school largely to the generosity of former pupils of Framlingham College. That, in itself constitutes a historical bond which is both emotional and financial. Brandeston Hall is a war memorial to those Old Framlinghamians who gave their lives for their country. Fellow Old Framlinghamians contributed generously to ensure that those lost lives were remembered and commemorated in a lasting memorial. Symbolically, the official opening of the Hall as a school took place on the same day as the War Memorial tablet at the College was dedicated. To that extent it can be asserted that those whose young lives are moulded at Brandeston are indeed indebted both to the generosity of past generations of Old Framlinghamians and to the memory of those OFs who laid down their lives in battle. This school does indeed honour the past by building the future. Its origins constitute an insoluble bond. Governors, particularly OFs, are guardians of a unique heritage. There is a structural umbilical cord: Brandeston Hall as a Junior School only came into existence to serve as a reminder of the sacrifices made by those leaving the Senior School.

Since the first pupils who moved to Brandeston came across from the former Junior House at the College, Brandeston Hall was in its conception the Junior House, helping to relieve the pressure on space and resources, but situated some four miles away from the four Senior Houses. It was of similar status to the four main Houses at the College. Indeed the Junior House was originally designed to be built on the Framlingham site. The Brandeston Headmaster found himself with responsibilities not dissimilar to those of a Housemaster, but with the advantage and challenge of finding himself on an independent site. Initially the Junior House housed boys predominantly of ten years and upwards. They would spend just two or three years at Brandeston, being prepared for 5 years at the College. Now that ratio has changed dramatically. It is quite possible for a pupil to spend close on 10 years at Brandeston, followed by 5 years at the College. Those years spent at Brandeston are not only crucially formative, they can constitute two thirds of the schooling of any pupil who attends both schools throughout. In 1948 Brandeston was about one fifth of the total establishment. In 2008 it constitutes one third. The responsibility of the Head of Brandeston is proportionally greater. The Junior School is no longer just one of five equally-sized units. Structurally the relationship has changed over 60 years.

The nature of Junior and Senior schools is distinctly different. There is a world of difference between educating a 3-year-old and an 18 year-old. The buildings, the ethos, the teaching methods, the activities have to reflect that. One school is a preparation for the other, not a young version of it. One school grows out of, and eases the transition from, the security of the family; the other launches young people into the insecurity of the wide and difficult world. That difference accentuates the sense of the one-time Junior House having become an educational entity in its own right. Every time the starting age moves downwards, the further the ethos moves away from that which is appropriate to an 18 year-old.

Inevitably, over the years, the separateness of the schools has brought advantages, disadvantages and problems. In the forties and fifties communications were difficult. Living-in staff at Brandeston rarely ventured very far. An assistant master with a car was a rarity. But the links were maintained. Once a week Brandestonians were bussed across to the College to enjoy the dubious benefits of the outdoor swimming pool. By contrast, many Senior School facilities – the indoor pool, the Astroturf hockey pitch, the theatre are nowadays readily accessible to Brandeston students. There have been collaborations in musical and dramatic productions at the College. Staff too, have moved backwards and forwards between the two schools. The talents of **Tony Lawrence**, now Second Master at The College, were first spotted when he was teaching at Brandeston. Conversely, the potential of the current Headmaster, **Martin Myers-Allen**, was first manifest in his work at the College. Staff cricket teams include players from both schools. CCF cadets have been route-marched across to Brandeston for field days, to shatter the rural calm with stentorian military commands and thunder flashes. Departments at the Senior School do their best to liaise with their Junior School counterparts and to ensure a smooth transition at the age of 13. Professional, sporting and social cross-fertilisation has been beneficial.

As communications, transport, telephones, then, finally, emailing improved contacts between the two schools, it became easier to maintain the structural link between them. Governors, the Head of the College, the Bursar, the Director of Operations, the Development Office – all have direct responsibility for operations at Brandeston. None of this is handled independently. An umbrella of

Headmaster praises parents' support

Pictured at Brandeston Hall speech day on Saturday: Mrs. L. Rimmer, Mr. R. G. Williams, acting headmaster; Mr. L. L. Rimmer, school governor and headmaster of Framlingham College; Jeremy Kemp, head boy; Mr. R. W. Jones, headmaster-elect, and Miss Jones.

Top: In the 40s and 50s Brandestonians were bussed across to the College to enjoy the dubious benefits of the outdoor swimming pool. The photo shows a pre-war pool gala.

At the official opening of Brandeston Hall as a school in 1949, Dr Rendall stated that "Brandeston Hall is indeed a very part of our Foundation and it would be impossible to think now of Framlingham without it."

Below: Brandeston held its own Speech Day in 1972 – parents enjoy tea on the south terrace – and a newspaper cutting covering the same event. l-r: Mrs Gillian Rimmer; Mr RG Williams, acting Headmaster; Mr L Rimmer, Headmaster of Framlingham College; Jeremy Kemp, Head Boy; Mr RW Jones, Headmaster-elect, and Mrs Joyce Jones.

administrative security is provided, and there is no need for duplication of effort. Overhead costs are spread too. This can, conversely, be a sensitive issue. It would be easy for such a relationship to be translated into a sense of subservience on the part of the junior partner. Brandeston would be far from unique in wishing to assert its independent viability. A degree of financial, administrative and professional independence confers a sense of self-worth. Some delegation is inevitable, given the four-mile distance between schools. A balance has to be struck. The Heads of both schools now attend all Governors' meetings. This was not always so. And it was not so long ago that Brandeston initiated its own Speech Day. Invariably, though, Speech Day is an occasion for mutual support, featuring Senior figures of both schools. The balance is evolving.

Some Junior Schools which are linked to Senior establishments are on the same campus. This can have both benefits and weaknesses. There are real advantages: continuity of curriculum, encouraging the two schools to dovetail their teaching programmes, shared facilities, teachers straddling the year groups, the sense of security that comes from familiarity, the understanding of a common ethos, and indeed the likelihood of ongoing friendships, so important to young people. This can, however, mean that a pupil beginning at the nursery stage might be on the same site for 15 years. The temptation to move on at 11, 13, or 16 could be strong – just for a change of surroundings. Present day youngsters – and we would not have it otherwise – have a spirit of adventure. They are not averse to risk. Brandeston and the College, from the point of view of pupils, offers the middle way. The two sites are loosely linked, but a move to Framlingham four miles away does constitute a significant change. For parents, such logistical challenges as have to be faced, are comparable on the two sites. No major upheaval is required.

Ideally the working relationship between the Head of the College and the Head of Brandeston is harmoniously constructive, working to mutual benefit. Contractually the Head of the College assumes responsibility for Brandeston, provider of at least 50% of the College intake. Conversely the majority of Brandeston leavers move on to the College. It is absolutely in the best interests of the two schools that cooperation should be close. It would, however, be foolish to pretend that there have not been, from time to time, tensions. There have been times perhaps when comparisons might be drawn with an overgrown cuckoo in the nest. The Head of the Junior School, enjoying a four mile buffer zone, has to strike a balance between compliance with the wishes of the Senior School, and the natural wish to lead and innovate. Fully compliant Heads rarely make an impact. Overly-independent Heads run the risk of fraying the tether. Good Heads create their own momentum and tend not to operate well within over-constraining frameworks. A balance has to be sought and achieved, and it has to be a balance which minimises the chances of personal friction.

Perhaps it is useful to bring in the historical analogy of Absolute Monarchy versus Constitutional Monarchy. Nations concluded that absolute monarchy was unacceptably despotic, and that constitutional monarchy provided a framework within which the monarch had his hands free if he/she wished to do good, but found himself constitutionally manacled if set on an harmful course. The Brandeston equivalent of the absolute monarch would be a maverick Head capable of spinning out of control to the detriment of both schools. Some constitutional control is not only necessary, but also cements the strong historical links between the schools and their inter-dependence.

60 years of history have been instructive and it seems that the right balance has been found. While a majority of leavers from Brandeston do still move on to the College, its independence is such that parents can now view it as a Prep School which may prepare pupils for Senior Schools other than Framlingham. Where once Framlingham used to set its own entrance exam, it now requires entrants to sit Common Entrance, an exam specifically intended to test entrants to a full range of independent schools.

So where are we now? The two schools together can and do provide continuity of education from the nursery stage through to A levels. The link that binds the schools together is evident not only in the administrative structures, aims and ethos but also in the publication of the Framlingham Yearbook which recognizes the strong links not only between the College and Brandeston but also with the Society of Old Framlinghamians. Strong though these links may be, they still permit that flexibility and those variations and opportunities which are so necessary when dealing with children and with parental aspirations for them. Young people with their evolving needs and personalities cannot be fitted into a fifteen-year strait-jacket. The strength of Brandeston lies in its history, in its independent siting, in its secure links with the College and in its own self-confidence. It is to be found in the awareness of staff, pupils and former pupils who share in, and take pride in its heritage. The two schools have moved forward together – in extending the age range, and in being, in 1976/7, amongst the first independent schools whole-heartedly to embrace full co-education. Beginning with the challenges of 1948, Brandeston and Framlingham have shown the resilience not only to meet those challenges and difficulties but to adapt and thrive, in partnership with one another.

Left: Birth of the River Deben at Debenham.
Right: The Tide Mill at Woodbridge indicates the Deben's use as a working river, before the tidal waters head out to the challenge of the open seas.

BRANDESTON HALL AND BEYOND

Children are so often unaware of much beyond their immediate surroundings. In the early days of Brandeston as a school, few ventured into the village. It might have been vaguely known that certain members of staff occasionally visited the 'Queens Head' public house, but generally the school and its grounds represented a haven of insulated security. It was not until the Headship of **Richard Broad** that boys were even allowed outside the grounds to visit the local Post Office.

In our security-conscious 21st century, schools are required to account for their charges throughout school hours. So the sense of containment within an educational cocoon probably remains. But Brandeston Hall is part of a historically rich county and at the heart of a typical Suffolk village. Its pupils come in from many miles around and, indeed, sometimes from overseas. Its former students move on from the security of a Prep School into the wider world, firstly for secondary education, then on to further education and to a wide range of careers. This chapter concludes by noting what has happened to just a few of Brandeston's former pupils. It also follows the evolution of the Austin family.

THE RIVER DEBEN – SYMBOL OF A WIDER WORLD

This river which flows through the grounds, symbolises very well the limited perspective of young schoolchildren. How many of them actually knew or know the name of the gently flowing river which borders one side of the school grounds? For many years it was a place to swim in, a place for fishing, a river which sometimes flooded – just a brief stretch of beautiful waterway.

As horizons widen, we become aware that it has its origins at Debenham, flows through Cretingham, swallowing up many an errant golf ball, Easton, Wickham Market, Rendlesham, Ufford, Eyke and on to Woodbridge. Here it becomes tidal and properly navigable and bridged for the first time. The Tide Mill indicates its use as a working river. Boat building and sailing have characterised this stretch of river. Here too on the northern bank the burial mounds of Sutton Hoo, and the treasure which they yielded, indicate the importance of this waterway to the Anglo-Saxons and other incomers from the continent of Europe. And then onwards, onwards to the sea, and the estuary at Bawdsey, winding along amidst green fields all the way. And it is here that the Deben, once a mere trickle at Debenham, flowing just a little faster at Brandeston, commercially important at Woodbridge, finally empties itself into the sea. That river which to young Brandestonians is just a short stretch of water in the grounds, exercising adventurous imaginations, has been witness to history, to invasion, to industry and serves as a gateway to a much wider world. The river is also an apposite metaphor for the development of the young lives of Brandestonians – small beginnings, gaining in vigour and confidence, increasingly concerned with the outside world of work, finally heading out to the challenge of the open seas.

THE WORLD BEYOND

The early owners of the Hall moved beyond it to earn a living. Their working lives often took them to London. Andrew Revett was not the only Suffolk resident in Tudor times to hold a significant position in London. Thomas Seckford and Cardinal Wolsey sought success and fortune in the capital. Charles Austin I too earned a fortune as an eminent lawyer in London.

Left: Professor Neville Marsh, acting Vice Chancellor at Adelaide University.
Right: (l-r) Alex Henney, John Barker and Emlyn Evans (Millfield) competed in the 2007 Race to the magnetic North Pole.

These men were owners of country seats as befitted gentlemen, but they moved in wider, cosmopolitan circles, and were well connected. Their world was not confined to Brandeston Hall.

The Austin line has moved on. From the early 20th century they lived in Brandeston, in The Broadhurst, while the Hall was tenanted. Eileen Austin married Gerry Hollebone during the war, but died recently, leaving Gerry living close to his daughter – still in Brandeston. Major 'Bunny' Austin, who sold the Hall to the College in 1947, had no children, but his brother, John Austin Senior was the father of the present John Austin who lives in Aldeburgh and is the last of the Austin line.

In the 80s John developed the very popular Cretingham golf course (a number of the Brandeston Hall staff were founder members) – and his mother, Liz (Buffy), the first class restaurant. This was on land that had been part of the estate and which they had previously farmed.

John has been very supportive of this endeavour – and indeed allowed us sight of an 1820s Survey of the Brandeston Estate –all in beautiful copperplate writing – which embellishes the inside covers of this book. John's sister, Jane, also lives in Aldeburgh, works in the bookshop – and will hopefully stock copies of this history. The link lives on.

Similarly Brandeston Hall pupils move on and away – many of them in the first instance to Framlingham College, whence to a range of careers. It seems appropriate to conclude this history by looking at the varied career paths of just a few of Brandeston's alumni. In 60 years some two or three thousand young men and women have moved on from Brandeston so it is somewhat invidious to make this selection. The list is based on those mentioned in the 'Distinguished' feature on the Old Framlinghamian website – www.oldframlinghamian.com

Academic

Professor Neville Marsh: Head of the Anatomy and Physiology Department in Brisbane before he then moved to Adelaide University as acting Vice Chancellor. His background is in cardiovascular physiology and his research interest is bleeding disorders caused by snake bite!

Professor David Hansell: appointed Professor of Thoracic Imaging, Imperial College, London in 1998. His primary specialty is radiology of the lungs. President of the European Society of Thoracic Imaging. Also author and co-author of medical books and papers.

Business/ Agriculture

Jonathan Adnams: Executive Chairman of Adnams brewery and a member of Southwold's lifeboat crew for 28 years. He became Chairman in 2006. In the 2009 New Years Honours List he was awarded an OBE for corporate social responsibility.

John Thurlow: he took over the family firm of George Thurlow and Sons. John was appointed High Sheriff of Suffolk in 2003. He is a Past President, Chairman and Hon. Director of the Suffolk Agricultural Association. He is also a Governor of the College.

The Services

Charles Blackmore: soldier, followed in the footsteps of Lawrence of Arabia, author, banker and security adviser.

Air Vice Marshal Simon Dougherty: appointed Air Vice Marshal at the time of becoming the Director-General of Medical Services (Royal Air Force) in September 2004. A Governor of the College.

Left: Alex (Sandy) Walker holding his prestigious Prince of Wales trophy.
Right: Laura Wright singing prior to kick-off at the Ipswich Town v Coventry City match played on Sunday 3rd May 2009.
(photo: Ipswich Town FC/Action Images)

Brigadier Miles Wade: late of the King's Royal Hussars, he was awarded the MBE following a tour in North Belfast in 1994 and a CBE for services to the Army in 2006. Took command of 145 (South) Brigade in January 2007.

Charles Carter: at Sandhurst he was awarded the Queen's Medal for passing out highest in the Order of Merit. He was part of the Army's operational and planning group for the recapture of the Falkland Islands in 1982. He was appointed OBE for his work with the United Nations in Cyprus.

Karen Buttenshaw: Head Girl in1988. She was tragically killed in an accident on 29 October 1994 during an Army exercise on Salisbury Plain. She was just 19 at the time. There is a memorial tree at Brandeston in her memory and the SOF has instituted a Karen Buttenshaw Memorial Prize.

Nick Innell was with the Intelligence Corps for 16 years. His tours of duty took him to Germany and Saudi Arabia, Iraq (UN Special Commission weapons inspection) and command of a Military Intelligence Battalion during the occupation of Kosovo. His subsequent career took him as Head of Security during the UN War Crimes Tribunal for the former Yugoslavia. This featured specific responsibility for Slobodan Milosevic.

Media, Entertainment and the Arts

Bruce Pearson: ecologist, film maker, writer and artist. Production Assistant in the RSPB Film Unit, before joining the British Antarctic Survey in 1975 as Biological Assistant. Wildlife Illustrator of the Year in 1983 and Bird Illustrator of the Year in 1984. He was elected President of the Society of Wildlife Artists in 1994.

Laura Wright: won BBC Radio 2 Young Chorister of the Year in 2006 and later that year became part of the all-girl group 'All Angels'. Nominated, with 'All Angels' for a Classic Brit award.

Chris Hall: distinguished as a collector of Chinese textiles. His collection is considered the foremost private collection of its kind in the world. Recipient of the Heritage Award from the Asian Civilizations Museum in Singapore.

David Bull: a doctor, before moving into broadcasting. Became the first person to broadcast to Children about their health issues on Newsround. Presenter of a number of high-profile TV shows. In 2000, he co-founded the creative communication agency Incredibull Ideas. Selected as Conservative Parliamentary Candidate for Brighton Pavilion.

Lucy Verasamy: became a well known weather presenter on Sky News and Channel 5.

Harry Mitchell: has worked for numerous BBC and commercial radio stations around the UK. Breakfast Show presenter for Radio Broadland in Norfolk and Suffolk. He has also served as the station's News Editor. He was named Journalist of the Year 2006 at the Creative East Awards and a finalist in the 2007 awards. He is also a contributor to Classic Newsnight on Classic FM.

Terry Hunt: appointed Editor of the East Anglian Daily Times.

Charlie Simpson: former guitarist with top pop group 'Busted', now fronting 'Fightstar'.

The Law

Sir Mark Hedley: He became a recorder in 1988, a circuit judge in 1992 and then a High Court Judge in the Family Division in 2001. In July 2005, he received an Honorary Fellowship from Liverpool John Moore University in recognition of his outstanding contribution to the legal profession.

Left: Norman Porter holds aloft the Scottish Hockey Cup, won in 1968
Right: Captain Nick Carlton aboard 'Grand Princess' in 2008 with Chris Essex (left), editor of the 'Distinguished' section of the SOF website.

Judge Rupert Overbury: appointed a Recorder on the South Eastern Circuit in 2003. In 2007 it was announced that he was to become a Circuit Judge on the South Eastern Circuit.

Sport

John Barker and Alex Henney: competed in the 2007 Race to the magnetic North Pole. They came 2nd overall out of 6 teams.
Alain de Cadenet: Former Le Mans driver and TV presenter for Top Gear and Speed Channel.
Jim Crosbie: awarded 51 Hockey Caps for Scotland between 1972 and 1978.
Nigel Janes: Ocean Racing: was in the winning boat in 1992/3 Round the World Race.
David (JDF) Larter: Played cricket for Northants and England, winning 10 caps between 1962 and 1965, and taking 37 wickets for 941 runs at an average of 25.43 runs per wicket.
Norman Porter: Played hockey for Scotland 12 times and was captain of Inverleith HC in 1968 when they won the Scottish Cup.
Jonathan Proud: represented England U.16 Hockey – 2006-07. Also U.18.
Richard Rowe: successfully sailed round the world as part of the BT Global Challenge in 1996/7.
Alex (Sandy) Walker: Shooting. Won the Prince of Wales Badge at Bisley in 2008. Selected for Great Britain.
Peter White: England U.21 Hockey and England Indoors International.
Richard Wilkins: Archery –in the English national squad.

Acts of Heroism

Nick Carlton: In August 2003 he was Captain of the P&O liner Pacific Sky. When the shout "man overboard" was made he immediately turned the ship around and headed back to search. After nearly 3 hours of searching in 25 knot winds and rough seas, the man was recovered.
Katy Wilks: In 1995, when only 19, she saved a 3 year old from drowning at Felixstowe and was awarded the Certificate for lifesaving by the Royal Humane Society.
Roger Sparrow: While still a pupil at Brandeston Hall in 1972-73, he dived to the bottom of the school Pool to rescue an unconscious pupil. He was first ever recipient of a Brandeston Hall Honours Tie.

Overseas

Ketto Okamoto: the Charlie Simpson of Japan! He is very big in the Pop scene there.
David Summers: Chartered Quantity Surveyor and Past President of the Australian Institute of Quantity Surveyors. He was involved in numerous major projects in Australia, including the redevelopment of Parliament House, Walsh Bay and Sydney Harbour Casino. Awarded the Order of Australia Medal (OAM) for 'Service to the Construction Industry'.

Presidents of the SOF: Neville Bromage (deceased) – also Governor; **Jim Blythe** – also Governor; **John Edwards** – also Governor; **Richard Overend**; **Norman Porter** – also Governor; **Brian Rosen** (Brandeston Staff); **Andrew Wright.**

So the range of achievement is wide. (*Anyone who would like to point out any omissions is invited to contact the author*). Having spent their formative years by the quiet banks of the Deben, these Brandestonians, on reaching the open sea, were equipped to embark on a wide range of career courses, and to make their mark. The next generation follows hard on their heels.

JIM BLYTHE
*Proposing the toast of Brandeston Hall at the 60th birthday celebrations
in a speech on 20th September 2008*

Well, who would have thought that so many of us would be gathered together sixty years on? May I ask you to raise your hand so that the assembled company can have a look at us, boys and staff. Perhaps during the evening we might share a moment for those who have not survived and those who are unable to attend.

Why me to propose this toast ? Well my love of Brandeston is well known, so it was with pride that I accepted this delightful task. Currently I am still alive, but the memory plays its tricks, so if I do get something wrong, please correct me later or I shall never get finished.

We will cast our mind back to the first day of that winter term of 1948, already first boy there was **Peter Murdoch Gordon Stewart**, shortly followed by myself. I was despatched early as I had two brothers at another place, who didn't have to be back till later. My embarrassment started early that first day. We had only two trunks in the family – though three tuck boxes – so I had use of my late Grandfather's sea chest, a great iron-bound thing from the 1850s, which could have accepted two wardrobes full of clothes, not just the limited amount that coupons gave us. I vividly recall Mother trading our sweet coupons for clothing ones just to get the Cash's name tags: 4 shirts, 12 collars, two sets of studs etc. We knew how to dress snappily. My trunk was the only one that wouldn't get into the loft because of its size and it had to rest in the linen room all term.

We were 77 boarders and 23 day boys. That first term we had a mumps epidemic and I was closeted with **George Gooderham**, **David Allars** and the one and only **John Walden Edwards**. The latter touched on Brandeston Hall as a school and the adventures we had there in his speech as prize-giver at Brandeston Hall last term and he scored a double first: he was mercifully short and funny. I shall try to live up to his example.

Above: A young Jim Blythe pictured c1948, gave a characteristically amusing speech, peppered with period anecdotes, on Brandeston's 60th, September 2008.

Games were for a while restricted to playing against the staff until the mumps had passed. We boxed twice a week and some of the older boys fought the masters which was as amusing as the film show given by the Blyth Valley Film Co.

When the weather was right we swam in the Deben and we climbed into the hollow trees and discovered secret passages and smoked the yewtree leaves, only if we could get bronco toilet paper. This probably cured many of us for good. What would Mr Elf and Mr Safety say now?

The staff was headed by **David Darlington Kittermaster**, our loco parentis – we did not have half terms and rarely exeats, petrol being on ration – and his wife **Rachel** and the blasted Corgi who bit you if it was your turn to ring the bell. Languages were taught by **PNY Craig**, and **JP Ferris** taught something else, and **Miss Brownsword** taught English and how to do beautifully curled handwriting, **Mrs Podd** taught form 1 probably everything. We borrowed, on occasions, **Bertie Manthorp** for Art from the College and also **Henry Hall**, who was assisted by **Marjorie Gillett** for music. Our physical well-being was seen to by the dashing **John Pemberton**, whose stock had shot up since marrying the delectable **Wendy Milne**. She along with Matron, **Dulcie Wilton**, administered to the injured, and their clothing, with help from the older sister brigade, and I do not remember in what order they came, but **Joy Winch, Pam De'ath** and **Marie Few** are just some I recall. **Doodie Day** – a grandfather figure built like a Russian Doll with his long white apron – his form of reward was allowing you to stir the gluepot, and his punishment was the bicycle ride, and then stirring the gluepot. And then **Peter Arbon**, not much older than some of us but who knew the way to a boy's heart was through his stomach mostly by apples.

We are thrilled to see so many from that first term here tonight. **Michael George Wright**, first Head Boy and Captain of most teams. Left arm round the wicket. **Andrew Gavin Wright**, his little brother, along with **Curtis John Capon**, a fine boxer, both not yet 70. Excellent achievements in boxing were from

Anthony James Martin, Robert James Blythe and Colin Geoffrey Wigg. You'd better believe it, it is in the Mag. Michael Anthony Cairns was outstanding and ready to fight anyone at any weight on any possible occasion, and on some impossible ones.

Academically the school was split into five forms that first term but subsequently became five forms over four years, there being 4A and 4B to cover the greater numbers in that age bracket. The first term the placings in form one were Michael John Ryder Allen and the third place was Andrew Gavin Wright, who was beaten for second place by, and he's here tonight, a current Governor and former High Sheriff of our County, John Geoffrey Thurlow. Robert James Blythe in the year above was yet to feature, mainly due to the incessant power cuts in the main hall.

Term 2 saw RJB rise to 3rd place behind Keith Edward Handley, 2nd, and Brian Anthony Scrivener 1st. Term 3: Blythe top from Scriv and Richard Leonard Havers, AG Wright still 3rd.

Order of merit GW Martin, 76, Juby and Tremlett 70, Blythe, Handley and RS Farman 4th 66.

Other sporting achievements were CG Wigg who won the high jump with 3 feet 8 inches and the same person beat the hot favourite for the table tennis, John Graham Rankin, who became wilder and wilder, looking for outright winners. JW Edwards, a left arm bowler, could deliver a dangerous ball, mainly because it was aimed at the head. Batting average 4.8 which beat JGR's 3.8. The last term of '49 saw RJB win house chess and snooker, only tenth in order of merit, no form prize – mixing with

Top: Pages from Jim's Autograph book of the 40s, from left: fellow pupils, Chelsea FC, the 'delectable' assistant matron Marie Few.
Above: A jubilant Jim Blythe at the SOF Annual Dinner 2008.

unsavoury company. No hands up?

On Sundays we had compulsory letter-writing home, always vetted so that 'Dear Father Mother tuck box empty send another' wouldn't do. We were allowed to listen to the wireless and at 9.30 it was Big Bill Campbell and his rocky mountain rhythm. He started with 'Howdy Pardners'.

To Brandestonians and all Old Framlinghamians may I remind you that Brandeston was a gift by your Society in memory of those lost in both world wars, who had passed through these portals – a sombre thought of a most generous gesture. Creative accounting saw the end result that OFs gifted the Hall to the College, and the College equipped it and staffed it, and how it has thrived and still encourages the children to be children and not machines to produce a regimented end-product. Your Society needs your support and not just financially, but with any time and expertise you are able to offer. The old become boring and fade away and the barrel needs plugging.

Finally I have in my pocket a document which doesn't just contain 30 Chelsea autographs, and that of Macdonald Bailey from 1948 and Leslie Welch, the memory man, but the autographs of 78 people from that first term. I will read you just one from the first Boy PMGS...

I am scanning the crowd for a person to do the toast for the third sixty years. I know you are there somewhere, I urge you to be more brief than I. Ladies and Gentlemen, my toast is to Brandeston Hall and Martin Myers-Allen.

On 27th February 2009, during the academic year which was 60 years on from the opening of Brandeston Hall as a school, The Headmaster, Martin Myers-Allen and his wife Helen, organised a special commemorative evening, in keeping with the early years of the school, and recreating for parents and grandparents memories of those years. Wartime costumes were worn in abundance, tickets were in the form of ration book covers, guests were greeted by army guards and camouflage netting, period music was played, and the evening hosted from the cockpit of a bomber. Dancing too was in keeping with the period, with demonstrations from experts. To cap it all, Herr Flick of the TV comedy programme 'Allo allo' hosted the high-speed draw with Gestapo precision and ruthlessness. In all, a particularly apt way of celebrating Brandeston's 60th birthday, and a good note on which to usher in the Headmaster's conclusion to this book.

THE HEADMASTER LOOKS BACK TO THE PAST – AND FORWARD TO THE FUTURE.

Brandeston Hall has been standing for over 450 years and I have every reason to suspect it will still be standing and will be just as cherished 450 years from now. It will remain nestled in glorious Suffolk country-side, surrounded by willows guarding the river Deben as it lazily meanders its way through meadows to the coast.

Since the 16th century it has seen war, peace, pestilence and fire. The rooms will have echoed with laughter, serious debate, rows, plotting and fireside chat. Throughout its impressive history it has been a family home and manor house, a seat of power, a military base and now flourishes as preparatory school and living war memorial to the 250 boys and masters at Framlingham College who fell in the two world wars. This year we celebrated its 60th year as an independent school and we are proud to be custodians of such a fine building and to play our part in its history.

This book celebrates much more and has been carefully crafted to show the great passion that everybody who has passed through its doors has for the place. The feeling of warmth and the sense that you have of belonging to Brandeston Hall is infectious and you feel obliged to take great care of it and preserve it for future generations. I am the ninth Headmaster and need to play my part in ensuring that Brandeston continues to be thought of fondly by the staff, parents, pupils, Old Framlinghamians, prospective parents, villagers, school Governors, the College and other great senior schools in the land.

We are often described as 'one of Suffolk's best kept secrets', but I don't mind if people cannot keep quiet. Norman Porter certainly has not and I applaud the hard work he and others have done to seal Brandeston Hall's history forever in words and pictures. Years from now somebody else will take up the same mantle and I'll wager that the next book will equally impressive. I hope that that next somebody will be a successful Old Brandestonian or Old Framlinghamian whose life has been shaped by his or her experiences, enjoying the best of days as a child at our glorious school.

Martin Myers-Allen

1948

1948-49   Michael Wright
1949-50   Michael Price

1950

1950-51   Michael Sparrow.
1951-52   Rodney Crabtree
1952-53   Andrew Wright and Keith Elmy
1953-54   Andrew Jackson
1954-55   Jim Butchart and Noel Hancock
1955-56   Alan Gates
1956-57   David Ballard
1957-58   Michael McGuire
1958-59   Robert Craig
1959-60   Mark Hedley

1960

1960-61   Michael Slessor
1961-62   David Seaton
1962-63   David Smith
1963-64   Jonathan McLeod
1964-65   Stewart Tighe
1965-66   Tony Knight
1966-67   David Kent
1967-68   David Morgan
1968-69   Piers Hedley
1969-70   Charles Blackmore

1970

1970-71   Andrew Jones
1971-72   Martin Robinson
1972-73   William Glasse
1973-74   Jeremy Kemp
1974-75   Tim Smart
1975-76   William Shirbon
1976-77   Julian Pollard and Stephen Mildenhall
1977-78   James Gubbins
1978-79   Simon Whittley
1979-80   Simon Newson and Joanna Law

1980

1980-81   Michael Pegg and Lisa Edwards
1981-82   Mark Twite and Susannah Pickstock
1982-83   Guy Chalkley and Lucy Graham
1983-84   Martin West
1984-85   Caroline Dixon
1985-86   Sarah Fulcher
1986-87   Simon Rolfe
1987-88   Karen Buttenshaw
1988-89   Katie Wilks
1989-90   James Kirk

1990

1990-91   Simon Roderick
1991-92   Joanna McIlveen
1992-93   Toby Hockley and Elizabeth Knight
1993-94   Paul Lewis
1994-95   Aniela Scattergood
1995-96   Hannah Woodgate
1996-97   Claire Sweetman
1997-98   David Mallett and Kirsty Wybar
1998-99   Patrick Cadell
1999-00   Roberta Organ

2000

2000-01   Graham Sweetman and Rosy Lawrence
2001-02   Henry Johnstone
2002-03   Freddie Hopkinson
2003-04   James Mee and Felicity Cobbold
2004-05   John Bird and Sarah Findlay
2005-06   Connor O'Leary and Charlotte Pring
2006-07   Eleanor Smith and George Kerridge
2007-08   Jack Scott and Lucy Pring

1540s-1902

1540s	Brandeston Hall built by Andrew Revett – Revett family in residence for 300 years.
1845	Hall sold to Charles Austin.
1847	Hall gutted by fire during renovation – (see a full account the Fire in the December 1949 Framlinghamian).
1864	Foundation of Framlingham College. Charles Austin is one of the Founders.
1902	The Austin family move to The Broadhurst in the village, renting out the Hall.

1940

'40-'47	Requisitioned by the British Army under the Emergency Powers Act.
'47/'48	Acquired for the College as the Junior School 23/9/48: Arrival of first pupils. 100 boys, 75 of them boarders.
'48-'49	Autumn: David Kittermaster's first set of 'School Notes' at Christmas, in the 'Framlinghamian', refer to: 'Periodic failure of electricity supplies, a mumps epidemic, and the discovery of crates of phosphorus bombs ('Molotov Cocktails') in the pond.' 2/7/49: Official opening by Princess Alice of Athlone (Full account of Opening Ceremony on p123 of the July '49 'Framlinghamian')
'49-'50	Autumn: First public drama presentation. 2 Form Plays: 'Mad Hatter's Tea Party' (Mrs Podd) and 'Captain Scuttleboom's Treasure (Mr Ferris).

1950

'50-'51	Autumn: Dec 16th - First School Carol Service held in Brandeston All Saints.
'51-'52	Aug 51:An Arts Council promotion (in conjunction with Suffolk Rural Music School) of an International Summer School for amateur musicians from Denmark, Switzerland, Portugal, Norway, Holland, Germany and India. The highlight was an unforgettable recital, by Benjamin Britten and Peter Pears, of English Songs.
'52	Death of King George VIth; Increase in numbers as 8/9 year olds are accepted.
'52-'53	Decision to allow Brandeston Hall boys to wear grey pullovers. New Heads's house under construction (completed Nov '53).
'53	June: Coronation of Queen Elizabeth II.
'53-'54	Summer: Memorable visiting lecturer: Freddie Grisewood - 'Behind the scenes at the BBC'.
'54-'55	Summer: Reginald Kirkman retired as Head of Framlingham.

	Matron Dulcie Wilton ('the Green Dragon') left BH (thence to the College).
'55-'56	Autumn: Stanley Porter in post as new College Head. Easter: First School Trip abroad: Paris (Messrs Hewitt and Pemberton i/c).
'56-'57	Easter: New Gym/Assembly Hall completed and used for 'PT classes and a new boxing ring for use in the evenings', replacing a Nissen Hut Gym facility.
'57-'58	Christmas... Asian Flu swept through Brandeston Hall and Framlingham College, affecting staff and pupils alike. Summer: David List (aged 12), a member of the Orchestra that played for the World Premiere of Britten's 'Noye's Fludde', at Orford, for the Aldeburgh Festival.
'58-'59	November: David List performing again, in 'Noye's Fludde', in Southwark Cathedral.
'59-'60	Summer: Village fete (in aid of Church and Village Hall) held in BH grounds for first time.

1960

'60-'61	Summer: Top Form taken to Portman Rd for Royal Visit of HM Queen Elizabeth II.
'61-'62	Autumn: Cherrie Middleton retired (having served as Head Matron and cook for differing spells). John Ferris retired (13 yrs)... Yellow Housemaster, Eng. and Hist.'48-'62. New changing room on site of old Naafi canteen.
'62-'63	Roger Radice left (BH Director of Music for 4 yrs).
'63-'64	Easter: A production of 'Pied Piper of Hamelin', the first of 3, Head of Drama – Philip Tushingham... brother of actress Rita Tushingham). Summer: Centenary Celebrations of founding of the College (June 26-28). Brandeston Hall senior Choristers took part in the Centenary Concert.
'64	Draining of playing fields.
'64-'65	Summer: Paul 'Daddy' Craig retired (17 yrs). Red Housemaster, Latin and French '48-'65
'66-'67	New Teaching Block under construction... in a sea of mud. (Opened Sept '67).
'67-'68	Mansell Beard's amateur cinematography making its mark... Films included: 'Witchfinder General', 'The Hon. Charles', 'Brandeston Hall: A Documentary', 'Beckett'... (featuring pupils Ivor Morgan, as Beckett and Patrick Candler, as King Henry and 'The Murder of King Arthur'. 'Beckett' was acclaimed in Prep Schools Review and 'The Murder of Prince Arthur' received a silver medal, in its category, at the Scottish Film Festival of 1968. Summer: Mrs Molly Podd retired. A long record of service: 20 years at Brandeston Hall and a fair number at Framlingham College prior to the move. Maths, Junior Class – and Hockey, Cricket and Soccer coach. David Kittermaster retired. DDK's Final School

	Notes in The Framlinghamian noted that the coveted House Cup (awarded termly, over the first 20 years of the school's history) had been won by Blue 27 times, Green 18, Yellow 11 and Red... only 4 times. (David also 'doubled' as Housemaster of Blue throughout this period.)
'68-'69	Autumn: Richard Broad's first term. Easter: Blizzard conditions. Peter Arbon seen operating an improvised snowplough, drawn by his BSA Bantam motor-bike, keeping the Front Drive and pitches clear. Summer: Simon Brunger stood down as Head Chorister after a remarkable thirteen terms' service as a choir member.
'69-'70	Autumn: Drama: First House Plays performed (Won by Blue: 'The Last Up Train'). Subject Rooms introduced. Choir now robed for Sunday Services. Parents Committee set up to fund-raise for projected new pool. Easter: Mansell Beard left for a post at Aysgarth Prep (8 yrs) - HoD Geog/Art, Blue/Boarding Housemaster. Summer: Inaugural Meeting of IAPS Area 9 Athletics Championships for Boys, at St Faith's. A July Ball at Brandeston Hall (in aid of Swimming Pool Appeal).

1970

'70-'71	Autumn: December - John Haslam (Maths and Drama) sadly died. Presentation to Frank Bedwell on his 70th Birthday... and still working. Summer: John Pemberton left for St Edmunds, Kesgrave - after 24 yrs (first appointed to Framlingham College in 1947). Second Master Latin, R.E., Geography, P.E.; coached 1st XI Soccer, Athletics, Swimming. Green/Boarding Housemaster. Graham Ireland left (8 yrs) - for Head of Music post at Caterham and, subsequently, Reading School - Director of Music - Red/ Boarding Housemaster. New Outdoor Swimming Pool opened by Chairman of Governors.
'71	'Survey of the Parish of Brandeston' published by the village Historical Society. Stanley Porter retired as Head of Framlingham.
'71-'72	Autumn: Laurie Rimmer in post as new College Head. Easter: Following the completion of the Brandeston Hall History Society's detailed Village Survey a request for a copy received from the British Museum, Oxford University Library, Cambridge University Library, National Library of Scotland, and Trinity College, Dublin, Library (Richard Broad's initiative). Summer: A Half Term holiday was introduced for the first time in the history of the College as a whole. First 'stand alone' Brandeston Hall Speech Day: Presentation of Prizes by Arthur Harrison (Former Chair, Secretary and Treasurer of IAPS and

Founding Chairman of IAPS Orchestra Committee.
Major Pryor retiring Chairman of Governors.
Heating unit installed for the Swimming Pool.

'72-'73 Autumn: The pattern of two End of Term Carol
Services introduced: a Day Pupils' and a Boarders'
Service.
Honours Tie introduced - Roger Sparrow first
recipient (for opportune life-saving)
Summer: P Arbon won 17 awards at the
Framlingham Flower Show.
July - Inaugural National IAPS Symphony
Orchestra Course at Brandeston Hall (80 boys
from 50 different IAPS schools).

'73 Last LEA Direct Grant boys start at Brandeston

'73-'74 Blazers no longer compulsory.
Easter: Tragic death of 2 former pupils (Brian
Arthur and Bryan Ellis) in the Turkish Airlines
Paris Air Disaster.
Easter: Richard Broad left (to King Edward's,
Witley)
Magazine references to John le Grove, pupil at
Framlingham College, returning to play the organ
for an evening School Service and Simon Cullum
producing 'commendable illustrations of engines':
Both portents of things to come, at Brandeston
Hall, on a more permanent basis.

'74-'75 Autumn: Ron Jones' first term.
Easter: First Brandeston Hall presence on an
IAPS Educational Cruise holiday - to the Eastern
Mediterranean.

'75-'76 End of Direct Grant status. New Independent
Status.
Junior Classroom Block built to North of the Gym.
Also a new additional Dormitory Block connected
to the Stable Block of Staff Flats.
Tony Lawrence (and his mother) appeared on
Bruce Forsyth's 'Generation Game' on national
TV… (A recording has recently been unearthed
from BBC archives.)
Summer: An Outdoor Speech Day (on Terrace and
Meadow). Gen. Sir Pat Howard-Dobson Chief
Guest.

'76-'77 Easter: First Brandeston Hall Ski holiday – to San
Valentino (Mike and Janet Anderson)
Summer: HM Queen Elizabeth II's Silver Jubilee
celebrated on a glorious day. Annual Sports Day
followed by a Jubilee Lunch for 500
parents/Staff/pupils.
Peter MacFarlane the first BH pupil to audition
successfully for a place with the National IAPS
Symphony Orchestra.
Another Outdoor Speech Day. General Jack Dye
Chief Guest. His theme was that of the Victoria
Cross, with particular reference to the
Framlingham awards.

'77-'78 Autumn: First girls at BH (14 for first intake).
Girls also started in College LVIth.
Summer: Opening of Jubilee Block (including new
Music/Drama Room and new Art Room/Ceramics
Studio) 16th June 78 by Lord Stradbroke.
New tarmac surface for The Drives/Front (thus
ending 30 years' use in what was often a sea of
mud).

30th Anniversary of founding of Brandeston Hall:
July 15th - 140 OFs attended a celebration buffet
lunch.
Malcolm Russell left (7 yrs)… Director of Music,
Green/Boarding Housemaster.

'78-'79 Easter: A number of Pupils and Staff snowed-in
for Half-Term break. Eventually tractored out to
Framlingham (Peter Arbon at controls) through
hedge-high drifts.
Summer: Brandeston Hall team win the National
IAPS Satipsathlon (Triathlon) title at
Charterhouse.

'79-'80 Summer: The first of a number of cultural
Eisteddfodds (Eisteddfoddau the Welsh plural!)
which flourished through the 80s/early 90s. (In-
House Competition featuring Music/Drama/Art/
Design and Technology/Poetry/Prose/Spoken Word).
Ron Jones retired through ill-health.

1980

'80-'81 Autumn: Paddy Newbery's first term.
Sad death of Janet Anderson – Junior Class,
Swimming. (Member of Staff and Mike's wife).

'81-'82 Easter: David Bull appears in Tony Lawrence's
production of 'The Royal Pardon.'
Brandeston Hall party on IAPS Mediterranean
Cruise that was curtailed at the half way point, in
Cairo, the S.S.'Uganda' having been requisitioned
for service in the Falklands.
Mike Anderson left for Deputy Headship of Wells
Cathedral Junior School – subsequently Head,
King's Ely Junior and, currently, Head of Taunton
Junior). HoD Hist./ Green/ Boarding Housemaster/
1st XV Rugby and 1st XI Cricket.
Summer: Brandeston Hall Golf team are runners
up in the National IAPS Stowe Putter
Competition.
David Kittermaster died.

'82 First computers installed.

'82-'83 Mike Rutterford appointed i/c Playing Fields.
Tony Lawrence left (9 yrs) – Yellow / Boarding
Housemaster and HoD of English/Drama, 1st XI
Soccer coach. Appointment to English Department
at The College.

'83-'84 New Multi-purpose All-weather Courts
(Hockey/Soccer/Netball/Tennis) on site of former
Vegetable Garden.
Boys' Boarding: Old metal 'hospital style' beds
replaced with wooden beds and bunks.
Summer: Tom Fleming retired after 30+ yrs
Brandeston Hall/Framlingham College service -
HoD Woodwork.
Joan Rix' second and final retirement as Head
Matron.
Riet Stuij retired (Housekeeper for 11 years)
Paddy Newbery left to take up Headship of
Hurstpierpoint Junior School.

'85-'86 Autumn: Nigel Johnson's first term.
Easter: Brandeston Hall take on the promotion of

the IAPS Area 9 Cross-country Championships, for
the Orwell Shield (the event run at FC) – and
continue their winning streak.
The popular Greshams Annual Hockey Festival
inaugurated.
Summer: Inaugural Meeting of IAPS Area 9
Athletics Championships for Girls, at Ely.
Chris Woodruff confirms his status as, historically,
probably best ever BH male athlete by winning
first and, thus far, only track title, over 800m, at
the National IAPS Athletics Championships in
Aldershot.
Andrew Twite, the boy soloist in Britten's opera,
'Albert Herring', at the Aldeburgh Festival.

'86-'87 Autumn: Robin Williams left (HoD of Maths/1st
XI Cricket coach and pioneering fledgling
Computer Studies.
New Girls' Boarding Wing opened, utilizing first
floor of Stable Block and new building.
November: First Brandeston Hall 'Open Day' (now
an important thrice yearly happening)
June 1st Adventure Week sortie to Skern Lodge,
Appledore, for Y8.
Nick Stafford (5yrs) left… HoD History,
Britten(Yellow)/ Boarding Housemaster, Rugby
coach.

'87-'88 Autumn '87 – Great Hurricane. More than 30
trees lost on the Brandeston Hall estate.
David Grace left (10 yrs) Junior Classics, P.E. for
post of Director of Sport at Hereford Cathedral
Prep.
Designation of Boys/Girls Boarding Houses as
'Kittermaster, Austin & Alice Halls'
Floodlighting installed on Hard Courts (facilitating
evening use throughout the year).

'88-'89 Summer: Sally Youngman (first Housemistress of
Alice Hall, left for Departmental Headship, St
Johns, Sidmouth). Junior Classics, Hockey,
Rounders and Athletics coach.
Laurie Rimmer retired as Head of Framlingham.

'89-'90 Autumn: James Miller in post as new College
Head.
Introduction of Cultural Tie as equivalent to Colour
Awards for Sport.

1990

'90-'91 Pre-Prep launched with 5 and 6 yr olds.
Continuous Education 5-18 now offered for first
time. Liz Tydeman and Anthea Smith key to its
success.
Summer: Nigel Cox left for Departmental
Headship at Maidwell Hall.

'91-'92 Easter – January '92: 'Official' retirement of Peter
Arbon. Presentation Ceremony and Tea for guests
in Drama/Music Room.
Brandeston Hall Girls team take 1st place (with
Eleanor Atkinson as individual champion) in the
Inaugural National IAPS Cross-country
Championships, at Marlborough College.

'92-'93   Brian Rosen retired. (14 yrs). HoD Woodwork (overseeing its change into CDT), French, Science, 1st XI Hockey, 1st Tennis squad, coaching Rugby and organizing innumerable winter skiing holidays. Former SOF President.

'Final' Peter Arbon retirement (nearly half a century of connections).

Penelope Kirk left. (7 yrs). Junior Department Co-ordinator and, latterly, Senior Mistress. Netball and 1st VIII Rounders and Netball coach. Appointed Head of Portsmouth High for Girls Junior School. Currently Head of Prince's Mead Prep School, Winchester.

Opening of the Queen's Room (old first floor Linen Room) as a new Music Teaching/Resource Centre with keyboard suite – and expensive red plush chairs.

'93-'94   BBC2 screening of 'Hard Facts' (much of it filmed in/around Brandeston Hall. In the programme Nigel Johnson has some salient points to make about the future of private education.)

Summer: July '94 – Simon Fuller, Melissa Wardle and Bob Williams lead a Year 7 party on a Pilgrimage/History Field Trip to the Normandy Beaches in recognition of the 50th Anniversary of D-Day.

Brandeston Hall hosts the inaugural IAPS Area 9 Golf Tournament – and win it.

Simon Fuller leaves (for a Head of History post at Edgarley Hall, Millfield Junior. Sadly, to die of cancer while still in post there). HoD History, Geography, Britten (Yellow)/Boarding Housemaster. James Miller's tenure as Head of Framlingham ends: Appointed Head of Newcastle RGS.

'94-'95   Autumn: Gwen Randall in post as new College Head.

Summer: 8th May: VE DAY Celebration. Jack Dye, Joan Rix and Peter Arbon - presented a special Morning Assembly, reflecting on their Wartime memories. Street Party on Terrace for whole school. Exhibition of memorabilia.

Brandeston Hall Golf team retain IAPS Area 9 Golf Championship and win prestigious National IAPS Stowe Putter competition - and Luke Miller the Laddie Lucas Spoon, at Sandwich.

Martyn Lane (Director of Music FC/BH) leaves.

Revd Roger Dixon retires as an outstanding School Chaplain (13 yrs) - emotional farewell at Speech Day.

'95-'96   Summer: Shirley Robinson retires (32 yrs). HoD Science, Maths - having started her Brandeston Hall career teaching Science, in spartan conditions with rudimentary equipment in a Nissen hut.

Mary Vellacott retires(18 yrs). Maths, R.E., Geography, 1st VIII Netball and 1st VII Rounders.

Margaret Kennon retires (c.15 yrs). Maths, Junior Class, Athletics and Cross-country coaching.

'96-'97   Autumn: First ever defeat of Greshams on the Rugby Field (43-3) – 'Away' at Holt at that! Demolition of old Woodwork Hut and move to new Technology Centre in old Gym. Spacious work area (including new mezzanine floor) with facilities to use CAD (Computer Aided Design) packages with an adjacent IT Centre (in former Day Pupils' Cloaks) with a total of 21 networked computers.

Billie Hopewell-Smith performs with her Group, 'Magenta Jazz', at the National Festival for Youth at the Royal Festival Hall.

Lady Rowley opens Rowley Hall.

First Speech Day in Rowley Hall (ability to seat 650)

First cohort of Year 8 pupils sit Common Entrance (rather than In-house College Entrance Exam)

Death of Ron Jones.

'97-'98   Autumn: Dominic Ross stars as 'Oliver' (with a bevy of Brandeston Hall 'Workhouse urchins') in Tony Lawrence's Framlingham College musical production.

Summer: Golden Jubilee Celebrations - 30th May: Thanksgiving Service/Memorabilia Exhibition/ Cricket and Tennis Tournaments/Birthday Tea/ Summer Ball. Rachel Kittermaster among invited guests.

29th June. Pupils' celebration Birthday Tea Party in Rowley Hall; cake cut by David Mallett and Kirsty Wybar, joint Heads of School. Guests include Lord Belstead (President of Corporation), John Clement (Chairman of Governors) and Gwen Randall. Lord Belstead and Emily Morgan bury a Time Capsule and Jubilee Tree. Whole school body of pupils photographed in House Shirts, in '50' formation on the Front and used as cover for BH98 Magazine.

John le Grove (Brandeston Hall man and boy) left for Music post at Yehudi Menuhin School.

Anthea Smith retires from Pre-Prep (8 yrs)

Alison Millington leaves (5 yrs) -Junior Department Co-ordinator, Hockey and Tennis.

'98-'99   Autumn: Matthew Sheeran (singing the part of the boy Nicholas) with Michael Romney, John Wybar and Ben Norton, as the 'Pickled Boys' featured in a production of 'St Nicolas', at Orford Church.

Summer: Annual Brandeston Hall Cricket Festival launched.

'99-'00   Easter: Jan 15th 2000 – Memorial Service for Joan Rix held at Brandeston All Saints Church. Terry Hunt OF (Editor EADT), Michael Vipond Hon.OF, Bob Williams Hon OF and Ivan Howlett (Managing Editor Radio Suffolk) deliver tributes.

Summer: Melissa Wardle left (14 yrs) Michael Baic (Brandeston Hall man and boy) retired (29 yrs) HoD Modern Languages, Gainsborough (Red)/ Boarding Housemaster.

2000

'00-'01   Autumn: Revival of Latin in the form of a Lunchtime Latin Club (for Yrs 4-8)

New School Uniform introduced - 'practical and comfortable' (no more ties on working days.)

October - New SOF Library opened (by Jon Ford SOF President and Gwen Randall) - linked with a successful Suffolk Supper at Brandeston Hall.

Michael Vipond retired (22 yrs) – Sometime HoD English/ Drama, Junior Class, 1st XV Rugby, Wolsey (Green) Housemaster and Senior Boarding Master.

Nigel Johnson left for Headship of Terra Nova Prep, Cheshire.

Easter: Stephen Player (officially) appointed Master.

Summer: Grace Hutson, in her final term, confirms her status as best ever all-round sportswoman by winning the Schools East of England Inter-Counties U15 1,500m title (the first 'sub-5 minute' time by a Brandeston Hall girl) and becomes the first ever pupil selected to represent Suffolk in the All-England Schools Championships, at Exeter.

Bob Williams retired (31 yrs) Second Master 28 Years. Constable (Blue) Housemaster. Senior Boarding Master 16 Yrs. HoD Geog and Art. 1st XI Soccer (until its demise, thereafter Junior Soccer) Athletics/Cross Country and sometime i/c Tennis, Table-Tennis, Golf and Colts Cricket.

'02-'03   Foundation House opened.

Brandeston Hall Boys win National IAPS Mini-hockey Championships at Millfield.

'03-'04   Summer: Stephen Player left (12 yrs) (for Headship of Spratton Hall Prep, Northampton) – Sometime Director of Studies, Senior Master, Boarding Housemaster, HoD Eng/Drama, Rugby/Hockey/Tennis/Athletics/Golf coach.

'04-'05   John Kelsall appointed caretaker Master.

'05-'06   Autumn: Nigel Woolnough's first term.

Easter: Brandeston Hall hosted Festival of Rugby, featuring youngsters from Rumania, Bulgaria and the Ukraine.

'06-'07   Summer: Nigel Woolnough left.

'07-'08   Autumn: Martin Myers-Allen appointed Master

Easter: Former pupil and 'All Angel', Laura Wright, features as 'Personality of the Month: Q&A' in January edition of EADT Suffolk magazine.

The School Library moved to its fourth location in 60 years... in fact reverting to its pre-2000 location, the Jones Room, which, since that date has served as the Master's Study. The Master has thus taken up residence again, in the original Study – the 'South Room' with his P.A. in close attendance in the bay behind the very fine glazed doors.

Claire Goodin left (c.6 yrs) - French, Drama

Chris Parker left (4 yrs) - Boarding Housemaster and Drama.

John Clough left (14 yrs) - Head of History, R.E., Hockey, Rugby and Cricket coaching.

A publication like this is only made possible by support which comes in various forms:

1
FINANCIAL SUPPORT

Both the Trustees of the Society of Old Framlinghamians and Framlingham College have given very generous financial support to this project.

It is also testimony to the affection in which Brandeston Hall is held that the following individuals have readily given financial support:

Chris Bellamy, Michael Beverley, Jim Blythe, Richard Brown, Jim Butchart, John Capon, David Carr, Bob Clayton, Jo Donsworth, Simon Dougherty, John Edwards, John Elliott, Paul Elliott, Andrew Fane, Jon Ford, John Gooderham, Paul Gooderham, Keith Handley, John Hanney, Michael Holden, Peter Howard-Dobson, Nick Jacob, Chris Keeble, Jeremy Kemp, Peter Liell, Neville Marsh, Michael McGuire, Tony Martin, John Maulden, Norman Mayhew, Robert Mayhew, David Mitchell, Tim Mitchell, Martin Myers-Allen, Roland Nice, Tosin Oguntayo, Richard Overend, Robin Podd, John Rankin, David Risk, Brian Rosen, Robert le Rougetel, Peter Smallpeice, Brian Smith, Michael Smy, Peter Stewart, Pam Sullivan, David Summers, Graham Taylor, Douglas Thomson, John Thurlow, Bill Wade, John Waugh, Roger Waugh, Colin Wigg, Andrew Wright, Michael Wright, and others who prefer to remain anonymous.

Without this financial support there would have been no publication.

2
SUPPORT IN THE FORM OF CONTRIBUTIONS TO THE CONTENT

The written contributions of many staff, past and present, recent and less recent pupils, make up the bulk of the text. To all who have dug into their memories and archives for anecdotes and reflexions, I am utterly indebted.

I am grateful to my daughter, Chantal, for early advice on the structure of the book, and to Emma Rutterford and Leigh Cunningham in the College Development Office for help with scanning and liaison, and to Lucy Bryanton at Brandeston Hall, for similar help.

Photographs too, have come from a wide range of sources, but I am particularly grateful to Bob Williams for a fine array of sports and action pictures, to the Brandeston archive albums for older shots, to Peter Arbon for a sight of his pre-war photo album and to Wilda Woodland for some marvellous early photographs. Others who have offered photographs are Lord and Lady Cunliffe, the Tank Museum, Bovington, the East Anglian Daily Times, James Ruddock-Broyd, Mike Slessor, Bruce Wilson, David Larter, The Britten Peers Foundation, Martin Myers-Allen, John Austin, Jim Blythe, Chris Bellamy, Simon Dougherty, Chris Keeble, Jeremy Kemp, Jack Dye, Sue Getting, Simon Stacpoole, Ipswich Town Football Club and a host of other individuals, with apologies for lack of individual mention.

3

SUPPORT IN THE PRODUCTION PROCESS

Without the expertise and commitment of Chris Keeble, the designer, there would have been no book. He has worked away, in true professional manner, for many hundreds of hours, taking in evenings and weekends, to ensure that this book is published on time. If photographs look enhanced, then it is because Chris has used his expertise to make them so. He is highly selective and sets the highest of standards. He has often taken on the job of sub-editor, knowing the material as he does, and tactfully suggesting amendments.

Bob Williams was at the heart of the action for half of the school's 60 years and has been not only a mine of information, but a researcher, chivvier of contributors and would-be purchasers, writer and proof-reader – in short a quite indispensable right-hand man.

Wilda Woodland, Brandeston's village recorder, has an invaluable archive of old documents and photographs upon which she has generously allowed me to draw. John Austin has allowed me privileged access to old documents. The late John Booth, Leslie Gillett and Simon Fuller have all written about the Hall and I have unashamedly drawn on their work, while paying all due tribute to it. Carole Maran has written a thesis on Brandeston, and has helped with aspects of the early days. Peter Howard-Dobson has been very helpful in

setting up our ISBN registration and advising about the sales process. I am grateful to them all.

Finally there is the support which has encouraged the author to see the task through to the end, a task which has taken almost three years to complete. That support has come from far and wide, and reflects more on Brandeston Hall than on the author, who has done his best to eliminate historical and factual error but has almost certainly failed to do so, in what has been a very complex enterprise.

To all of those acknowledged, I can but offer my thanks. To none of the above can any of the shortcomings of the book, or possible inaccuracies be attributed. For these the author/editor assumes total responsibility.

Above: John Austin in 2009 – not only carrying on the family name – but also brandishing a copy of the Flyer promoting this book.

be for some years of not the least benefit to her it can be not
t perverseness that can induce her to keep the Estate in this
apidated and wasteful state the buildings of the different far
all now in a bad state the Mansion House called Brandes
ll now in the occupation of Mrs Revett together with the Par
nds and woods about 50 acres —

he roof of the House appears to want repairing the laths fr
Oldness of them have sunk in very much and the tiling is
ry uneven state in parts consequently the water must get
times as it appears by looking thro' the window in the
awing room a part of the wainscot is decayed and the
wing got down not being allowed by Mr Burrows to g
side the house I concluded this damage to the wainscott
the Drawing room must be caused from the wet gettin
the top of the house and in such a house as this if
ing is not kept tight the whole will very soon go to dec
found the water spouts stopt up and the water runn
er and damaging the Walls of the house and I should
t be surprized if I could have got inside to have se
at some of the rafters are decayed from the uneve
anner a part of the roof appears to be in — The
tbuildings are large and Numerous, The Granary ov
ach house and Cart house wants some repairs the Raf
we some of them sunk and the Ceiling giving way
aces owing to the laths being rotten — The Fowl hou
which there are two rows are going fast to decay for
ant of being repaired in time — The Pig Stys are al
thing into the same state there being no doors to th
will houses and part of the Tiling of which causes t
et to damage and rot the Timber. The net house o
w house is in a very bad state — The tiling has a